IS THE AGE OF THE ANTICHRIST, MARTYRDOM, RAPTURE *AND* THE MILLENNIAL KINGDOM *COMING?* (II)

IS THE AGE OF THE ANTICHRIST, MARTYRDOM, RAPTURE *AND* THE MILLENNIAL KINGDOM *COMING?* (II)

PAUL C. JONG

Hephzibah Publishing House

A Ministry of THE NEW LIFE MISSION
SEOUL, KOREA

Is the Age of the Antichrist, Martyrdom, Rapture and
the Millennial Kingdom Coming? (II)
Copyright © 2003 by Hephzibah Publishing House

Scripture quotations are from *the New King James Version.*

ISBN 89-8314-285-5
Cover Art by Min-soo Kim
Illustration by Young-ae Kim
Printed in Korea

Hephzibah Publishing House
A Ministry of THE NEW LIFE MISSION
48 Bon-dong, Dongjack-gu
Seoul, Korea 156-060

♠ Website: http://www.bjnewlife.org
♠ E-mail: newlife@bjnewlife.org
♠ Phone: 82(Korea)-16-392-2954
♠ Fax: 82-33-651-2954

Acknowledgements

It is by the grace of God that the second volume of the *Commentaries and Sermons on the Book of Revelation* is published.

First of all, I would like to thank God for allowing me to spread the Word of Revelation throughout the world, illuminated by the whole Scripture and the guidance of the Holy Spirit, in this time of the impending arrival of the era of the pale horse. I believe that now is the pressing time for every soul to be born again by the gospel of the water and the Spirit, to hear what the Word of Revelation says about the end times, and to obey its teachings in faith.

Words cannot express my deepest gratitude for all the servants and members of The New Life Mission, who have labored together to put out this book, and who have, to this very moment, united their hearts all along to spread the gospel. Each and every one of them is the actual publisher of this book.

I would like to also thank Rev. Samuel Kim and Rev. John Shin, my fellow workers who have faithfully carried out all the tasks for the publication of this book. I extend my heartfelt thanks to Mr. Youngwon Cho as well for his translation. It is only regrettable that I cannot give my individual thanks to all my fellow workers involved in the editing and printing of this book.

I give all glory to God, who has allowed us to be born again in the gospel of the water and the Spirit, and who has made us, by spreading the Word of Revelation in this evil generation, keep our hope for the Millennial Kingdom and the New Heaven and Earth, and defend our faith. ✉

PAUL C. JONG

CONTENTS

CHAPTER 17

CHAPTER 18

CHAPTER 19

CHAPTER 20

CHAPTER 21

CHAPTER 22

Appendix

Foreword

Do You Know When the Rapture of the Saints Will Occur?

In my first volume on the Book of Revelation, I wrote that God has planned seven eras in His Providence, that the era of the pale horse would be fast approaching us, and that people would suffer greatly under the tyranny of the Antichrist; but the born-again saints would be able to overcome him and attain the Millennial Kingdom and the New Heaven and Earth through their genuine faith given by God.

With this sequel volume, you will be able to discover the correct and detailed knowledge on the Word of the remaining parts of Revelation, from chapter 8 to 22.

First of all, I advise you to have strong faith in the truth that all the prophecies of Revelation will be literally realized: There will soon be the plagues of the seven trumpets; the emergence of the Antichrist; the massive martyrdom of the saints by the Antichrist; the resurrection and the rapture of the born-again saints in the middle of the Great Tribulation; the plagues of the seven bowls pouring upon the enemies of God; the coming of the Millennial Kingdom; the second resurrection of the sinners for their eternal punishment; the saints' dwelling with God in the eternal Kingdom of Heaven.

Among these things to come, the rapture of the saints must be a matter of concern for all Christians. When will it indeed happen, and who will certainly participate in this blessing?

Christians of the old times believed in the theory of post-tribulation rapture, but most Christians in these days advocate the theory of pre-tribulation rapture. But the truth is that the rapture of the saints will surely take place just after the first three and a half years of the seven-year Great Tribulation.

In chapter 10 of Revelation, when the Lord spoke to John through His angel who stood on the sea and the earth, and when John tried to write them down, God told him not to write. This was the very mystery that He would reveal only to us, the saints of the end times.

This mystery is none other than our rapture. To know exactly at what point our rapture would happen, we must first realize that the seventh trumpet of God is the decisive clue to solving this mystery. Revelation 10:7 states that when the seventh angel is about to sound, *"the mystery of God would be finished."* When, then, will the seventh trumpet sound? It will sound when the first three and a half years of the seven-year period of the Great Tribulation are slightly passed by. This is the very point when the saints' resurrection and rapture will come true. And when the rapture is over, the plagues of the seven bowls will shortly follow.

Therefore, now is the time for all sinners to repent and believe in the gospel of the water and the Spirit, for only the born-again will overcome the Antichrist and participate in the first resurrection and the rapture. Even though the persecution of the Beast will be extremely terrible, the born-again saints will not receive the mark of this Beast, and they will be martyred to defend their true faith. They will then be raptured by the Lord and enter the marriage supper of the Lamb.

Our Lord Jesus invites you to the Word of truth, saying, *"He who has an ear, let him hear what the Spirit says to the churches (Revelation 2:29)."*

May the blessings of our Lord be with you! ✉

Paul C. Jong

CHAPTER

8

The Trumpets That Announce The Seven Plagues

< Revelation 8:1-13 >

"When He opened the seventh seal, there was silence in heaven for about half an hour. And I saw the seven angels who stand before God, and to them were given seven trumpets. Then another angel, having a golden censer, came and stood at the altar. He was given much incense, that he should offer it with the prayers of all the saints upon the golden altar which was before the throne. And the smoke of the incense, with the prayers of the saints, ascended before God from the angel's hand. Then the angel took the censer, filled it with fire from the altar, and threw it to the earth. And there were noises, thunderings, lightnings, and an earthquake. So the seven angels who had the seven trumpets prepared themselves to sound. The first angel sounded: And hail and fire followed, mingled with blood, and they were thrown to the earth. And a third of the trees were burned up, and all green grass was burned up. Then the second angel sounded: And something like a great mountain burning with fire was thrown into the sea, and a third of the sea became blood. And a third of the living creatures in the sea died, and a third of the ships were destroyed. Then the third angel sounded: And a great star fell from heaven, burning like a torch, and it fell on a third of the rivers and on the springs of water. The name of the star is Wormwood. A third of the waters became wormwood, and many men died from the water, because it was made bitter. Then the fourth angel sounded: And a third of the sun was struck, a third of the moon, and a third of the stars, so that a third of them were darkened. A third of the day did not shine, and likewise the night. And I looked, and I heard an angel flying through the midst of heaven, saying with a loud voice, 'Woe, woe, woe to the inhabitants of the earth, because of the remaining blasts of the trumpet of the three angels who are about to sound!'"

Exegesis

Revelation 8 records the plagues that God will bring to this earth. One of the most critical questions here is whether or not the saints will be included among those who would suffer under these plagues. The Bible tells us that the saints, too, will go through the plagues of the seven trumpets. Of the seven plagues, they will go through all but the last plague. These plagues of the seven trumpets that appear in this chapter are the actual plagues that God will bring to this earth. God tells us that He will punish the world with the plagues that would begin with the angels' sounding of the seven trumpets.

Verse 1: When He opened the seventh seal, there was silence in heaven for about half an hour.
This refers to the calm just before the wrath of God is poured on the mankind. God will keep silence for a while before brining His terrifying plagues on the earth. This shows us how horrible and fierce His plagues of the seven trumpets will be. When the mankind stands before God after going

through these plagues, those who are saved will receive eternal life, but those who are not will receive eternal punishment. Thus, realizing what kind of era this time is, we must be awake and do the work of the evangelists.

Verse 2: And I saw the seven angels who stand before God, and to them were given seven trumpets.

God used the seven angels to do His works. But let us not forget that in today's era, God works through the righteous who believe in the Word of the gospel of the water and the Spirit.

Verse 3: Then another angel, having a golden censer, came and stood at the altar. He was given much incense, that he should offer it with the prayers of all the saints upon the golden altar which was before the throne.

This shows us that God, having heard of the prayers of the saints offered in the midst of their persecution and tribulations by Satan and his followers, will bring all His plagues to the earth. The "golden censer" here refers to the prayers of all the saints, meaning that as their prayers are delivered to God, all His works will be fulfilled. God works by hearing the prayers of the saints.

Verse 4: And the smoke of the incense, with the prayers of the saints, ascended before God from the angel's hand.

This shows just how much the Antichrist has tormented the saints on this earth. Because of the tribulations of the end times, the saints will pray to God to drive away the Antichrist, to let the tribulations pass by them soon, and to show their murders just how fierce the wrath of God is for them. The verse here shows that God will thus receive all the saints' prayers. Having received these prayers of the saints, God will begin to judge the Antichrist and his followers with the plagues of the seven trumpets and the seven bowls. God's judgment of the Antichrist and his followers is His final answer to the prayers of the saints.

Verse 5-6: Then the angel took the censer, filled it with fire from the altar, and threw it to the earth. And there were noises, thunderings, lightnings, and an earthquake. So the seven angels who had the seven trumpets prepared themselves to sound.

God is preparing the plagues of the seven trumpets on this earth. Therefore, this world will not escape from noises, thunderings, lightenings, and earthquakes.

Verse 7: The first angel sounded: And hail and fire followed, mingled with blood, and they were thrown to the earth. And a third of the trees were burned up, and all green grass was burned up.

The first plague is the burning of a third of the earth, where one-third of the trees and all grass will be burnt down. This plague will fall on the forests of this world.

Why would God bring down this kind of plague? Because people, though they have seen the beauty of God's creation with their own eyes, did not recognize the Creator as God and worship Him, but instead "worshipped and served the creations rather than the Creator" (Romans 1:25). God therefore brings the plagues of the seven trumpets to those who do not give glory to God but instead stand against Him.

Verses 8-9: Then the second angel sounded: And something like a great mountain burning with fire was thrown into the sea, and a third of the sea became blood. And a third of the living creatures in the sea died, and a third of the ships were destroyed.

The plague of the second trumpet is of a falling star crashing down on the earth. This asteroid will fall into the sea and turn a third of the sea into blood, killing a third of the living creatures in the sea and destroying a third of the ships. Through the God-created nature, the mankind has received many blessings. But instead of thanking God for the blessings of the nature, they became arrogant and turned against God. The second plague punishes them for this sin.

Verses 10: Then the third angel sounded: And a great star fell from heaven, burning like a torch, and it fell on a third of the rivers and on the springs of water.

Why did God allow the asteroid to fall "on a third of the rivers and on the springs of water?" Because the mankind, though it lives by the Lord who is the host of life, did not worship and thank Him, but instead disdained this Lord of life.

Verse 11: The name of the star is Wormwood. A third of the waters became wormwood, and many men died from the water, because it was made bitter.

From this plague a third of the rivers and springs will turn into wormwood, and many will die from drinking their water. This is the plague of punishment for the sinners who had tormented God and the hearts of the saints. God will never fail to thus bring avenge to the sinners for all their deeds committed against the righteous. When the sinners bring suffering to the righteous, God will judge them. The third plague is yet another plague on the nature; it was brought down for the people's sin of disobedience in not believing in the gospel of the water and the Spirit given by God. The

"Wormwood" in the Bible always refers to the judgment of those who disobey and oppose God.

Verse 12: Then the fourth angel sounded: And a third of the sun was struck, a third of the moon, and a third of the stars, so that a third of them were darkened. A third of the day did not shine, and likewise the night.

The fourth plague is the darkening of a third of the sun, the moon, and the stars. All this time, the mankind has been following Satan and has loved darkness. They thus disliked the light of salvation shone by the gospel of the water and the Spirit given by Jesus Christ. As such, to teach them just how terrifying and accursed the world of darkness really is, God would bring them this plague of darkness. The plague is also to show how fierce the wrath of God is for their sin of hating Jesus Christ and loving the darkness. As a result, a third of the sun, the moon, and the stars of this world will lose their light and be darkened.

Verse 13: And I looked, and I heard an angel flying through the midst of heaven, saying with a loud voice, "Woe, woe, woe to the inhabitants of the earth, because of the remaining blasts of the trumpet of the three angels who are about to sound!"

This verse tells us that there are still three more woes to come to all those who live on this earth. Therefore, all the sinners and all those who stand against God should be delivered from their sins by believing in the gospel of the water and the Spirit as soon as possible. ⊠

Are the Plagues of the Seven Trumpets Literal?

< Revelation 8:1-13 >

In Revelation 5 appears a scroll sealed with seven seals, which Jesus took. This meant that Jesus thus was entrusted with all authority and power of God, and that He would lead the world according to God's plan from then on. Revelation 8 opens with the passage, *"When He opened the seventh seal, there was silence in heaven for about half an hour. And I saw the seven angels who stand before God, and to them were given seven trumpets."* Jesus thus opens the seventh seal of the scroll, and shows us things to come.

Chapter 8 begins by telling us that the plagues of the seven trumpets will begin with the prayers of the saints. From verse 6 and on, the chapter then speaks of the plagues of the seven trumpets that will be brought to this world.

The Plague of the First Trumpet

The First Trumpet—Verse 7: *"The first angel sounded: And hail and fire followed, mingled with blood, and they were thrown to the earth. And a third of the trees were burned up, and all green grass was burned up."*

The first thing that we must find out is whether or not we the saints will be in the midst of the plagues of the seven trumpets when these are bought to the earth.

Here come seven angles blowing seven trumpets. We must realize that, of these seven plagues, we will remain on this earth and go through the first six plagues. We must also realize that when the seventh trumpet sounds, we will be raptured, and that this will be followed by the plagues of the seven bowls.

Verse 7 tells us that when the first angel sounded his trumpet, hail and fire mingled with blood rained on the earth, scorching a third of the earth and a third of the trees. A third of the world and the nature, in other words, were burnt down.

Could we live on when the nature is thus burnt up in smoke? With hail and fire mixed with blood raining down on us, and the trees turned into ashes, could we really live surrounded by this kind natural environments that have been burnt to the ground? When we actually confront the stark reality of losing our homes to this rain of hail and fire mixed blood, and of the smoldering of thick forests and hills, none of us will have any desire left to live on, nor, for that matter, could we do so even if we wanted to.

Don't forget that you and I have to go through this first plague. When it dawns on us that we are entering this enormous plague, we must also realize that the Antichrist already exists on this earth by then. Because such plagues will begin before the Antichrist fully emerges to seek his absolute domination of the world, the leaders of the world will begin to form a united front to battle the plagues, and a certain ruler will gather together seven other rulers to produce a great power.

The Antichrist will then emerge quite naturally as the absolute ruler in this process. As the Antichrist shows a great ability in managing and recovering from the destruction of the nature, many, impressed by his power, will begin to follow him, thinking of him as a divine being, and his adherents will emerge, gradually but for sure.

The Bible tells us that when the first angel sounds his trumpet, it will bring the first of the plagues of the seven trumpets that will scorch a third of the earth. Both we the saints and the people of the world will be living on this earth when this plague strikes. What, then, will happen to the world? Chaos will run rampant in the world, with ruins, corpses, and the injured lying everywhere; the atmosphere will be covered by the smoke and toxic gas produced by the lake of fire that engulfs the whole world; and the air will lack oxygen as the global desertification caused by the fire would drastically cut the planet's capacity to regenerate oxygen. The first plague alone will reduce this world to ashes, devastating enough to take away even our desire to live.

From this plague, we must make a wise choice. Living in a normal world now, we may become fearful of the great plagues and tribulations to come. But we can be freed from this fear and be bold instead, for when a third of the nature of the world goes up in flame and people are wailing everywhere, long before this we would have already known that the plague was due all along, and that there are even more plagues to come. Because we have hope, we can be filled by it, but because we also have the flesh, we can at times be struck by fear. But because we know the future of this earth, we place our hope not on this earth, but in the Kingdom of God. With such faith, and by the indwelling of the Holy Spirit, we can be courageous and brave.

The wailing cries of the people of the world will get ever louder, and we, too, might be mourning if our own families are among those who have not received the remission of their sins. Some of our own families of the flesh, unredeemed of their sins, might even sell us out to the Antichrist for scraps of food. Others, on the other hand, might come to us to ask us how they can receive the remission of their sins. This is more than possible, for the opportunities for their redemption are still available then. The Bible tells us that when the plagues of the seven trumpets come, a third of the whole world will die. This also means that a two-third of the world will survive. When a third of the world's population are actually burnt to death, we should realize that the time of our martyrdom and the return of the Lord is not far away. God said that He will rain down hail and fire mixed with blood from the sky.

When God brings down fire and hail on us, we will be helpless to avoid them. It will be impossible, even with scientific progress, to develop and put a defensive shield in the atmosphere that can cover the whole world from the pouring fire and hail. Even if we were to come up with such a device, it would be no match for the power of the plague coming from the Lord. We must accept into our hearts the fact that these plagues will indeed come to us in reality, and live our present lives by believing in all the Word of God's promises with our hearts.

Recently, I heard in the news that hailstones as large as a man's head, measuring 45 cm in diameter, fell in China. Accelerating from the fall, these ice chunks, in the size of a man's head, fell with an amazing force, piercing through rooftops and destroying everything in their path. What will fall with the first plague is even greater in force. We must believe in our hearts that the fire that will consume a third of this earth, far more destructive than these hailstones in China, will indeed come down; we must keep this faith in our hearts; and we must act by this faith when this plague actually arrives. We must believe that this world is soon to be destroyed. And we must also be determined to face the plague with such faith, and resolve ourselves to be martyred. When the seven trumpets sound, the seven plagues will in fact be brought to this world. This is the first of these plagues.

The Plague of the Second Trumpet Brought by God

The second trumpet—Verses 8-9: *"Then the second angel sounded: And something like a great mountain burning with fire was thrown into the sea, and a third of the sea became blood. And a third of the living creatures in the sea died, and a third of the ships were destroyed."*

We have to pay attention to the fact that the saints will also live through this second plague.

It says here that something like a great mountain was thrown into the sea, turning a third of the sea into blood and killing a third of its living creatures. When the end times come, the order of the universe will break down, undermining the constellation of stars and causing them to collide with one another and break apart, and from this many meteors will fly toward the earth on a collision course. Some of these meteors will make through the atmosphere and fall into the sea with the full brunt of their force, turning a third of the sea into blood, killing a third of its living creatures, and destroying a third of the ships. This is the plague of the second trumpet among the seven trumpets' plagues.

Will we then be able to eat fish from the sea, or even swim in it, when this happens? Neither would be possible any longer. When an asteroid like a great mountain falls into the sea, a third of the sea will be turned into blood, a third of its living creatures will be killed, rotting the sea will their dead carcasses, and tidal waves and earthquakes will not only destroy the ships but also kill many people.

I remember seeing a movie where an asteroid falls into the sea and causes great tidal waves that cover the earth. The movie producers, I am sure, had the vivid picture of the end times in their minds when they made this movie. That great disasters will strike the earth is the truth that even the unbelievers can easily recognize. Countless people will be killed by the plague of the falling meteors. But as only a third of the world is destroyed, you and I will continue to live on this earth until the plagues of the seven bowls are poured.

People used to believe before that the rapture would happen after the Great Tribulation is over, but with the emergence of the theory of pre-tribulation rapture, many theologians began to believe in this pre-tribulation rapture instead. Even worse, even amillennialism, which denies the Millennial Kingdom, has now made its appearance. Theologians, in their inability to tackle the whole Word of Revelation, are now only trying to run away from all its Word. Those who would have lost their hope on this earth because of the plagues to come will provide a stark contrast to the born-again saints who will endure the situation instead, having placed their hope only in the Millennial Kingdom and the New Heaven and Earth promised by the Lord.

We should be preparing our faith as the end times comes nearer to us, but instead of doing so, many people prefer talking about pre-tribulation rapture or amillennialism, trying to avoid facing the real faith. Because they believe that Jesus will return in clouds as they go about their daily, undisturbed lives, and because they believe that they will be directly lifted up to the Kingdom of God without going through any of the plagues, they are not preparing their faith for the Great Tribulation at all.

At first glance, those who are relaxed and not preparing for the Great Tribulation may even appear to be quite bold. The reason why the sinners who are not born again seem so bold before the Great Tribulation is because their souls, having already drunk from the false prophets' lies, are dead, and have no spiritual desires left in them anymore. For the same reason, that is, because their souls are already dead, people do not hear and even reject the gospel of the water and the Spirit, which enables them to be born again of water and the Spirit and enter the Kingdom of God (John 3:5).

But the born-again must prepare their faith for the tribulations of the end times, no matter how comfortable their present lives may be. They must prepare for the future in advance by keeping in their minds the desire to preach the gospel to those who would be faithful to God, so that they may be able to save as many souls as possible during the time of the Tribulation.

Ignoring the imminent arrival of the Great Tribulation is incredibly foolish. Those who do so will be helpless before the plagues, akin to what had happened with the Korean War. Before the Korean War broke out, the United States had detected the massive mobilization of the North Korean army and warned South Korea of a possible sudden invasion, but the South Korean government and military completely ignored the warning, going as far as to sending troops away for vacation and letting the frontline officers enjoy their weekend on the actual day of invasion.

Because they had not prepared for war even when the intelligence on the North Korean invasion was made available to them, they were unable to repel the North's attack and were pushed, in no time, all the way down to the last front in the southernmost corner. By the time South Korea hurriedly recalled its troops back from their vacation and tried to organize the army for war, its frontline had already been penetrated, and it had no choice but to keep retreating with massive casualties.

This is the kind of woe that will befall on us if we do not believe in the Word that God spoke to us about the end times. But if we sincerely believe in it, we can escape from such a woe. Revelation talks about a refuge in the time of the Tribulation, but it does not tell us about its exact location. Nevertheless, it tells us that the saints will be sheltered and nurtured in a refuge. This refuge refers to none other than the church. Where can one find a shelter in this world? Some people say that they can survive if they flee to Israel. But in Israel they will actually face even more severe tribulations. You should realize that since the Antichrist himself will be headquartered in Israel, the plagues will be even more intense over there.

Even though this Word of tribulations may not immediately appear as realistic right now, but you must nevertheless know it in your hearts and prepare for the future. You must believe in it with your heart, and with this faith you must preach the gospel to people as if you were already living in this time of the Great Tribulation. You must prepare people's hearts and lead them to their shelter by preaching the gospel of the water and the Spirit to them. God has kept us in His churches so that we would preach to the people of such things to come and help them prepare their faith for the end times.

This is why we are doing what we are doing—that is, preaching the gospel of the water and the Spirit with our whole strength. We are preaching the Word of Revelation in this time not to boast of our own, but because it is the Word that is so necessary to today's era, for both the believers and unbelievers alike. Only by preparing this faith from now can our hearts be unshaken when the tribulations and plagues descend on us.

God will, of course, give us His special protection, but because we are living in a horrible, hard, and difficult world, if we know what is to come in the end times and prepare our faith to overcome the tribulations, we can spread the gospel even more. Also, because we will place even greater and more confident hope in the Kingdom of God, we will never be swept away by the current of the world, or sell out our faith, but instead do even more works of faith. This is why we preach the Word of Revelation and serve the many works of faith.

The Plague of the Third Trumpet

The third trumpet—Verses 10-11: *"Then the third angel sounded: And a great star fell from heaven, burning like a torch, and it fell on a third of the rivers and on the springs of water. The name of the star is Wormwood. A third of the waters became wormwood, and many men died from the water, because it was made bitter."*

The saints will also live through this third plague. The plague of the second trumpet was brought on the sea, but this time the third trumpet will bring the plague on the rivers and springs. The great star falling from heaven here refers to a comet. The rivers and the springs that are hit by the comet will turn bitter, as they turn into wormwood. In the old times, people used to ground wormwood and eat its sap for medicinal purposes, which was bitter beyond any imagination. The Bible tells us that as this biter wormwood spreads throughout the water supplies of the world, many people will die from drinking it.

As a third of the world's fresh water turns into wormwood, many people will die from it, but the Lord will protect His people throughout this plague. The most likely cause of the massive death will be some waterborne diseases, probably from some kind of biochemical changes in water triggered by the fall of the comet. People do not die, in other words, just because water turn bitter, but because of something else. We know and believe that all these things are real, and that they will infallibly come to pass in the future.

The Plague of the Fourth Trumpet

The fourth trumpet—Verse 12: *"Then the fourth angel sounded: And a third of the sun was struck, a third of the moon, and a third of the stars, so that a third of them were darkened. A third of the day did not shine, and likewise the night."*
Don't forget that the saints will still be living on this earth through this fourth plague.

If a third of the day does not shine, it means that the daylight is reduced to about four hours from the average of seven to eight hours. Since the moon and the stars will also lose a third of their light, the whole world will turn dark. When it should be broad daylight, in other words, darkness will fall all of a sudden. The movie *Rapture* follows the theory of pre-tribulation rapture, but in it you can see the whole world turning dark in broad daylight, causing everyone to scream and panic. Think about it yourself: it's supposed to be 11 o'clock in the morning, and yet all of a sudden the sun disappears and there is no light anymore. You, too, will be struck by fear, as if you were visited by the angel of death.

We know that we will have to live through such a

disastrous time, but you should not fear. God will protect and bless us even more. By this time, your faith would have turned so strong that God will answer your prayers and work for you the moment you pray to Him. Because God promised us to always be with us until the end of the world, God will never leave us alone in the Great Tribulation of the end times. Without a trace of doubt, He will always be with us. As such, because God will thus be with us all the time, we must believe that He will protect us and allow us to survive, and we must spread this faith to others and prepare their faith as well.

Three More Plagues to Come

Verse 13 says, *"And I looked, and I heard an angel flying through the midst of heaven, saying with a loud voice, 'Woe, woe, woe to the inhabitants of the earth, because of the remaining blasts of the trumpet of the three angels who are about to sound!'"*

As the angel shouts woe for three more times, there will be three more plagues to follow on this earth. Of the plagues of the seven trumpets, in other words, three more plagues still remain. We should realize that by the seventh trumpet our rapture would be realized. When the plagues of the first six trumpets all end, and the seventh angel blows his trumpet, the saints will be immediately resurrected and raptured. When all the saints are lifted up and meet the Lord in the air, the plagues of the seven bowls will then be poured on this earth.

We must realize that this earth will soon enter into the beginning of the plagues of the seven trumpets and of the seven bowls, the latter of which will be poured with the seventh trumpet's plague according to God's will. And we must believe in them with all our hearts, and nurture our faith now so that our faith may grow strong enough to persevere through all these plagues. If people believe without any prior knowledge of the end times, they will be so shocked when the Tribulation actually comes that they may even end up apostatizing.

As such, for us to triumph in the end, our faith in these things must be accompanied by the accurate knowledge of the end times. Today, when the end is nearing us so close, we must therefore never neglect the church or fall from it too far. All our hearts must be united in the church, and, no matter what, we must all believe in the Word of God as preached to us through the church, holding each other by and living in faith.

When these plagues come, some of the unsaved from even your own family, relatives, or friends might come after you. Even in ordinary times, when asked who our relatives, brothers, and parents are, our Lord told us that only those who follow the will of the Father are our family, parents, and brothers. When the world of tribulations comes, the born-again will realize even more certainly who really are their true brothers, sisters, and family. Because we understand and help each other now with this faith, and because God has already delivered you and me alike from all these plagues, He will watch over us, protect us from the plagues, and nurture us in His church as His children. This faith must be firmly planted in us.

Those who sell us out to the Antichrist in the end times could very well turn out to be from our own family of the flesh. As such, even though they are our family and relatives, if they are not born again by the water and the Spirit, our faith must be strong enough to consider them as strangers from the very beginning. They are, in other words, capable of doing far worse things to us than even the real strangers. It does not matter that they are our own family of the flesh—if they are not saved, then we must realize that they are our enemies regardless. We must open our hearts to what we often heard from the Word of God on this issue and believe in its as the truth.

Just as God turned Sodom and Gomorra into a lake of fire by raining down on them brimstone and fire, He will also bring such a plague in the end times to the sinners. God's destruction of Sodom and Gomorra is a fact proven by archeological evidences.

In these days, many movies whose plot relies on the destruction of the mankind by the collision of the earth with asteroids have come out. Such movies have been made based on the Word of the Bible that records the plagues of the last days that will descend on this earth. The probability of meteors falling on the earth is actually quite high, making it more than likely for these plagues to materialize into reality in this world.

A good example is paleontological evidence from the fossils of dinosaurs, which shows that that the earth went through some great changes in ancient times. Extinct life forms tell us of their previous existence through their fossils. Some scientists suggest that this extinction of the ancient life forms, including dinosaurs, is explained by a catastrophic collision of the earth with an asteroid. The plagues of meteors written in Revelation 8, therefore, are more than possible to be realized in this world.

In Not Too Distant Future...

We must realize that such plagues will come to this earth in not too distant future. Some scientists have already tried the human cloning, which must be a most formidable challenge to God. Thus, all these plagues are ready to be brought by God in this era. The mankind must not forget God in their reliance on the power of science.

The mankind is now trying to respond to all the plagues of the world by the power of its scientific knowledge. But no scientific breakthrough can ever prevent God's plagues, for they are far worse than any other disasters that the mankind has ever gone through before. When we look at today's man-made scientific progress, we can see that the mankind is challenging the authority of God, wanting to become like Him. But no matter how far its scientific advancement is made, no one can stop the plagues brought by God. All these plagues have been asked by none other than the mankind itself.

The only way to escape from the plagues brought by God is to discover the truth of salvation through the gospel of the water and the Spirit, and take refuge in the Lord's arms by believing in it. Escape from these plagues by realizing and believing that the only way to avoid the terrifying judgment of God is your faith in the gospel of the water and the Spirit.

All blessings and curses are held in God's hands. If God decides to keep this earth, then the earth will live on; if not, then it can only be destroyed. Living in such an era, if you believe and follow the Word of God more purely and fear Him even more, God will lead you to the gospel of the water and the Spirit that can shelter you from these horrendous plagues to come.

Even right now, many people throughout the world are dying and trembling in fear from the earthquakes, typhoons, and diseases. Moreover, there is no end to war everywhere, with nations standing against nations and states against states. As such, when the Antichrist emerges in the near future and resolves the urgent problems of such chaotic situation, many people will follow him. This will then be accompanied by the descending of the most fearful plagues on this earth, and, in the end, this world will be completely destroyed by these plagues brought by God.

God will create the New Heaven and Earth and give it to those who have been delivered from sin. The purpose in God's creation of the New Heaven and Earth is to bestow it to those who have been born again by believing in the gospel of the water and the Spirit. Before long, God will destroy the first world and open the second world. Just as the ancient dinosaurs disappeared, so will this world of modern scientific civilization vanish, and we will bear witness with our own eyes to the new beginning of a new world brought by God.

We must then think about how we should live now. We must believe in all the plagues to come as recorded in the present passage, and live the rest of our remaining lives for the righteousness of God, preparing for the next world with faith. We must be knowledgeable of Revelation's Word of prophecy. I say this now because when the day comes, all the knowledge that you have thus attained will prove to be hugely beneficial for your faith.

All the space objects that have the potential to collide with the earth, from the asteroids scattered between Mars and Jupiter to the countless comets with unknown cycles, are collectively called as "Near Earth Objects (NEOs)." NASA once unveiled a list identifying 893 known NEOs in the solar system alone. If any one of these NEOs were to collide with the earth, the devastation brought by this collision would be beyond any imagination. The disastrous impact would probably be greater than that of thousands of nuclear bombs combined.

Imagine what would happen to this world then. That the world's forests, water, and ships would be destroyed is a given. All the mankind, therefore, must believe in the gospel of the water and the Spirit and live their lives preparing for eternal life.

The Lord has told us that when the natural plagues come to this earth, a third of the sun, the moon, and the stars will lose their light. But few people know this, and even fewer believe in it. As such, only a small number of people believe in the gospel of the water and the Spirit and are preaching its truth.

Our minds must be awake. These plagues will indeed come. We must find out with what kind of faith and determination we should live the rest of our lives. You and I must realize that today's era is only a step away from the Great Tribulation, and we must live our remaining lives in faith, without a trace of doubt whatsoever in our hearts.

If we do not live by believing in the Word of prophecy for this Tribulation now, our hearts will turn empty, our purposes will be lost, and we will be crippled by the worries of life. This must not happen. At the same time, far less should we live by placing our hope in this world, as if we would never leave this world behind. Many who have a modicum of scientific knowledge know very well that there is no hope for this world. God will certainly lay this world to waste.

God will make the new Kingdom of Jesus and allow the righteous to live in it. And He will allow those who believe in the gospel of the water and the Spirit to live with Him forever.

We should cast down our own will and thoughts before God, and in humility accept and believe in His Word of prophecy. We must be preaching the gospel of the water and the Spirit, and then meet the Lord when He comes. Let us live for this work of God. When the Lord returns to this earth, we will receive a new life, our bodies will be transformed like His, and we will live again in His new world, all as He has told us.

We do not know the exact day and time of the Lord's

return. But from looking at the signs of the world, we do know that all the plagues recorded in the Word of God are nearing very close to us. We thus believe in God who has prophesied all these things, and who has shown us the way of salvation. ⊠

CHAPTER

9

The Plague from the Bottomless Pit

< Revelation 9:1-21 >
"Then the fifth angel sounded: And I saw a star fallen from heaven to the earth. To him was given the key to the bottomless pit. And he opened the bottomless pit, and smoke arose out of the pit like the smoke of a great furnace. So the sun and the air were darkened because of the smoke of the pit. Then out of the smoke locusts came upon the earth. And to them was given power, as the scorpions of the earth have power. They were commanded not to harm the grass of the earth, or any green thing, or any tree, but only those men who do not have the seal of God on their foreheads. And they were not given authority to kill them, but to torment them for five months. Their torment was like the torment of a scorpion when it strikes a man. In those days men will seek death and will not find it; they will desire to die, and death will flee from them. The shape of the locusts was like horses prepared for battle. On their heads were crowns of something like gold, and their faces were like the faces of men. They had hair like women's hair, and their teeth were like lions' teeth. And they had breastplates like breastplates of iron, and the sound of their wings was like the sound of chariots with many horses running into battle. They had tails like scorpions, and there were stings in their tails. Their power was to hurt men five months. And they had as king over them the angel of the bottomless pit, whose name in Hebrew is Abaddon, but in

Greek he has the name Apollyon. One woe is past. Behold, still two more woes are coming after these things.

Then the sixth angel sounded: And I heard a voice from the four horns of the golden altar which is before God, saying to the sixth angel who had the trumpet, 'Release the four angels who are bound at the great river Euphrates.' So the four angels, who had been prepared for the hour and day and month and year, were released to kill a third of mankind. Now the number of the army of the horsemen was two hundred million; I heard the number of them. And thus I saw the horses in the vision: those who sat on them had breastplates of fiery red, hyacinth blue, and sulfur yellow; and the heads of the horses were like the heads of lions; and out of their mouths came fire, smoke, and brimstone. By these three plagues a third of mankind was killed—by the fire and the smoke and the brimstone which came out of their mouths. For their power is in their mouth and in their tails; for their tails are like serpents, having heads; and with them they do harm. But the rest of mankind, who were not killed by these plagues, did not repent of the works of their hands, that they should not worship demons, and idols of gold, silver, brass, stone, and wood, which can neither see nor hear nor walk. And they did not repent of their murders or their sorceries or their sexual immorality or their thefts."

Exegesis

Verse 1: Then the fifth angel sounded: And I saw a star fallen from heaven to the earth. To him was given the key to the bottomless pit.

That God gave the angel the key to the bottomless pit means that He decided to bring a plague as terrible as hell on the mankind.

The bottomless pit is also called as the abyss, meaning a place of endless depth. To bring suffering to the Antichrist living on the earth, his followers, and those who stand against the righteous, God will open the bottomless pit. The key to this bottomless pit was given to the fifth angel. This is a terrifying plague that is as horrendous as hell itself.

Verse 2: And he opened the bottomless pit, and smoke arose out of the pit like the smoke of a great furnace. So the sun and the air were darkened because of the smoke of the pit.

When God allowed the opening of the bottomless pit, the whole world was filled by dusts like volcanic ashes, bringing in the plague of darkness. This plague of darkness is reserved for those who love darkness. God is the God of light who shines on us, giving the gospel of the water and the Spirit to everyone. To those who believe in this truth, God gave the grace of salvation and allowed them to live in His bright light. But those who do not accept the truth face the righteous retribution of God, for He will bring on them the plague of darkness and His just judgment.

People are fundamentally born as sinners, and they prefer darkness over light in their lives. They thus deserve to receive the plague of darkness from God for rejecting and not believing in the gospel of the water and the Spirit given by the Lord.

Verse 3: Then out of the smoke locusts came upon the earth. And to them was given power, as the scorpions of the earth have power.

God will send locusts to this earth and punish the sins of

those who oppose the truth of God in their instinctive thoughts. This plague of locusts is capable of bringing a pain as excruciating as that of a scorpion's sting. Therefore all the sinners of this world must believe in the true love of God. And those who do not, they must get the first-hand experience of seeing just how big and painful the sins of their rejection of the love of God and their stand against Him are.

God sent the locusts to this earth and made the people pay the wages of their sins in standing against the God of truth with their instinctive thoughts. This price of sin is their suffering from the plague of the locusts.

Verse 4: They were commanded not to harm the grass of the earth, or any green thing, or any tree, but only those men who do not have the seal of God on their foreheads.

When God brings the terrible plague of locusts, He does not forget to show His mercy for those who are sealed by Him. He also commands the locust not to harm the nature.

Verse 5: And they were not given authority to kill them, but to torment them for five months. Their torment was like the torment of a scorpion when it strikes a man.

In Song of Solomon 8:6, God speaks of His love and wrath, saying, *"For love is as strong as death, Jealousy as cruel as the grave; Its flames are flames of fire, A most vehement flame."* Likewise, this plague tells us just how much more terrible the punishment will be for those who reject God's love shown through His gospel of the water and the Spirit. This plague will torment people for five months.

Verse 6: In those days men will seek death and will not find it; they will desire to die, and death will flee from them.

The plague of locusts will bring such great sufferings that people will prefer to die than to live in this pain, and yet they will not be able to die no matter how much they so desire. This plague came because people ignored God. Thinking that the end of the life of the flesh is the end of all, they ignored God, who reigns over both life and death. But through this plague of locusts, God shows us that even death cannot come but by the permission of God.

Verses 7-12: The shape of the locusts was like horses prepared for battle. On their heads were crowns of something like gold, and their faces were like the faces of men. They had hair like women's hair, and their teeth were like lions' teeth. And they had breastplates like breastplates of iron, and the sound of their wings was like the sound of chariots with many horses running into battle. They had tails like scorpions, and there were stings in their tails. Their power was to hurt men five months. And they had as king over them the angel of the bottomless pit, whose name in Hebrew is Abaddon, but in Greek he has the name Apollyon. One woe is past. Behold, still two more woes are coming after these things.

The tails of the locusts from the bottomless pit have the power to hurt people for five months. Although in their appearance they look like women, these locusts are extremely fearsome and cruel beings. This shows how big of a sin men have committed by pursuing women more than God. We must not forget that Satan seeks to make us fall into sexual immorality and tear us away from God by bringing such sins of the lust of the flesh deep into our lives.

Verse 13-15: Then the sixth angel sounded: And I heard a voice from the four horns of the golden altar which is before

God, saying to the sixth angel who had the trumpet, "Release the four angels who are bound at the great river Euphrates." So the four angels, who had been prepared for the hour and day and month and year, were released to kill a third of mankind.

God's judgment of sin, which He had long waited in patience for the sake of the mankind, has finally begun. Now is the time of the plague of war that will kill a third of the mankind at the Euphrates River.

Verse 16: Now the number of the army of the horsemen was two hundred million; I heard the number of them.

Here, the number of the army of the horsemen is spelled out. This war refers to a modern electronic warfare. Though a third of the mankind is killed in this war, the surviving people will still continue to worship idols, stand against God, and refuse to repent of their sins. This shows us just how hardened everyone's heart will be with his/her sins in the end times.

Verse 17: And thus I saw the horses in the vision: those who sat on them had breastplates of fiery red, hyacinth blue, and sulfur yellow; and the heads of the horses were like the heads of lions; and out of their mouths came fire, smoke, and brimstone.

What the Apostle John saw were the terrifyingly destructive weapons of the 21st century, such as tanks, fighter planes, and other modern-day arms.

Verse 18-19: By these three plagues a third of mankind was killed—by the fire and the smoke and the brimstone which came out of their mouths. For their power is in their mouth and in their tails; for their tails are like serpents, having heads; and with them they do harm.

A huge warfare fought with modern weaponry will come at the end times. And a third of the mankind will die from the plague of the fire and the smoke and the brimstone came out of such weaponry.

Verse 20: But the rest of mankind, who were not killed by these plagues, did not repent of the works of their hands, that they should not worship demons, and idols of gold, silver, brass, stone, and wood, which can neither see nor hear nor walk.

Despite these plagues, those who survived the war worshipped idols even more and continued to bow before them, for these people were set to be destroyed.

Verse 21: And they did not repent of their murders or their sorceries or their sexual immorality or their thefts.

This shows us that in the end times, the mankind will never repent of their sins before God. God will therefore judge these sinners, but permit a new and blessed world to the righteous. ⊠

Have Bold Faith in the End Times

< Revelation 9:1-21 >

Of the plagues of the seven trumpets, we have just gone over the plagues of the fifth and the sixth trumpets in the above passage. The fifth trumpet sounds the plague of locusts, and the sixth trumpet announces the plague of war at the Euphrates River.

The first thing we need to find out is whether or not the saints will go through these plagues of the seven trumpets. This is the first thing that we must hear, know, and believe in.

Will the saints find themselves in the middle of the plagues of the seven trumpets? The saints, too, will surely find themselves in the middle of these plagues. A third of the world's forests will be burnt out, a third of the sea and the rivers will turn into blood, and the sun, the moon, and the stars will be struck and lose a third of their light. Although a third of the nature of the whole world will either turn into blood or lose light, this also means that the other two-thirds would still remain.

The Word tells us that we, the saints who have been saved, will find ourselves in the midst of the first six plagues that will destroy a third of the world. However, we do not fear these plague, because as God commanded the locusts to harm "only those men who do not have the seal of God on their foreheads" in His fifth plague, He will protect the saints sealed by Him in the midst of these plagues of the seven trumpets.

But this still means that the saints will go through all these plagues. You and I, as the ones who have been redeemed by believing in the gospel of the water and the Spirit, will find ourselves in the middle of the first plague, which will burn off a third of the world with the fire rained down by God, as well as the second plague, turning a third of the sea into blood with the fall of a blazing mountain, and also the third, which will turn a third of the rivers and springs into wormwood with the fall of a great star from the sky.

We will live through the fourth plague as well, bringing darkness by striking a third of the sun, the moon, and the stars; we will go through the fifth plague also, when locusts harm people with scorpion-like power; and, when the sixth plague brings a world war at the Euphrates River, we will still find ourselves living through the whole plague. No one can do anything about it, because this is the providence of God waiting to be realized. That we will live through these six horrendous plagues is the written fact of God's Word.

Our Lord has redeemed you from all your sins. He has taken away all our sins through His baptism, His blood on the Cross, and His resurrection from death. We received our atonement by believing in what Jesus Christ has done for us. To those who have received the remission of all their sins by believing in the gospel of the water and the Spirit, even as they live through the six horrible plagues, God's special protection will be with them. The Word tells us, in other words, that God's special grace will allow us to live on. We must realize just how worthy our God is to receive all our thanks for giving these special privilege and protection in the midst of the plagues to those of us who are saved.

When the fifth angel sounded his trumpet, John saw "a star fallen from heaven to the earth," which "was given the key to the bottomless pit." The star here refers to an angel; the spiritual meaning of God's stars is that they are all His servants and saints. When this angel who fell to the earth received the key to the bottomless pit and opened it with its key, smoke arose out of the pit like the smoke of a great furnace.

The "bottomless pit" refers to a place that has, quite literally, no bottom or end. Also known as the Abyss, it is a pit of endless depth. When the fifth angel sounded his trumpet, he, having received the key to this bottomless pit, opened the pit with this key. From the pit came out great smoke, as if from a great fire. This smoke from the abyss covered the sun and the sky, darkening the whole world.

Smoke was not the only thing that came out when the bottomless pit was opened; also arising out of the pit with the smoke were locusts. These "locusts" that climbed on to the earth were given power like that of scorpions of the earth, stinging people with their tails. The Bible describes them as having faces that look like the faces of men, their shape like the horses prepared for battle, their teeth like lion's teeth, and their hair like women's hair.

By using the plural word "locusts" instead of the singular locust, the Bible also tells us that we are not talking about just one or even a few locusts, but a huge cloud of locusts, like those that plague the tropical regions from time to time, consuming all the plants on its path of destruction and leaving nothing behind but their roots. Such locusts will arise out of the bottomless pit and torment the people for five months.

Those who will be struck by the fifth of the plagues of the seven trumpets are only those who are not born again. This plague of locusts will pass by the born-again. Our Lord will not bring the plague of locusts on us, for He knows that the born-again, if were they stung by the locusts, will spit out the gospel of salvation, wondering, "why was I saved at all?" We can ascertain this with verse 4: *"They were commanded not to harm the grass of the earth, or any green thing, or any tree, but only those men who do not have the seal of God on their foreheads."*

We know that 144,000 of the people of Israel will be sealed by the seal of God, but the Bible makes no mention of the Gentiles. Does this then mean that we will be tormented by the locusts just like the sinners? Not at all! As 144,000 Israelites are sealed, so are we—that is, the hearts of those who have received the remission of their sins are sealed before God by the Holy Spirit. Do you not have the Holy Spirit in your heart? Because those whose hearts are dwelt by the Holy Spirit have been sealed as the children of God, we, along with 144,000 Israel, will escape from the plague of locusts as His people.

Because the plague of locusts will harm only those who are not born again, people will probably hate and persecute us even more. During the five-month period of the plague, only those who are not born again will be stung by the locusts, tormented in great pain and yet unable to die. The faces of these locusts look like the faces of men, their hair like women's hair, their teeth as ferocious as lions' canine teeth, and their shape like horses prepared for battle, with tails of scorpions. These locusts will threaten everyone in their path with their heads, bite them everywhere with their teeth, and sting them with their poisonous tails, bringing indescribably excruciating pain to their victims.

A single sting will be enough to bring incredible pain, perhaps akin to being shocked by high voltage electricity, which will last for five months. And people will not be able to die, no matter how much they are tormented by the locusts or how much they themselves want to rather die than to live with such suffering. Because the plague of the undead is included in this plague of locusts, there will be no death on the earth for five months. This plague will torment the world for five months.

We have not seen such plagues with our own eyes, but they are nevertheless all planned by God. God tells us that He will bring these plagues on this earth, to the people of this world—that is, to those who do not believe in God, neither in His love and salvation, nor in His gospel of redemption. All these have been planned by God. Because God has planned to do all these things, we must believe that God will indeed bring all of them to pass.

All that we can do is only believing in God, for no man can ever argue about what God plans and does. Even in this situation where people are suffering from the locusts, God will not allow the locusts to bite or sting us and protect us from this plague, for He will commanded them not to harm those who have the seal of God on their foreheads.

Why Does God Bring the Plagues of the Seven Trumpets?

God's purposes in bringing the plagues of the seven trumpets are, for the born-again, to receive glory from them; for those who are yet to be born-again, to give them another chance to be born again; and for every and each one in this world whom God created, to show them that the Lord is God, the Creator of this world, the Savior, and the Judge of all.

First, by bringing suffering to the sinners through the plagues and allowing the righteous to escape from them, God makes the righteous to praise the Lord's greatness, His grace, blessings and glory.

Second, God allows the plagues for His last harvest. He brings the plagues of the seven trumpets to save, for the last time, those who have known the gospel of the water and the Spirit but have not believe in it. It is to give through the Tribulation all whom God created, both the Gentiles and the Israelites, their last chance to return to the Lord and be saved.

Third, as nothing in this world came into its existence without the Lord, Jesus Christ—who came to this earth in the flesh of a man, took upon the sins of the world on Himself with His baptism, and wiped out all sins with His death on the Cross—will show, through these terrifying plagues, His majestic power to those who have not accepted His love and the love of His Father, and not believed in the gospel of salvation. To those who are not born again, He will bring both their suffering in this world and their eternal condemnation to hell in afterlife.

God brings the plagues to this world with such purposes and plans. We must know and believe that these plagues will indeed come. Though we will be especially exempt from the plague of locusts, we must realize that we will nevertheless live through all these plagues. The plague of fire that burns down a third of the nature and the forests of the whole world, the plague of water that turns a third of the sea into blood and a third of the rivers and springs into wormwood, the plague of darkness that darkens the sun, the moon, and the stars, and the plague of war that destroys the world—we will all be right in the middle of all these plagues. But we must also realize that even as we live through such plagues, we will still be filled by ever greater joy.

With the plagues of the seven trumpets, we will lose all

interests in earthly life. Let's assume, for a moment, that volcanoes are erupting everywhere, earthquakes are uprooting the ground, mountains are burning up in smoke, and a third of the sea, the rivers, and springs have turned into blood and wormwood. Dust, smoke, and ashes cover the whole world; the sun rises around 10 in the morning and sets by 4 in the afternoon; and the moon and the stars have lost their light that we can't even see them anymore. Would you feel excited about your earthly life in such a world? Of course not!

This is why the saints will look only at God and place their hope only in His Kingdom at this time. All our hope, 100 percent of it, is found in God alone. Neither would we have any interest in living on this earth anymore, nor could we ever do so, even if we were given all the riches of the world to live for a thousand years. Because all these plagues have been planned and permitted by God, no one can stop them. As God has planned these plagues, so will He allow them.

Why are the plagues planned by God recorded in the Bible? Why did God lift up John to Heaven, let him hear and see all the plagues that would happen with the sounding of the seven trumpets, and make him write down what he heard and saw? In showing what would happen to this world, it was to make the saints place their hope only in the Kingdom of God, to make them preach the gospel on this earth, and to make everyone believe in Jesus Christ.

God has planned and permitted all these things so that through these plagues, people would think again and not suffer in the lake of fire and brimstone burning in hell. God has given them, in other words, a refuge to escape from the plagues. Because God does not want any of us to end up in hell, He wants the sinners' hearts to return to Him through the plagues. I believe that the Word was written and shown to us so that everyone would be led to Heaven.

The plagues that God brings to us, in other words, are not just to make us suffer. God brings these plagues to the world and to us so that we would place our hope not on this earth but in His Kingdom. We must also realize that He permits all these things to make us preach His love of salvation to the countless lost souls who are bound to the eternal flames of hell, so that they, too, may believe in the Word of salvation, be saved, and escape from this Tribulation.

Some kinds of catfish are renowned, among other things, for the pain that they can cause with their stings. If you are not careful in handling these fish, your hand can get stung by their poisonous fins, and then excruciating pain will follow, as if you were shocked by electricity. This pain is nothing compared to the pain of being stung by the locusts.

Now imagine having such pain for five months. It will be the worst pain possible, for even as people would rather die than live in their agony, they will not be able to do so. They will not even be able to kill themselves, as the Word tells us, *"They will desire to die, and death will flee from them."* But because we have become God's children by believing in the gospel of the water and the Spirit, and because we thus have the Holy Spirit in us, God will protect us from this plague so that we would not suffer the pain brought by the locusts. We are protected even amidst such a plague because we have received the remission of sins by believing in the gospel of the water and the Spirit.

We should not regard the Book of Revelation with only fear, but through the Word of Revelation, we must realize how God would give us His special protection from the plagues, how He would be glorified through us, and how we, too, would be clothed in glory by God. By knowing these things, we can be bolder, preach the gospel more, and give even more glory to God when the time of the Tribulation comes. As such, we must live this era without any fear in our hearts, nor any greed for our earthly lives. God teaches us all these things beforehand, so that we would have the courage. We must therefore have the faith of boldness.

God classifies the seven plagues into two categories, the first four catastrophes and the last three woes, and He clarifies that the latter will be far more horrible and terrible in scale and intensity. So, He announces especially, when the fifth plague is over, *"One woe is past. Behold, still two more woes are coming after these things."*

The second woe is the plague of the sixth trumpet: *"saying to the sixth angel who had the trumpet, 'Release the four angels who are bound at the great river Euphrates.' So the four angels, who had been prepared for the hour and day and month and year, were released to kill a third of mankind."* In verse 16, it says, *"the number of the army of the horsemen was two hundred million."* It shows that a massive war will break out, and a third of all mankind will be killed by this warfare. God will bring, in other words, a horrendous plague of war to this earth.

Verses 17-18 say, *"And thus I saw the horses in the vision: those who sat on them had breastplates of fiery red, hyacinth blue, and sulfur yellow; and the heads of the horses were like the heads of lions; and out of their mouths came fire, smoke, and brimstone. By these three plagues a third of mankind was killed—by the fire and the smoke and the brimstone which came out of their mouths."* God will allow that a countless number of people will be actually brought to death to by the massive army of the horsemen. This is the plague that will come with the sounding of the sixth angel's trumpet.

What happens when the seventh trumpet sounds? Resurrection and rapture will come. Up to the sixth trumpet, all the preceding plagues would be brought either as natural disasters or as a war that would directly bring death to people. Because all these are including in the plagues of the seven trumpets and recorded in the Bible, I believe in this Word. But what about you? Do you also believe in this truth?

Have you received the remission of your sins by believing in the gospel of the water and the Spirit? Though included in these plagues, for you to escape from the suffering of the eternal plague and to never enter hell, you must believe in the gospel of the water and the Spirit now, which God gave you to make all your sins disappear, to deliver you from the Great Tribulation, and to give you His Kingdom, the New Heaven and Earth. You must have faith that believes in this gospel. You must know and believe in this gospel. There is no other way to Heaven but by your faith in this gospel of the water and the Spirit.

Jesus told Peter, *"And I will give you the keys of the kingdom of heaven."* The keys of the Kingdom of Heaven are given to us when we believe in Jesus Christ as our Savior—that He came to this earth, that He took upon all the sins of the mankind and of the world on Himself with His baptism received from John the Baptist at the Jordan River, that He carried all these sins and died on the Cross, and that He rose from the dead again. We can enter Heaven and be protected from these plagues only when we have this faith—faith that believes that all our sins have been blotted out.

With the sounding of the seventh trumpet comes the rapture, together with the martyrdom described in Revelation 13. When the Antichrist emerges, we will face our righteous death, martyred for the gospel.

You must realize just how precious and important is this gospel that you know and believe in. Believe in this gospel of the water and the Spirit. You will then be able to overcome the end times in boldness and dwell in the Millennial Kingdom and the New Heaven and Earth promised by the Lord. To worship the Lord as one of the 24 elders standing around Jesus Christ, who is God, there is no other way but to boldly overcome the Tribulation by believing in the gospel of the water and the Spirit.

I hope and pray that you will, as the saints born again by believing in this gospel with your hearts, all overcome the end times and inherit God's Millennial Kingdom and His eternal Heaven. ✉

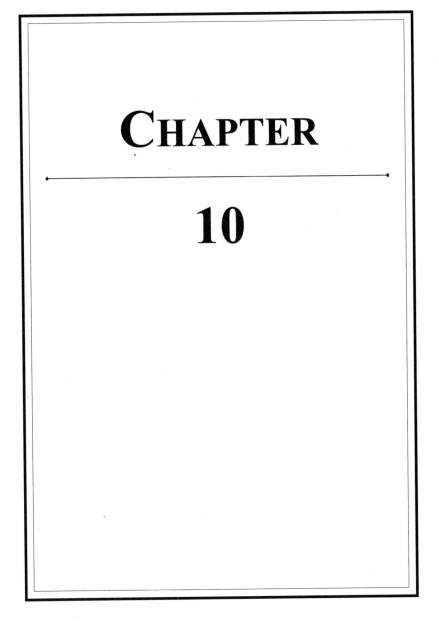

CHAPTER

10

Do You Know When the Time of Rapture Is?

< Revelation 10:1-11 >
"I saw still another mighty angel coming down from heaven, clothed with a cloud. And a rainbow was on his head, his face was like the sun, and his feet like pillars of fire. He had a little book open in his hand. And he set his right foot on the sea and his left foot on the land, and cried with a loud voice, as when a lion roars. When he cried out, seven thunders uttered their voices. Now when the seven thunders uttered their voices, I was about to write; but I heard a voice from heaven saying to me, 'Seal up the things which the seven thunders uttered, and do not write them.' The angel whom I saw standing on the sea and on the land raised up his hand to heaven and swore by Him who lives forever and ever, who created heaven and the things that are in it, the earth and the things that are in it, and the sea and the things that are in it, that there should be delay no longer, but in the days of the sounding of the seventh angel, when he is about to sound, the mystery of God would be finished, as He declared to His servants the prophets. Then the voice which I heard from heaven spoke to me again and said, 'Go, take the little book which is open in the hand of the angel who stands on the sea and on the earth.' So I went to the angel and said to him, 'Give me the little book.' And he said to me, 'Take and eat it; and it will make your stomach bitter, but it will be as sweet as honey in your mouth.' Then I took the little book out of the angel's hand

and ate it, and it was as sweet as honey in my mouth. But when I had eaten it, my stomach became bitter. And he said to me, 'You must prophesy again about many peoples, nations, tongues, and kings.'"

Exegesis

The highlight of this chapter is found in verse 7: *"but in the days of the sounding of the seventh angel, when he is about to sound, the mystery of God would be finished, as He declared to His servants the prophets."* Rapture, in other words, will happen at this time.

Verse 1: I saw still another mighty angel coming down from heaven, clothed with a cloud. And a rainbow was on his head, his face was like the sun, and his feet like pillars of fire.

The mighty angel that appears in chapter 10 is God's executor who bears witness to His works to come. The appearance of this angel is to show just how great God's majesty and power are. It is also to show that God will destroy the seas of this world, and resurrect and rapture the saints up to heaven.

Verse 2-3: He had a little book open in his hand. And he set his right foot on the sea and his left foot on the land, and cried with a loud voice, as when a lion roars. When he cried out, seven thunders uttered their voices.

God does all things according to His plans. He will destroy both the land and the sea when the last day comes. Our Lord, in other words, will destroy the first sea and the first land.

This passage shows God's indomitable will to fulfill all

things as He has planned, and the completion of His works. In the Bible, the number seven carries the meaning of completion. God used this number when He completed all His works and rested. Likewise, this passage tells us that God will, in the end times, deliver many from their destruction, but destroy this world for sure, on the other hand.

Verse 4: Now when the seven thunders uttered their voices, I was about to write; but I heard a voice from heaven saying to me, "Seal up the things which the seven thunders uttered, and do not write them."

God commanded John not to record what the seven thunders uttered, to hide the rapture of the saints from the unsaved. At times, God hides His works from the unbelievers, because they, as the enemies of God, hates and persecutes His saints.

In Noah's time also, when God destroyed the world with water, He revealed the coming flood only to Noah. Even as now, God preaches the gospel of the water and the Spirit to all over the world, and gives the Kingdom of Heaven to those who believe in it. But apart from these who have the true faith, He has not revealed to anyone else when the rapture is coming. For the righteous, God has created a new world in His Kingdom, and He desires to live in it with them.

Verse 5-6: The angel whom I saw standing on the sea and on the land raised up his hand to heaven and swore by Him who lives forever and ever, who created heaven and the things that are in it, the earth and the things that are in it, and the sea and the things that are in it, that there should be delay no longer;

All these things can be sworn by the name of God, as the

last vow in everything is taken not by one's own name, but by the name of someone greater. As such, God is the last guarantor for both the saints of the last times and all those who have already become His saints.

Here, the mighty angel swears by the Almighty that the rapture will come for certainty. This vow tells us that God will create the New Heaven and Earth and live with His saints in this new world. It shows that God does not delay His creation of the new world, but will shortly complete it for His saints.

Verse 7: but in the days of the sounding of the seventh angel, when he is about to sound, the mystery of God would be finished, as He declared to His servants the prophets.

This verse tells us that when the last seventh trumpet sounds in the final tribulations, all the saints will be raptured. What people on this earth wonder the most is when the rapture of the saints will come.

Revelation 10:7 tells us, *"but in the days of the sounding of the seventh angel, when he is about to sound, the mystery of God would be finished, as He declared to His servants the prophets."* What does the phrase *"the mystery of God would be finished, as He declared to His servants the prophets"* mean here? It means that just as the gospel of the water and the Spirit is the true gospel, and as whoever believes in it receives atonement and the Holy Spirit into his/her heart, the rapture of the saints will likewise surely come when the seventh trumpet sounds.

After the plague of the sixth of the seven trumpets is over, the saints will be martyred as the Antichrist, having made his appearance in the world and established his dominion over it, demands everyone to receive the mark of the Beast. Shortly after, when the seventh angel sounds his trumpet, both the martyred and the surviving saints who defended their faith will be resurrected and raptured simultaneously. Then the plagues of the seven bowls, the last plague on the mankind, will begin. By this time, the saints would no longer be on the earth, but in heaven with the Lord after their rapture. The saints must know that their rapture will happen when the seventh angel sounds the last trumpet.

The Apostle Paul, too, tells us in 1 Thessalonians 4 that the Lord will descend from heaven with the trumpet of an archangel. Many Christians think that the Lord will come down to this earth when the rapture happens, but this is not the case. When the rapture happens, our Lord does not come down onto this earth, but to the air. He completes the rapture, in other words, by lifting the saints up to and receiving them in the air.

As such, these Christians who mistakenly think that the Lord would come down to this earth when the rapture of the true saints comes should discard their wrong understanding, and they should know the truth and believe in it properly by remembering that the rapture of the saints will come when the seventh angel sounds his trumpet.

"The mystery of God would be finished, as He declared to His servants the prophets." You must realize that the mystery of God here refers to the rapture of the saints that will come with the sounding of the plague of the seventh trumpet. Now, in short, God destroys the first world, and founds the second world. This is for God to dwell and live with those who, while on this earth, have been born again by believing in the gospel of the water and the Spirit, and also to faithfully fulfill all the promises that the Almighty has made to His people. This is the will of God, the Creator of the whole universe, which He set in Himself for the saints.

When the angel sounds the seventh trumpet, the plagues

of the seven trumpets will be over, and the final plagues of the seven bowls will be ushered in. The Word tells us, *"in the days of the sounding of the seventh angel, when he is about to sound, the mystery of God would be finished, as He declared to His servants the prophets."* The mystery of God here is that the saints will be raptured with the sounding of the seventh angel's trumpet.

The saints are now living on this earth, but for them to live in a new, better world, they must be martyred, resurrected, and raptured. Only then will they be invited to the marriage supper of the Lamb with the Lord and reign with Him for a thousand years. After this millennium, the Antichrist, Satan, and all his followers will receive the eternal judgment of God. And from then on, the saints will be blessed to live with the Lord in His Heaven of eternal blessings. This is the mystery of God. We can only thank God for having revealed this mystery to those of us who have the true faith. God tells us that He will fulfill all these promises when the seventh angel sounds his trumpet.

Verse 8: Then the voice which I heard from heaven spoke to me again and said, "Go, take the little book which is open in the hand of the angel who stands on the sea and on the earth."

God tells us that the saints and the servants of God must continue to preach the gospel of the water and the Spirit until the last day comes. This gospel is about the truth of the remission of sins, martyrdom, resurrection, rapture, and the marriage supper of the Lamb. For the saints and God's servants to preach the gospel until the end, they must first feed on the Word of God with their faith before the advent of the Great Tribulation. God demands two kinds of faith from us. The first is the faith to be born again, and the second is the faith to embrace martyrdom to defend our true faith.

Verse 9: So I went to the angel and said to him, "Give me the little book." And he said to me, "Take and eat it; and it will make your stomach bitter, but it will be as sweet as honey in your mouth."

The saints and the servants of God must first feed on the Word of God and then spread it to many others. This verse teaches us that although the hearts of those who believe in the Word of God are sweetened, preaching this Word of faith to the lost souls is not such an easy task, accompanied by sacrifices. This is what God is showing us here.

Verse 10: Then I took the little book out of the angel's hand and ate it, and it was as sweet as honey in my mouth. But when I had eaten it, my stomach became bitter.

When John ate the Word of God in faith, his heart was filled with joy. But in preaching the truth testified by the Word of God to those who do not believe in the truth, John faced many hardships.

Verse 11: And he said to me, "You must prophesy again about many peoples, nations, tongues, and kings."

The saints must prophesy again to everyone that God's blessings come through the gospel of the water and the Spirit. They must prophesy again that the purpose of our Lord for this world in the end times is for everyone to come into God's blessings by believing in the gospel of the water and the Spirit. What God commanded John to prophesy is to preach the Word of truth—that a new world is coming soon, brought by God, and that whoever wants to enter it must be justified by believing in the gospel of the water and the Spirit. For this work, the saints and the servants of God must preach the Word of God from the beginning all over again, so that everyone in this world will have the faith that will allow them to enter and live in the Kingdom of our Lord. ✉

Do You Know When the Rapture of the Saints Will Occur?

< Revelation 10:1-11 >

Let us now turn our attention to the issue of when the rapture will happen. There are many passages in the Bible that are talking about the rapture. The New Testament has many passages that discuss it, and so does the Old Testament, where we can find, for instance, Elijah who ascended to heaven in a chariot of fire, and Enoch who walked with God and was taken away by Him. As can be seen, the Bible speaks of the rapture in many places. Rapture means 'to lift up.' It refers to God's lifting up His people to heaven by His power.

However, what is the most puzzling of the Bible is also this question of rapture. When will God lift up His people? This question on the rapture's time is one of the most frequently asked questions within Christianity.

Let us turn to 1 Thessalonians 4:14-17 and see what God has told us through the Apostle Paul: *"For if we believe that Jesus died and rose again, even so God will bring with Him those who sleep in Jesus. For this we say to you by the word of the Lord, that we who are alive and remain until the coming of the Lord will by no means precede those who are asleep. For the Lord Himself will descend from heaven with a shout, with the voice of an archangel, and with the trumpet of God. And the dead in Christ will rise first. Then we who are alive and remain shall be caught up together with them in the clouds to meet the Lord in the air. And thus we shall always be with the Lord."*

In Jude 1:14, God also tells us, *"Now Enoch, the seventh from Adam, prophesied about these men also, saying, 'Behold, the Lord comes with ten thousands of His saints.'"* The saints, in other words, will be lifted up to the air by our God with the sounding of the archangel's trumpet, remain in the air for a while, and then descend on earth again with our Lord. This is the biblically sound description of rapture.

The reason why we looked at the above passages beforehand is because Revelation 10 tells us when the rapture will come. As I mentioned before, the core passage of this chapter is found in verse 7, *"but in the days of the sounding of the seventh angel, when he is about to sound, the mystery of God would be finished, as He declared to His servants the prophets."* This verse is the key to answer all our questions and queries about the rapture, for it tells us when the rapture will happen.

God sends a mighty angel to John in vision, and He shows what He will do through this angel by having him act as if the Lord had come to this earth. This angel, raising his hand to heaven, *"swore by Him who lives forever and ever, who created heaven and the things that are in it, the earth and the things that are in it, and the sea and the things that are in it, that there should be delay no longer."* That there should be no more delay means that there is no longer any reason to delay anymore. It means "there is no time." That there is no time, in turn, means that on the day of the sounding of the seventh angel, the mystery of God will be fulfilled as God declared to His servants the prophets.

Of the plagues of the seven trumpets, when the last

trumpet sounds, the world will enter into the plagues of the seven bowls. We must realize that by then, there will no longer be any time remaining for this world. As such, the Word of God in verse 7, that on the day of *"the sounding of the seventh angel, when he is about to sound, the mystery of God would be finished, as He declared to His servants the prophets,"* refers to the time of rapture. Elsewhere, Paul, too, said that the rapture would happen with the voice of an archangel and the sounding of God's trumpet. This is what Paul had in mind, and this is the starting point for all other references of the Bible to rapture as well.

"But in the days of the sounding of the seventh angel, when he is about to sound, the mystery of God would be finished, as He declared to His servants the prophets." This Word tells us that the rapture of the saints will happen when the seventh angel sounds his trumpet, lifting them up to the air. When the servants of God spread of the gospel of the water and the Spirit to the lost souls, the Holy Spirit actually descended on the hearts of the believers who accepted the true gospel, and they actually became the children of God. It is all the same to us that the rapture, the mystery of God, will also turn into reality, lifting up the saints to the air.

After this, God will completely destroy this world by pouring on it the last plagues of the seven bowls, bring the Kingdom of God on this earth where we will reign with Christ for a thousand years, and then move us to the New Heaven and Earth where we will live forever.

After telling John about the coming rapture, God commanded him to eat the little book and prophesy again. The most important lesson that the servants of God must teach the saints living in these last days is of the event of rapture and its exact time. They should teach these lessons in biblically sound terms. They must also preach the gospel of the water and the Spirit accurately. These are what the servants of God and His saints, who are living through the end times, must do. God has thus entrusted the saints with these works, as well as revealing His mystery to them. God tells us that He will not delay, but fulfill His works without fail. When the time comes, God will fulfill everything into reality.

In chapter 11, there appear two olive trees, that is, two prophets. These two servants of God, symbolized as the two olive trees, will be killed by the Antichrist in their fight against him, but they will be raised from the dead again and be raptured in three and a half days. In other words, God shows us, on different occasions, that that the rapture will happen when the saints are martyred in this time of the Antichrist.

What we must know beforehand is that the saints will live through the Great Tribulation, remaining on this earth until the first six plagues of the seven trumpets' plagues come to pass. And God will protect the saints from these plagues of the seven trumpets—that is, God will protect them until the sixth plague, but the Antichrist will finally kill them at the height of his tyranny as he makes his last-ditch struggle against God. The death that the saints will embrace at this time is their martyrdom. Because they will die the righteous death to defend their faith, we call this "martyrdom." We must therefore believe that the rapture will come after this martyrdom, and also preach this faith to others.

Many people have been greatly confused about whether the rapture will happen before or after the Great Tribulation. People in the old days used to think that Christ will return after the Tribulation, and that the saints will be lifted up with this second coming of Jesus. But nowadays, most Christians believe that the rapture will come before the Great Tribulation.

They think that they will have nothing to do with the plagues of the seven trumpets or of the seven bowls, and that they will be lifted up when they are going about their everyday, normal, and fine lives. But we must not be deceived by this false teaching. These people are hugely mistaken in their knowledge and understanding of the time of rapture; as the end times get nearer and nearer, their piety will slacken and their faith will disappear.

When I tell you that the rapture will come in the middle of the Great Tribulation, I am not saying this to make you become even more pious. I just want you to have clear understanding on the time of the rapture and flee from the false teaching of the pre-tribulation rapture, for in verse 7 God tells us in detail: *"in the days of the sounding of the seventh angel, when he is about to sound, the mystery of God would be finished, as He declared to His servants the prophets."* When the plagues of the seven bowls are poured, unlike the preceding plagues of the seven trumpets, they will be poured one after another continuously. We, the saints, must realize this.

Revelation 16:1-2 tells us, *"Then I heard a loud voice from the temple saying to the seven angels, 'Go and pour out the bowls of the wrath of God on the earth.' So the first went and poured out his bowl upon the earth, and a foul and loathsome sore came upon the men who had the mark of the beast and those who worshiped his image."* The pouring of the remaining bowls in a row then follows this first plague, as if the plagues are in an auto-pilot mode, with the seven angels emptying their bowls one after another, with no sounding of trumpets nor anything else. By pouring the seven bowls in a row, in other words, God will completely destroy this world. Why? Because everything will end with the pouring of the plagues of the seven bowls, which, together, are all included in the plague of the seventh trumpet.

When the plagues of the seven trumpets are brought, there are at least some pauses between one plague and the next, but with the plagues of the seven bowls, there is no such a pause. Because these plagues of the seven bowls are reserved for the final moment, after the plagues of the seven trumpets are brought in their order, when the last trumpet finally sounds, the world shifts onto a whole new level where everything will end.

This is why Revelation 11:15-18 record: *"Then the seventh angel sounded: And there were loud voices in heaven, saying, 'The kingdoms of this world have become the kingdoms of our Lord and of His Christ, and He shall reign forever and ever!' And the twenty-four elders who sat before God on their thrones fell on their faces and worshiped God, saying: 'We give You thanks, O Lord God Almighty, The One who is and who was and who is to come, Because You have taken Your great power and reigned. The nations were angry, and Your wrath has come, And the time of the dead, that they should be judged, And that You should reward Your servants the prophets and the saints, And those who fear Your name, small and great, And should destroy those who destroy the earth.'"*

It is said here that when the seventh angel sounded his trumpet, loud voices were heard, saying, *"The kingdoms of this world have become the kingdoms of our Lord and of His Christ, and He shall reign forever and ever!"* But there is no mention of a plague. Why? Because immediately following the sounding of the seventh trumpet was not the seventh plague, but the rapture. God will resurrect and lift up the saints, both those still living on the earth and those who are already asleep, and when their rapture is over, He will pour the plagues of the seven bowls and completely destroy the world.

If we want to find out when exactly our rapture will

happen, we only have to look at the Word of God found in Revelation 10:7. The mystery of God will most certainly be finished at this time, as He declared to His servants the prophets. The mystery of God here refers to the rapture—not of anyone, but of the saints.

Here, I present another passage for your clear understanding and correct faith. Again, the Bible says, *"Behold, I tell you a mystery: We shall not all sleep, but we shall all be changed—in a moment, in the twinkling of an eye, at the last trumpet. For the trumpet will sound, and the dead will be raised incorruptible, and we shall be changed (1 Corinthians 15:51-52)."* Doesn't the Bible clearly say that the resurrection of the saints will occur at the last trumpet? When the trumpet sounds, the dead in Christ will be raised incorruptible, and we also shall be changed in a moment to be raptured.

The angel that appears in chapter 11 is a mighty angel sent by God, different from the other angels who sound the first six trumpets. When we look at what this mighty angel does, he appears so much like God that we might even mistake him for God: *"And a rainbow was on his head, his face was like the sun, and his feet like pillars of fire. He had a little book open in his hand. And he set his right foot on the sea and his left foot on the land, and cried with a loud voice, as when a lion roars. When he cried out, seven thunders uttered their voices."*

We might mistake this angel for God, in other words, because this mighty angel executes all the things that Jesus Christ is to do, on His behalf. This tells us that God will do all these things through this mighty angel. It tells us that this angel, setting his foot on the sea and the land, will destroy them both, and that when the thunders come, he will complete everything that God has planned in Jesus Christ since the very beginning of the creation of the universe and the mankind.

Of the plagues of the seven trumpets, we the saints will live through and experience the first six plagues, and we will continue to preach the gospel until then. God told John to take and eat the little book and to prophesy again, but this Word is also directed at you and me—that is, until the final day, we must continue in our faith and live on. As our rapture will come true when the seventh trumpet sounds, we must recognize this truth of our rapture, hold fast to it in faith, and hear the Word and preach the gospel until this day comes.

Up until the seventh trumpet sounds, the Antichrist will be active amidst this plague, the saints will be martyred with it, and they will be raptured shortly thereafter. As such, even in this time, when the faith of many believers in Jesus is shaken to its core and losing its vitality, you and I must still live by faith. We must believe, in other words, that our rapture will come exactly after the sounding of the seventh trumpet, and live our lives by this faith.

We will soon see the plagues of the seven trumpets with our own eyes. We will see and count these plagues, from the very first to the sixth, with our own eyes. After this, when we the saints intuitively feel that the time for our martyrdom has come, we will in fact be martyred accordingly. This is neither a fairy tale nor a science-fiction. Nor is it something that you can believe or not at your own whims. This is what will actually happen to you and me.

Revelation 10:7, the verse that shows the rapture most clearly from the Book of Revelation, tells us that the rapture of the saints will come with the sounding of the seventh trumpet, and that the world will end with the plagues of the seven bowls. After lifting up the saints, God will bring the whole world to its demise. When all the saints are raptured, they will praise the Lord in the air. But on this earth, the plagues of the seven bowls will be poured, completely destroying the world, and when these plagues of the seven bowls end, the saints will descend on the renewed earth with the Lord. And the Millennial Kingdom, the Kingdom of Christ, will then be built on this earth.

Today's Christians mostly support the pre-tribulation rapture, and nowadays some of them have gone as far as to advocate even amillennialism—that is, that there is no such thing as the Millennial Kingdom. Is the Millennial Kingdom not a reality then? There are many who believe so in these days. Some of them, who minister in some of the biggest churches in Korea, even declare that everything in Revelation, from the mark of 666 to the rapture, is not factual but only symbolic. As our Lord once asked, "when the Son of Man comes, will He really find faith on the earth?" it surely is very hard to find true believers in these end times.

But the Lord tells us that our rapture will indeed happen as reality. When we are raptured, we will meet the Lord in the air and praise Him, be taken care of and comforted by Him, and return to this earth again with Him. Coming down to the Millennial Kingdom, we will live new lives in our resurrected and transformed bodies, in the midst of everything that is renewed, from our changed lives to the changed blessings. We will live in such glory clothed by God. You and I must live with this faith and this hope. And when the Millennial Kingdom is over, we will enter the New Heaven and Earth, and reign with Christ forever in eternal honor and glory.

When we enter the Millennial Kingdom and the New Heaven and Earth, all the angels will be our servants. To whom will all spiritual beings, the whole world created by God and Jesus Christ, and everything in it belong? They will all be ours. This is why the Bible says that the ones who will inherit all things are the saints. Because you and I are the saints who were born again by the gospel of the water and the Spirit, we are the heirs of God and joint heirs with Christ, to whom all things will be inherited. As such, you and I must overcome the hardships on this earth by faith, and persevere by looking at the day of our inheritance. We must also have the battling faith as the elite troops of God.

God has told us that all these things will soon be fulfilled without any delay. They will, in other words, most certainly be fulfilled shortly. Some may then wonder why God did not tell us about it in more detail. The answer to this question is that hiding the works of God is His wisdom (Proverbs 25:2, Luke 10:21).

Were God's plan written down in detail, it would be a cause for much agitation in this world. The saints will then not be able to live until the last day. Almost all the saints will be killed by the unbelievers, and not a single saint will survive. If every detail about the end times is written in the Bible, those who are not born again by the water and the Spirit will slaughter all the born-again believers. Having hidden His purposes, God reveals them to only those who deserve, and otherwise keeps them as mysteries from the rest—this is the wisdom of God. God has revealed His plan to us and allowed us to know it, only because it is so necessary to the saints of this era.

That the born-again churches of God are now speaking of the end times in detail means that the last days are nearing us. Because the era of the Tribulation is imminent, the Word of Revelation is preached so that the saints would have the proper knowledge of the end times to persevere through and overcome this nearing Tribulation. Even the born-again, if they face the Tribulation without any knowledge, will not know what to do and be thrown into great confusion when the Tribulation actually arrives. This confusion will be even greater for those who rely only on their own individual faith.

We can imagine that many unprepared souls, in their ignorance and confusion, will start to go off on the wrong track when the end time comes. "Did God tell you something?" "Didn't He show you a vision when you were praying?" Many will be agitated to seek visions from God, and many will claim to have seen such visions in the end times. "Didn't God tell you something when you were praying?" If the saints remain ignorant, this will be quite a common question raised among the saints of the end times.

But God never works in such a way, for He has already commanded us, *"He who has an ear, let him hear what the Spirit says to the churches."* The saint, in other words, must hear only what the Holy Spirit says through the churches. Because the Holy Spirit, guaranteeing the Word of God, testifies only what is true and correct, when the plagues ringing the end of the world come, we the saints will not be caught by surprise from the following tribulations, but live by faith—for by then we would have already heard the Word of truth and carved it into our hearts in faith beforehand.

This is why John revealed to us what will happen in the future beforehand, and why the servants of God preach the truth within the bounds of this written Word. Prophesying is none other than knowing and preaching what will come from the written Word of God; claiming to have seen visions in dreams or prayers is not!

Never forget that our rapture will indeed come, and that we are the saints of God. Nor forget that you have now become a saint, who will be with Christ in the air when your rapture comes, who will come down onto the renewed earth again to live for a thousand years, and who will live forever in the New Heaven and Earth. If you hear people talking about pre-tribulation rapture or post-tribulation rapture, or claiming that there is no Millennial Kingdom at all, tell them the truth by referring to the passage that we have been discussing here. You should also refer them to 1 Thessalonians 4 and 1 Corinthians 15, and tell them that the Lord will descend with the voice of an archangel and the sounding of the last trumpet, and lift up the saints to the air to be with Him. Only when you believe in this rapture can you defend your faith.

To be raptured, there must be martyrdom by faith and the resurrection of the body. Because the rapture will come simultaneous to the resurrection, as soon as we are resurrected, we will be raptured and lifted up to the air. The rapture and the resurrection, therefore, are the same. Taking part in the first resurrection means to live with the Lord in the Millennial Kingdom. Being raptured, too, means to live with the Lord for a thousand years on this earth.

Why, then, will we be raptured? Because God will destroy everything on this earth by pouring the plagues of the seven bowls—that is, He will rapture the saints beforehand in order to deliver His children from these plagues of termination. To separate the saints from the sinners, and to show their different destinations, He will rapture the saints. As such, we must believe in all these things—in our rapture, in our resurrection, and in our martyrdom.

To some, the gospel of the water and the Spirit is revealed in detail, while to others, it remains as a completely hidden secret. Likewise, the saints' martyrdom, resurrection, rapture, and their reign over the Millennial Kingdom and the New Heaven and Earth are all God's secrets. Only to the born-again has God revealed and shown these secrets. And by making them believe in these secrets He has enabled them to live through the end times and overcome all their hardships with their hope in the rapture and the Kingdom of Heaven.

You and I must have this kind of faith. Without this kind of faith—that is, without believing that we will be raptured, that we will live in the New Heaven and Earth, that the Lord will raise us from the dead when we are slaughtered by the Antichrist, rapture us, allow us to dwell in the air, and then return us to this earth to reign with Him for a thousand years—we will not be able to persevere through the difficult and depressing life of this last era.

The saints have a beautiful dream, and no one else but our Lord can make this dream come true. Without this hope, we will live only in sadness and suffering in this depressing world.

Paul told Timothy to keep the beautiful thing that was entrusted to him. This gospel is beautiful; so are our martyrdom, resurrection and rapture; and so is living in the Millennial Kingdom and the New Heaven and Earth. These are all good and beautiful things. They belong only to the saints, and they are all realizable faith and hope, not illusions or imaginations. These are our hope and faith given by the Lord. With faith in all these, we must live this era hoping for the day when the Millennial Kingdom and the New Heaven and Earth will be brought to us.

Those who will be raptured are none other than you and I. We must live by faith, waiting for the day when we will be raptured to stand before the Lord and reign in the Millennial Kingdom and the New Heaven and Earth.

God tells us that the One who is to come will soon come. The plagues that will come during the first half of the seven-year period of the Great Tribulation are quite mild and short-lasting. Were the plagues to continue throughout the seven years of the Great Tribulation, how could anyone stand them? The early plagues are short, and as time gets nearer to the final end, there will be far more to see. When the plague of the seventh trumpet comes, it will reach a spectacular proportion.

When Satan tries to shake the saints' faith, he will make examples out of a few church leaders by murdering them. Satan might say, "I'll spare your life if you deny God!" Even if the world were to turn better, one would still think twice about Satan's offer. Who in his right mind, then, would deny the Lord when he knows very well that the Lord would pour down the plagues of the seven bowls, and that he would go through all the sufferings brought by these plagues? The saints who know the end of the world neither deny the Lord nor betray their faith. Also, because in our hearts is the Holy Spirit, He will give us the courage.

Because all God's plans will be quickly fulfilled in the end times, there will be no room for boredom. When the short-lasting plagues are over, there will be the resurrection, and after this will come the rapture, which will lift us up to the air. Imagine our bodies of the flesh transformed into spiritual bodies, praising the Lord. In the Kingdom of God, we can enjoy a whole different world, beautiful and elegant, the likes of which we have never experienced before on this earth. As spiritual bodies are free from the limitations of time and space, we would live in a wondrous and marvelous world where we can go anywhere we want.

I give my true thanks to God for giving us such great blessings. I thank God for revealing to us in detail, through His Word, the Great Tribulation, its plagues, our martyrdom, resurrection and rapture. And I pray that our hearts will always live by knowing this last era and believing in it. ✉

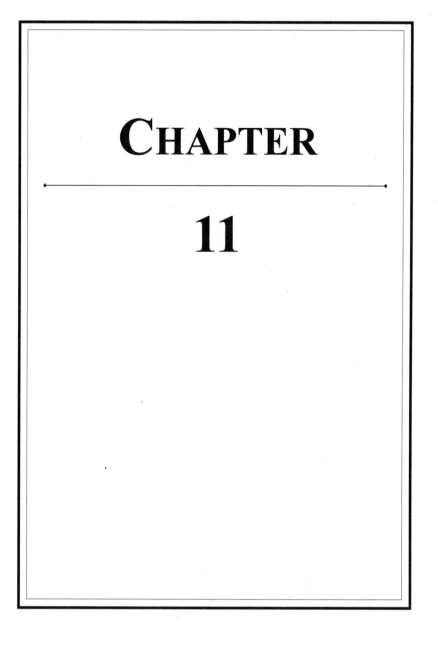

CHAPTER

11

Who Are the Two Olive Trees and The Two Prophets?

< Revelation 11:1-19 >

"Then I was given a reed like a measuring rod. And the angel stood, saying, 'Rise and measure the temple of God, the altar, and those who worship there. But leave out the court which is outside the temple, and do not measure it, for it has been given to the Gentiles. And they will tread the holy city underfoot for forty-two months. And I will give power to my two witnesses, and they will prophesy one thousand two hundred and sixty days, clothed in sackcloth.' These are the two olive trees and the two lampstands standing before the God of the earth. And if anyone wants to harm them, fire proceeds from their mouth and devours their enemies. And if anyone wants to harm them, he must be killed in this manner. These have power to shut heaven, so that no rain falls in the days of their prophecy; and they have power over waters to turn them to blood, and to strike the earth with all plagues, as often as they desire. When they finish their testimony, the beast that ascends out of the bottomless pit will make war against them, overcome them, and kill them. And their dead bodies will lie in the street of the great city which spiritually is called Sodom and Egypt, where also our Lord was crucified. Then those from the peoples, tribes, tongues, and nations will see their dead bodies three-and-a-half days, and not allow their dead bodies to be put into graves. And those who dwell on the earth will rejoice over them, make merry, and send gifts to one another, because these two prophets tormented those who dwell on the earth. Now after the three-and-a-half days the breath of life from God entered them, and they stood on their feet, and great fear fell on those who saw them. And they heard a loud voice from heaven saying to them, 'Come up here.' And they ascended to heaven in a cloud, and their enemies saw them. In the same hour there was a great earthquake, and a tenth of the city fell. In the earthquake seven thousand people were killed, and the rest were afraid and gave glory to the God of heaven. The second woe is past. Behold, the third woe is coming quickly. Then the seventh angel sounded: And there were loud voices in heaven, saying, 'The kingdoms of this world have become the kingdoms of our Lord and of His Christ, and He shall reign forever and ever!' And the twenty-four elders who sat before God on their thrones fell on their faces and worshiped God, saying:

'We give You thanks, O Lord God Almighty,
The One who is and who was and who is to come,
Because You have taken Your great power and reigned.
The nations were angry, and Your wrath has come,
And the time of the dead, that they should be judged,
And that You should reward Your servants the prophets and the saints,
And those who fear Your name, small and great,
And should destroy those who destroy the earth.'

Then the temple of God was opened in heaven, and the ark of His covenant was seen in His temple. And there were lightnings, noises, thunderings, an earthquake, and great hail."

The Word of Revelation 11 is very important to us, as is all the Word of God. To destroy the world, there is a critical work that God needs to do beforehand. This is harvesting the people of Israel for the last time. God also has another work to do for both the Israelites and the Gentiles, and this is to make them participate in the first resurrection and the rapture by having them martyred.

As the Bible provides an overall account on these issues, we need to find out how God's salvation of the remission of sin is fulfilled in the New Testament. The Scripture speaks to us on these topics because if we do not examine them closely, we would get confused about the saints, the servants of God, and the people of Israel appearing in the Book of Revelation.

Exegesis

Verse 1: Then I was given a reed like a measuring rod. And the angel stood, saying, "Rise and measure the temple of God, the altar, and those who worship there."

This tells us that the work of saving the Israelites from sin by the grace of God is now set to begin. "Measuring" here means that God will personally intervene to save the people of Israel from their sins in the end times.

In the main passage of chapter 11, we must place our focus on the salvation of the Israelites from sin. This Word tells us that the gospel of the water and the Spirit will be spread to the people of Israel from then on, signifying the beginning of God's work that turns the Israelites into God's people delivered from all their sins through the grace of salvation given by Jesus Christ. God recorded Revelation 11 to also give His remission of sin to the Israelites in the end times. The "measuring" in verses 1 and 2 means setting the standard for all things. The purpose of God in measuring His Temple is to find out, having already planned to save the Israelites, whether or not their hearts are ready to receive their salvation. And if their hearts are not ready, then it is to make them ready, so that their hearts may stand upright.

Verse 2: "But leave out the court which is outside the temple, and do not measure it, for it has been given to the Gentiles. And they will tread the holy city underfoot for forty-two months."

God gave Satan power to trample on the Gentiles for three and a half years. Therefore, all the Gentiles must receive into their hearts the gospel of the water and the Spirit, the Word of redemption, as soon as possible within the first three and a half years of the seven-year period of the Great Tribulation. The history of this world will end as the Great Tribulation passes its midpoint and enters into its second half-period. Soon, the time will come in the near future when all the Gentiles, as well as the saints who have already been saved from all their sins, will be trampled on by Satan.

The Gentiles thus must receive the remission of their sins and prepare their faith of martyrdom before the first three and a half years of the Tribulation pass by them. At this time, the people of Israel will also suffer under the fearful Tribulation during the first three and a half years. But they will also accept the fact that Jesus is their Savior at this time. In the end, the people of Israel will receive their salvation from all their sins during the first three and a half years of the Great Tribulation. We must realize that God will allow the remission of sin to the Israelites even during the period of the Great Tribulation.

Verse 3: "And I will give power to my two witnesses, and they will prophesy one thousand two hundred and sixty days, clothed in sackcloth."

God will especially raise two witnesses as His servants for the people of Israel. The two prophets that God will raise for the Israelites are given twice as great power as that of the old prophets, and through the words of their testimony, God will begin to work among the people of Israel so that they would accept Jesus Christ as their Savior. Through the works of these two prophets, many Israelites will become the truly born-again people of God.

By having the two prophet, whom God would send in the end times to save the Israelites from their sins, perform miracles and wonders, He will make the Israelites, who would then be led by these prophets, return to Christ and believe in Him as their Savior. These two prophets will feed the Word of God to the people of Israel for 1,260 days during Great Tribulation's first three and a half years. By giving the gospel of the water and the Spirit to the Israelites and making them believe in it, God will allow them the same salvation that had saved the Gentiles of the New Testament's times from all theirs sins through faith.

Verse 4: These are the two olive trees and the two lampstands standing before the God of the earth.

The "two olive trees" here refer to the two prophets of God (Revelation 11:10). The "two lampstands," on the other hand, refer to God's Church that He founded among the Gentiles, and the Church that He permitted to the people of Israel. God has built His Church among both the Jews and us the Gentiles, and He will continue to do His work of saving souls from sin until the very last day.

By the "two olive trees" and the "two lampstands," God tells us that just as He had raised up His prophets in the Old Testament's times to save the Israelites from their sins and had worked through these prophets by speaking to them, when the end times come, He will also raise up from the people of Israel two prophets who would preach His Word, and lead the Israelites to Jesus through these prophets.

The Israelites have failed to take seriously the servants of God who are of the Gentile origin, and they do not listen to what these servants of God have to say to them. As they know everything about the sacrificial system and the prophecies of the Old Testament, the end times' prophets of God need to be raised from their own people of Israel. The Israelites are so well-versed in the Scripture that they might as well recite the whole Torah even as they are running. This is why they never believe in what the Gentile servants of God say to them.

But God's servants, hearing the gospel of the water and the Spirit that you and I are now preaching, will rise from their own people. When the believers in the gospel of the water and the Spirit rise from their own, and from them rise the two prophets established by God who would explain and preach the Word of God to them, only then will the Israelites come to believe.

The people of Israel will know that these two witnesses are the prophets sent and raised by God Himself to save them from their sins in the end times. These prophets will exercise their mighty power, just as the servants of God in the Old Testament, whom the Israelites know well and believe in, had exercised before. The Israelites will therefore see with their own eyes the powerful wonders that two witnesses would actually perform. From this, the people of Israel will return to Jesus Christ and believe in the Lord. When they recognize

Jesus Christ as the Son of God and their Savior, just as we do, they will have the same faith as ours—that is, they, too, will be saved by believing in the gospel of the water and the Spirit.

These two witnesses will explain the Word of God and feed it to the people of Israel for 1,260 days during the Great Tribulation of seven years. Just as you and I, who are the Gentiles of the New Testament's times, have been saved by believing in the gospel of the water and the Spirit, God will also allow the Israelites to be saved in the end times by believing in this gospel of the water and the Spirit.

As verse 4 tells us, *"these are the two olive trees and the two lampstands standing before the God of the earth,"* the Bible calls these two witnesses as "the two olive trees." The two olive trees refer to the two prophets of the end times. In verse 10, it is written, *"And those who dwell on the earth will rejoice over them, make merry, and send gifts to one another, because these two prophets tormented those who dwell on the earth."* Here, we must solve this Word by focusing on who the two olive trees are.

Olive trees were used in the age of the Old Testament to consecrate the furnishings of the sanctuary and the altar in the Temple of God by anointing them with their oil. This olive oil was used for other purposes as well, such as in lighting the Temple's lamps. They had to use only the pure olive oil in the Temple. God did not allow whatever oil to be used in His Temple, but He made sure that only the olive oil would be used. Thus, we have to know that the olive tree, as well as the fig tree, represents the people of Israel.

There are many interpretations on these two olive trees and two lampstands. Some people even claim that they themselves are the olive trees. But the two olive trees refer to the anointed ones. In the Old Testament's times, people were anointed when they were established as a prophet, a king, or a priest. When one was thus anointed, the Holy Spirit descended on him/her. As such, the olive tree refers to Jesus Christ who was conceived by the Holy Spirit (Romans 11:24). But people have many misunderstandings on this point.

Nevertheless, the two olive trees, who are the two witnesses mentioned throughout the main passage, refer to the two servants of God whom He would especially raise in the end times for the salvation of the Israelites.

This is what verse 4 is telling us. And the two lampstands here refer to God's Church that He allowed among the Gentiles, and the Church permitted to the people of Israel. In the age of the Old Testament, the Israelites had God's Church originally. But from the age of the New Testament, they no longer have had this Church of God. Why? Because they are yet to recognize Jesus Christ, and also do not have the Holy Spirit in their hearts.

As they have accepted neither the gospel of the water and the Spirit nor Jesus Christ, God's Church is no longer found among them. However, before the final end of the world, during the first three and half years of the Great Tribulation, God will allow His Church to the people of Israel also. This is why the Bible tells us about the two olive trees, who are the two witnesses.

The Lord will establish His Church and do His work of saving souls from sin among both the Jews and us the Gentiles. And through these churches, He will make them serve this spiritual work of saving souls from sin until the appearance of the Antichrist. This means that God will make the vessels out of the saints, the members of His Church, to have them serve the ministry of saving the souls lost in sin. We must therefore diligently carry out our remaining ministry in faith.

Verse 5: And if anyone wants to harm them, fire proceeds from their mouth and devours their enemies. And if anyone wants to harm them, he must be killed in this manner.

God gave this power to the two prophets so that they may carry out their special mission. To make the people of Israel repent and overcome Satan in the end times, God shows us that whoever tries to kill the two witnesses will themselves be harmed, and that the power of His Word will be with these two witnesses.

As such, the people of Israel, believing in the teachings of these two prophets, will return to Jesus Christ. This is why God would permit the two olives—that is, the two witnesses—to the Israelites, so that they may be saved from their sins during the end times.

Verse 6: These have power to shut heaven, so that no rain falls in the days of their prophecy; and they have power over waters to turn them to blood, and to strike the earth with all plagues, as often as they desire.

Because the people of Israel would not repent unless the servants of God whom He would raised for them perform these acts of power, God will permit the two witnesses to work with His power. The two prophets will not only lead the Israelites to Jesus, but they will also overcome God's enemies with power and fulfill all the works of their calling. God will give them special power so that they may preach all the Word of prophecy to the people of Israel, testify that Jesus Christ is their long-awaited Messiah, and make them believe.

Verse 7: When they finish their testimony, the beast that ascends out of the bottomless pit will make war against them, overcome them, and kill them.

This Word tells us that the Antichrist will appear in this world when the first three and a half years of the seven-year period of the Great Tribulation pass by. It is at this time that those who believe in Jesus Christ as their awaited Messiah would finally rise from the people of Israel. But many of them will be martyred to defend their faith from the Beast, who is the Antichrist, and his followers. The two prophets of God will also be martyred when they complete the works of their calling.

That these two witnesses would be killed by the Antichrist is according to the will of God. Why? Because God also wants to give them His reward for the martyrs. This reward is for them to participate in the first resurrection, join the Lord in the marriage supper of the Lamb, rejoice forever, and receive eternal life. To give this blessing to all the saints, God wants them to be martyred for their faith. All the saints, therefore, must neither fear nor avoid their martyrdom, but instead embrace it in affirmative faith and receive their blessed reward.

Verse 8: And their dead bodies will lie in the street of the great city which spiritually is called Sodom and Egypt, where also our Lord was crucified.

This verse tells us that the "two witnesses" are exactly from the people of Israel. The two servants that God will raise for the Israelites are not from the Gentiles, but from their own people of Israel. As such, the two witnesses are killed in the same place where Jesus was crucified. This fact tells us clearly that these two witnesses are Israelites. For the people of Israel, they are the servants of God.

To the people of Israel, who are spiritually like the people of Sodom and Egypt, God will establish His two prophets, give them power, and make them testify that Jesus is the Messiah for whom the Israelites have waited, so that the people of Israel may repent and believe in Jesus.

The Antichrist will kill the two servants of God on the place of Golgotha, where Jesus was crucified. Because the followers of the Antichrist have evil spirits, they will hate to death these two witnesses who believe in Jesus and testify for Him. Like the Roman soldiers who crucified Jesus and pierced His side with a spear before, those with evil spirits will hate not only Jesus, but they will also hate the two witnesses of God and kill them.

Verse 9: Then those from the peoples, tribes, tongues, and nations will see their dead bodies three-and-a-half days, and not allow their dead bodies to be put into graves.

Among the people of Israel also, there are those who do not believe in Jesus Christ as their Savior. Seeing the death of the flesh of the two servants (two olive trees), these people will get overwhelmed by their sense of triumph, and to enhance this sense of victory, they will not even give their victims a proper burial. But their victory will be shattered to pieces when God brings the "two witnesses" to life again, and they will therefore come to fear God.

They may congratulate themselves for the death of the two servants of God, but this will not last long, for they will soon realize that the Antichrist is no match for Jesus Christ— disappointment and emptiness will thus overwhelm them.

These people dislike God's Word of prophecy preached by the two prophets. By standing against these two servants whom God would raise, they will eventually be cut off from the last harvest of salvation and end up turning into Satan's followers.

Verse 10: And those who dwell on the earth will rejoice over them, make merry, and send gifts to one another, because these two prophets tormented those who dwell on the earth.

As they would preach God's Word of prophecy, the two witnesses raised for the salvation of the Israelites would be a great pain in the neck for the followers of Satan. As such, they will all rejoice with the death of these two witnesses and send gifts to each other to congratulate themselves.

We, too, are happy when those who had been bothering us disappear. The Antichrist and his followers will hate it when the two witnesses raised by God preach His Word. Every time they hear the Word of God, their spirits would be overwhelmed by agony. Because they would thus have been so tormented whenever the two witnesses spoke to them about Jesus, they would rejoice when they see them put to death by the Antichrist. This is why they would exchange gifts and congratulate each other.

Verse 11: Now after the three-and-a-half days the breath of life from God entered them, and they stood on their feet, and great fear fell on those who saw them.

God, however, will make the two witnesses participate in the first resurrection. This Word is the evidence of the fact that the saints, who are martyred to defend their faith after having been saved from sin by believing in the Word of salvation given by the Lord, will participate in the first resurrection.

That the breath of life entered them in "three and a half days" tells us that the Lord will allow their resurrection in a short while, just as He Himself was resurrected from His death of the flesh. That God has allowed all the saints this faith of the first resurrection is, for the saints themselves, a great blessing of God, but for all the sinners, it will bring them great disheartenment and fear. The first resurrection of the saints is the promise of God and His reward for their faith.

Verse 12: And they heard a loud voice from heaven saying to them, "Come up here." And they ascended to heaven in a cloud, and their enemies saw them.

This Word points out the resurrection and rapture of all the saints. Having believed in the Lord's Word of prophecy, those who have been saved from all their sins would have no choice but to be martyred to defend their faith. This verse shows us that the Lord will resurrect all these saints and rapture them. The saints and the servants of God who are martyred in their faithfulness to Him will be blessed by being lifted up to the air (rapture) because of their faith in the Lord. We cannot help but thank the Lord for giving us our resurrection and rapture as the reward for being martyred after being saved by believing in the remission of sin that He has given us.

God the Father will allow the resurrection and rapture to all those who stand against the Antichrist and are martyred by believing in the gospel of the water and the Spirit given by Jesus Christ. We must believe in this fact. The saints' resurrection and rapture are the blessings that flow from their salvation through their faith in the gospel of the water and the Spirit given by God. Satan and his followers of the end times would find all their efforts evaporating into thin air when they see the saints, whom they had so persecuted and killed, are resurrected and raptured.

God will resurrect and rapture the martyred saints, but He will destroy those who still remain on this earth by pouring the plagues of the seven bowls. When this work is quickly completed, He will come down to this earth with the saints and invite the righteous to the marriage supper of Christ. Our Lord will have this feast last for a thousand years. When this millennium is over, He will allow Satan to rise from the bottomless pit briefly and fight against God and His saints, but

He will eventually destroy Satan and His followers and judge them to be thrown into the eternal fire. The righteous, however, will enter the Lord's Kingdom of Heaven and live with Him forever.

Verse 13: In the same hour there was a great earthquake, and a tenth of the city fell. In the earthquake seven thousand people were killed, and the rest were afraid and gave glory to the God of heaven.

After the martyrdom, resurrection, and rapture of the two prophets whom God would raise for the salvation of the Israelites, He will allow His angels to freely pour down the plagues of the seven bowls on this earth. Those who still remain on this earth after the saints' rapture will receive these plagues of the seven bowls as their gifts. Only then will they be grappled by fear and give glory to God, but this would be no use for them, for it would not be an act of the true faith in God's love.

When this world is destroyed, the righteous would have their eternal Heaven, eternal resurrection, and eternal blessings, but for the sinners, only the suffering of the eternal fire in hell would await them. This is why everyone must receive the remission of their sins by believing in the gospel of the water and the Spirit. And because those who have thus been redeemed of their sins believe in the new world that God promised them, they preach the gospel of the water and the Spirit to everyone.

Verse 14: The second woe is past. Behold, the third woe is coming quickly.

For both the Gentiles and the Israelites, the third woe from God would await everyone except those who have participated in their resurrection and rapture by being saved and martyred.

The plague that lasts from the angel's sounding of the sixth trumpet to the beginning of the plagues of the seven bowls with the sounding of the seventh trumpet is called the second woe. The plagues of the seven trumpets are divided into three periods—the early, the middle, and the late periods. The natural plagues and the saints' martyrdom by the Antichrist are included in the first and second woes. The third woe, on the other hand, is the plagues that will destroy the world completely. This third woe is the bowls of the wrath of God that will be poured on the sinners still remaining on this earth.

Verse 15: Then the seventh angel sounded: And there were loud voices in heaven, saying, "The kingdoms of this world have become the kingdoms of our Lord and of His Christ, and He shall reign forever and ever!"

The phrase *"there were loud voices in heaven"* shows us that the saints and servants who have been saved from all the sins would already be in Heaven by the time the plagues of the seven bowls begin in this world. As such, God's people will no longer be found in this world by this time. We must realize this. *"The kingdoms of this world have become the kingdoms of our Lord and of His Christ, and He shall reign forever and ever!"*

At this time, the saints will praise the Lord in Heaven, but after all the plagues of the seven bowls are poured down, they will also descend to the renewed earth with the Lord and reign with Him for a thousand years in this world. This will then be followed by the Lord and the saints reigning forever in the New Heaven and Earth.

To deliver us from sin, our Lord has served us as a servant all this while, instead of reigning over us as the King. He has bestowed us with His grace of making those who believe in the gospel of the water and the Spirit as their salvation into God's children. As our Lord is the eternal King for us, He would also make His people reign forever. Hallelujah! Thank the Lord!

Verse 16: And the twenty-four elders who sat before God on their thrones fell on their faces and worshiped God,
God is worthy to receive all glory. It is only proper for those who have been saved from all the sins to fall on their faces, and worship and praise God. Our Lord, who has done all these works of saving the sinners, is worthy to receive praise and worship from all the saints and all the creations forever and ever.

Verse 17: saying: "We give You thanks, O Lord God Almighty, The One who is and who was and who is to come, Because You have taken Your great power and reigned."
To reign with His people forever from then on, our Lord would conquer Satan and receive great power from God the Father. As such, the Lord would reign forever. He is worthy to do so. I give glory to Him, for the Lord who has made all the sins of the world disappear, who has saved all those who believe in the gospel of the water and the Spirit, and who has judged His enemies, is worthy to take His majestic power and reign forever. As such, all those who recognize God's sovereignty will be clothed in the glory of praising God forever with the Lord's almighty power and love.

Verse 18: "The nations were angry, and Your wrath has come, And the time of the dead, that they should be judged, And that You should reward Your servants the prophets and the saints, And those who fear Your name, small and great, And should destroy those who destroy the earth."

Simultaneous to the pouring of the plagues of the seven bowls will now come the destruction of the flesh of those who remain spiritually Gentiles. This Word tells us that then would be the time for God to judge everyone as the Judge of all, rewarding His servants and prophets, the saints, and those who revere Him, and destroying those who stand against and disobey His will. The Lord will bring the judgment of His wrath on those who do not recognize His sovereignty, but He will allow the saints to be glorified with Him. This means that the Lord has become the Judge of all, good and evil.

When the Lord sits on His throne as the King of the born-again and judges everyone, all the sinners and the righteous of the world will receive their fair judgment. At this time, as the verdict of His judgment, the Lord will give Heaven and eternal life to the saints, but to the sinners He will bring their eternal destruction and the punishment of hell. The sovereignty of Jesus Christ and the blessing of His people's reign will go on forever. The first world will end at this time, and the second world, the Kingdom of Christ, will thus begin.

Verse 19: Then the temple of God was opened in heaven, and the ark of His covenant was seen in His temple. And there were lightnings, noises, thunderings, an earthquake, and great hail.

God will allow His saints, the righteous, His blessing of living in His Temple. All these things are fulfilled according to God's Word of promise to the mankind in Jesus Christ. The Kingdom of God begins with God's Word of prophecy, and it is completed by the fulfillment of this prophecy.

All the promises of God, from the resurrection and rapture of the saints to their participation in the marriage supper of the Lamb with Jesus Christ and their blessing to reign forever as kings, are given equally to both the people of Israel and us the Gentiles. Also, He treats the salvation of the Israelites during the end times and our salvation in the same way, makes us both to be martyred at this period, allows us the same resurrection and the same rapture thereafter, and clothes us in the same glory. The Word tells us that though the Israelites and we the Gentiles are different peoples in the flesh, we are nevertheless the same people of God spiritually.

Many people claim and believe that the born-again will be raptured before the Great Tribulation of seven years properly begins. But this is not the case. Biblically speaking, people will continue to hear the true gospel and be saved throughout the first three and a half years of the seven-year period of the Great Tribulation. The Antichrist will then emerge, the saints will be martyred, and after their resurrection and rapture will come Christ's marriage supper of the Lamb, allowing the saints to reign with Him for a thousand years.

The saints must have the exact knowledge of the time of their martyrdom, resurrection and rapture. Without knowing this time, they will continue to wander in their confusion and die spiritually in it.

Those who have the exact knowledge of God's Providence about the end times hope for their resurrection and rapture, and will diligently serve the gospel. Those who know that there is no hope on this earth must have the same hope as that of the born-again by believing in the gospel of the water and the Spirit. And the saints are martyred by believing in the Word of God.

The faith that can discern the times is indispensably needed in this age. The time has almost come for the fearful plagues and tribulations to descend on the whole world and for the Antichrist to emerge. Now is the time to wake up from your sleep. We must keep it in mind that we have to go through almost all the tribulations of the Great Tribulation. And it is imperative that we believe in Christ's return, in our resurrection and rapture, and in our participation in the marriage supper of the Lamb with Christ. For us to have the most appropriate faith for this era, we must enter the ark of the gospel of the water and the Spirit.

I hope and pray that by knowing this present era, you will have the faith that is most urgently required and the most proper for this age. ⊠

The Salvation of
The People of Israel

< Revelation 11:1-19 >

Why would God send the two prophets to the people of Israel? God would do so to save the people of Israel in particular. The main passage tells us that God would make His two witnesses prophesy for 1,260 days. This is to save the Israelites for the last time. That God would thus save the people of Israel also means that the time for the end of the world would have come.

Verse 2 says, *"But leave out the court which is outside the temple, and do not measure it, for it has been given to the Gentiles. And they will tread the holy city underfoot for forty-two months."* This means that when the horrendous plagues come to the Gentiles, when the seven-year period of the Great Tribulation begins and gradually brings great confusion and plagues, when those among the Gentiles who have heard and believed in the gospel are martyred, God will raise the two prophets for the people of Israel, make them testify that Jesus is God and the Savior, and thus save the Israelites. It tells us that these are the works of God to come.

We must teach this Word to those who, deceived by Satan, claim that the leaders of their denominations are the two olive trees of the end times, or that the founder of their sect is the Elijah prophesized for the end times. Whenever the worldly churches talk about Revelation, they exploit this passage on the two olive trees the most. Of all the people deceived by heretical cults whom I have met in my life of faith so far, none has ever failed to make the outlandish claim that the leader of his/her cult is one of the two olive trees mentioned here. Every heretic that I know has made such a claim eventually.

But the two olive trees and the two lampstands of Revelation are not what these heretics claim to be. In truth, these olive trees actually refer to the two prophets whom God would raise from the Israelites to save them.

Chapter 11 tells us in detail how God would save the people of Israel. Like the Book of Romans, each chapter of the Book of Revelation has its special theme. Only by knowing this theme can we understand what this chapter is all about. Reading that the Gentiles would tread the holy city underfoot for forty-two months, some people claim, without knowing this theme, that the era of the Gentiles would be over, the era of the salvation of the Israelites would instead open, and so from then on only the Israelites would be saved.

But this is far from the truth. Chapter 7 tells us that a countless multitude from the Gentiles would also come out of the Tribulation saved—that is, both the Gentiles and the Israelites would be saved throughout the Tribulation, not just the Israelites. As such, what chapter 11 tells us is that God would thus raise the two prophets to save the people of Israel in the end times, but this does not mean that the Gentiles would no longer be saved.

Some will ask in return, then, "Were not 144,000 Israelites already saved, as chapter 7 tells us that this was the number of the Israelites sealed by God?" Being sealed is not the same as being saved. There is no one who can be saved without going through Jesus Christ. Salvation comes only by believing that Jesus Christ became our Savior by coming to this earth, being baptized to assume all our sins, carrying all these sins of the world to the Cross and dying on it, and rising from the dead again.

Though we know that we are bound to sin until our death, we were nevertheless saved by believing that Jesus Christ made all our sins completely disappear and thus became our Savior. While 144,000 Israelites would be sealed, God would also raise up His two prophets, and through them preach His gospel to these Israelites. What the Word tells us, in other words, is that the two prophets would preach the gospel to the Israelites, and that 144,000 of them would thus be saved.

The Bible is never prejudiced or discriminatory. There is no one who can be saved without going through Jesus Christ. God does not say, without going through Jesus Christ, "You are save, but you are not."

The two prophets, who are the two olive trees mentioned in the main passage, will be killed at the place called Golgotha. Their dead bodies will be left in the open without burial, and those who neither believe nor accept Jesus will rejoice over their death and send gifts to each other. But verses 11 and 12 tell us, *"Now after the three-and-a-half days the breath of life from God entered them, and they stood on their feet, and great fear fell on those who saw them. And they heard a loud voice from heaven saying to them, 'Come up here.' And they ascended to heaven in a cloud, and their enemies saw them."*

This tells us straightforwardly that we—that is, you and I who are Gentiles—will also be martyred by faith when the time comes, and that shortly after our martyrdom will come our resurrection and rapture. This subject continues to make its appearance throughout the whole Book of Revelation. There are also passages that tell us that when the plagues of the seven bowls are poured on this earth, the raptured saints would be praising God in the air.

Chapter 14 also speaks of the 144,000 saved, who praise God with a song that no one else but the firstfruits of salvation can sing. What this tells us that when the people of Israel are saved, they will be martyred everywhere, and shortly after their martyrdom will come their resurrection and rapture.

The same applies to the Gentiles. In the end times, you and I will go through many hardships of the plagues of the seven trumpets, but God will still protect us from these plagues. When the Great Tribulation of seven years reaches its height with the passing of the first three and a half years, the persecution of the saints will also reach its peak. But this extreme persecution will last only for a short time. Many saints and servants of God will shortly be martyred, and quickly after their martyrdom will come their rapture.

Why? Because Revelation repeatedly records that by the time the plagues of the seven bowls are poured on this earth, the saints would already be in heaven praising God. The Word describes this as marvelous.

Revelation 10:7 says, *"but in the days of the sounding of the seventh angel, when he is about to sound, the mystery of God would be finished, as He declared to His servants the prophets."* This refers to none other than the rapture, the mystery hidden by God. In 1 Thessalonians 4:16, the Apostle Paul also tells us, *"For the Lord Himself will descend from heaven with a shout, with the voice of an archangel, and with the trumpet of God."*

That the Lord will descend from Heaven, however, does not mean that He will come down to this earth immediately. He will descend from Heaven to the air, and when the first resurrection that raises the asleep and transforms the born-again alive happens, the rapture with which the saints receive the Lord in the air will follow right away. After the marriage supper of the Lamb is held in the air and this world is completed destroyed by the pouring of all the remaining seven bowls' plagues on this earth, the Lord will descend on the renewed earth with us and make His appearance before those who would still be alive.

Interpreting the Word of Revelation and the Bible based on one's own individual opinions is to embark on the road to destruction. It is simply wrong to just believe in mere hypotheses proposed by some theologians and advocate these claims without properly understanding the Word.

Among the theologians who are highly respected and renowned in the conservative Christian communities, some scholars such as L. Berkhof and Abraham Kuyper espoused amillennialism. Of the theories of pre-tribulation rapture, post-tribulation rapture, and amillennialism, believing in this last doctrine of amillennialism is the same as not believing in the Bible itself.

The time when people used to believe in the theory of post-tribulation rapture has now gone by, and in these days virtually everyone believes in the theory of pre-tribulation rapture. But this theory, too, is not biblically sound. Yet people still like it very much whenever they are told about the pre-tribulation rapture. Why? Because according to this theory of pre-tribulation rapture, Christians would have nothing to worry about the Great Tribulation of seven years.

As such, it becomes acceptable for the believers to live a life of faith that is neither hot nor cold, and for the churches to worry only about increasing the size of their congregations. People's faith thus grows lax. Because they think that there is no need for them to worry about going through the Great Tribulation, their faith becomes all rosy and lax just when their faith must in fact get stronger with the nearing of the end times.

People used to believe in amillennialism long ago, and then in the theory of post-tribulation rapture for a while, and they now believe in the theory of pre-tribulation rapture.

In 1830's, Rev. Scofield, a professor at the Moody Bible Institute, began to write his reference Bible. Scofield was highly influenced by a world-renowned theologian named Darby.

Darby, Scofield's spiritual mentor, who used to be a Catholic priest before, was a highly intelligent and widely knowledgeable man. He left the Catholic Church after realizing its fallacies, joined a small Christian organization, and became its leader. Though Darby constantly read and studied the Bible, he could not figure out from Revelation whether the rapture would happen before or after the Great Tribulation. So he went on a trip in search of more clear evidences on this issue.

During this trip he met a teenaged female who was a leader of pneumatology. This girl claimed to have seen through her vision that the rapture would happen before the Great Tribulation. Believing what she told him and convinced that the rapture would come before the Tribulation, Darby concluded His biblical studies with the theory of pre-tribulation rapture.

However, because the people of this time had mainly believed in the theory of post-tribulation rapture, Darby's theory of pre-tribulation rapture was not received well.

Darby claimed that what is written in the Book of Revelation is about the salvation of the people of Israel, and that it had nothing to do with the salvation of the Gentiles. And by *"You must prophesy again (10:11),"* he interpreted this not as the preaching of the gospel of the water and the Spirit, but of the gospel of the Kingdom that proclaims its coming arrival.

Scofield, who accepted such hypotheses of Darby intact

and incorporated this theory of pre-tribulation rapture into his reference Bible, came to create his own hypothesis on the seven eras. Such claims of Scofield met the demands of his time and fit rather well to his background, causing a great stir among the religious throughout the world and becoming widely accepted.

But what does God say in the Bible? In the Scripture we see Jesus taking and opening the scroll sealed with seven seals before the throne of God, who has divided history into His seven eras with the seven seals.

The first era is the era of the white horse. This is the era of salvation, the era in which God decided to save us from the very moment that He created this universe and man, and has indeed saved us accordingly. As Revelation 6:2 tells us, *"And I looked, and behold, a white horse. He who sat on it had a bow; and a crown was given to him, and he went out conquering and to conquer,"* the Lord have triumphed and will continue to triumph. Even before the creation, the gospel was already in existence and salvation had already begun.

The second era is the era of the red horse, the era of Satan. This is the Devil's era in which he would take away peace from the mankind, making them wage war against each other, hate one another, and engage in religious conflicts.

The third era is the era of the black horse, which is a time of spiritual and physical famine, and the fourth era is the era of the pale horse, the era of martyrdom. The fifth era is the era of rapture—God has set the saints' rapture as one of His eras. The sixth era is that of the seven bowls, entailing the destruction of this world, and the following era is that of the Millennial Kingdom and the New Heaven and Earth. God has thus set this world's time into these seven eras, within the scroll sealed by the seven seals.

Scofield's division of time into seven eras was set on his own. In contrast, the seven eras that are prophesized in Revelation 6 through the seven seals of the scroll held on God's hand have been set by God Himself. Yet people speak of the man-made theory of pre-tribulation rapture, and the many who believed in it conclude that there is no need for them to believe in the Lord earnestly.

They have decided in their hearts, "Since we'd be raptured before the Great Tribulation, we would already in God's presence when the Great Tribulation of seven years comes. So we got nothing to worry about!" Had the Word of God told us that we were to be raptured before the Tribulation, there would indeed be no need to prepare our faith, and attending the church once or twice a year would suffice. But this is not what God has told us.

"They will prophesy one thousand two hundred and sixty days." "They will tread the holy city underfoot for forty-two months." Such Word of God tells us that the Gentiles, too, will be saved in the time of the Tribulation. God will raise up His two prophets to spread the gospel of the water and the Spirit. There is no one who can stand before God without going through the first three and a half years of the seven-year period of the Great Tribulation set by Him, when the time of hardships comes. God also tells us that many martyrs will come out from the Tribulation at this time.

To believe in Jesus correctly, one must learn the Bible exactly and believe in what are exactly correct. If people preach and believe on their own without reading each page of the Bible carefully, they will end up as heretics. The reason why there are innumerable denominations in this world is also because of the fact that many people base their faith on their own interpretation of the Bible.

That the people of Israel would be saved tells us that God's plan will be fulfilled according to His Word of promise. This also tells us that God will never break His Word of promise spoken to us but fulfill them all. This is why we have such a great hope.

The two prophets of Israel will be resurrected in three and a half days after their death and ascend to Heaven. This is the rapture. It provides a model for how the martyrs of the Great Tribulation would be raptured, and is shown to us as a precursor to our own rapture. The Bible tells us that after the sounding of the seventh trumpet, this earth will become the Kingdom of Christ and He will reign over it forever. So, too, will those who have trusted in Jesus Christ reign with Him.

God will wholly destroy this earth after rapturing the saints. We don't know if the destruction will be for 100 percent, as this detail is not recorded in the Bible, but God does tell us in Revelation 11:18, *"The nations were angry, and Your wrath has come, And the time of the dead, that they should be judged, And that You should reward Your servants the prophets and the saints, And those who fear Your name, small and great, And should destroy those who destroy the earth."*

The rapture will most certainly happen as the Great Tribulation passes over its peak of three and a half years—not at the exact reaching of the first three and a half years, but slightly past it. The midpoint of the seven-year period is when the Tribulation reaches its height. This is when the saints from the people of Israel will be martyred, and the rapture will come shortly thereafter. When the rapture happens, we will all join the marriage supper of the Lamb in the air.

While we are participating in the marriage supper of the Lamb in the air, as Matthew 25 tells us that we will, the plagues of the seven bowls will descend on this earth. Praising

God in the air and seeing all the things that are happening on this earth, we will thank God for His grace all the more.

I hope and pray that through the Word of Revelation, you would be able to discern the times when the last days come, believe in the Word properly, live your life diligently by faith, and prepare for the future. To give praise, honor, and worship to the Lord as you are taking part in the marriage supper of the Lamb with Him, you must prepare your faith.

I hope that the Word of Revelation will prove to be a great guide for you in the days to come, reminding your heart once again that you must live diligently and truthfully by your faith in the gospel of the water and the Spirit. ⊠

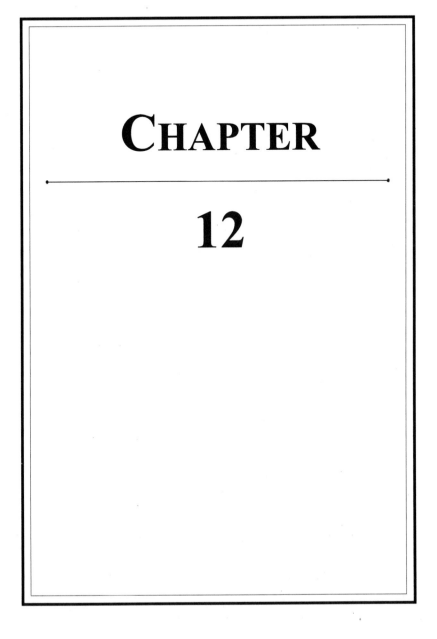

CHAPTER

12

God's Church That Will Be Greatly Harmed in the Future

< Revelation 12:1-17 >

"Now a great sign appeared in heaven: a woman clothed with the sun, with the moon under her feet, and on her head a garland of twelve stars. Then being with child, she cried out in labor and in pain to give birth. And another sign appeared in heaven: behold, a great, fiery red dragon having seven heads and ten horns, and seven diadems on his heads. His tail drew a third of the stars of heaven and threw them to the earth. And the dragon stood before the woman who was ready to give birth, to devour her Child as soon as it was born. She bore a male Child who was to rule all nations with a rod of iron. And her Child was caught up to God and His throne. Then the woman fled into the wilderness, where she has a place prepared by God, that they should feed her there one thousand two hundred and sixty days. And war broke out in heaven: Michael and his angels fought with the dragon; and the dragon and his angels fought, but they did not prevail, nor was a place found for them in heaven any longer. So the great dragon was cast out, that serpent of old, called the Devil and Satan, who deceives the whole world; he was cast to the earth, and his angels were cast out with him. Then I heard a loud voice saying in heaven, 'Now salvation, and strength, and the kingdom of our God, and the power of His Christ have come, for the accuser of our brethren, who accused them before our God day and night, has been cast down. And they overcame him by the blood of the Lamb and by the word of their testimony, and they did not love their lives to the death. Therefore rejoice, O heavens, and you who dwell in them! Woe to the inhabitants of the earth and the sea! For the devil has come down to you, having great wrath, because he knows that he has a short time.' Now when the dragon saw that he had been cast to the earth, he persecuted the woman who gave birth to the male Child. But the woman was given two wings of a great eagle, that she might fly into the wilderness to her place, where she is nourished for a time and times and half a time, from the presence of the serpent. So the serpent spewed water out of his mouth like a flood after the woman, that he might cause her to be carried away by the flood. But the earth helped the woman, and the earth opened its mouth and swallowed up the flood which the dragon had spewed out of his mouth. And the dragon was enraged with the woman, and he went to make war with the rest of her offspring, who keep the commandments of God and have the testimony of Jesus Christ."

Exegesis

Verse 1: Now a great sign appeared in heaven: a woman clothed with the sun, with the moon under her feet, and on her head a garland of twelve stars.

This tells us of God's Church giving glory to Him through martyrdom. The "woman clothed with the sun" refers to God's Church on this earth, and the phrase "with the moon under her feet" means that the Church is still under the rule of the world. The phrase "on her head a garland of twelve stars," on the other hand, means that His Church will overcome Satan's persecution and threats with its martyrdom.

This verse refers to God's Church in the midst of the Great Tribulation. His Church will suffer great harms from Satan and be martyred in the end times, but it will nevertheless overcome Satan with its faith and be glorified by God. Even in the Tribulation's time, the saints of God's Church will overcome the Antichrist and triumph with their martyrdom by believing in the gospel of the water and the Spirit.

The children of God who have been born again by the water and the Spirit will most certainly be martyred in the end times. Those who would have already believed and served God before the advent of the Tribulation, and those who would believe in the gospel and rise up like so many mushrooms amidst the Tribulation, will both have the faith of martyrdom that can enable them to stand against and overcome the Antichrist.

Those who are excluded from martyrdom by betraying Him will also be excluded from Heaven, and fall into the hell of Hades along with Satan. And we should be prepared to embrace our martyrdom with bold faith lest we lose our eternal blessings prepared for us. And we have to know that all the born-again will face the threatening of Satan. Martyrdom will last only momentarily, and when this brief moment is over, the Millennial Kingdom and Heaven will be ours.

As such, we must live this present era knowing that when the end times come, we will be martyred by faith and through the Holy Spirit. The Holy Spirit will then give us the words with which to speak in this time of martyrdom, enabling us to courageously overcome our persecution and willingly embrace our martyrdom without betraying our faith.

Even in the midst of the fearful Tribulation, God's Church will still fight against Satan and overcome him by being martyred. It is most clear that the Church will receive its rewards from God by overcoming the Antichrist with its martyrdom, believing in the Lord's Word even in the last era of Satan.

Verse 2: Then being with child, she cried out in labor and in pain to give birth.

This verse tells us of God's Church in tribulations. It tells us of the whole Church persevering through the persecutions and tribulations of the end times brought by Satan. God's Church will pass through the Great Tribulation, the time of its struggle against the Antichrist. The saints would thus call upon God only when they go through the Tribulation. They would pray, "God, give us Your grace so that we may quickly pass through all these tribulations. Help us by abating all these tribulations. Allow us to overcome our tribulations. Make us overcome Satan!"

Verse 3: And another sign appeared in heaven: behold, a great, fiery red dragon having seven heads and ten horns, and seven diadems on his heads.

When Satan makes his appearance on this earth in the future, he will act as if he were God, and that He will garner together all the nations of the world and use them as his instruments to fulfill his purposes. Also, he will most certainly kill the saints and reign the world like God and a king.

The phrase, *"Behold, a great, fiery red dragon having seven heads and ten horns, and seven diadems on his heads,"* shows that Satan, the peace-breaker, will move seven kings and ten nations at his own disposal. It tells us that Satan, in his very essence, stands against God fundamentally.

Verse 4: His tail drew a third of the stars of heaven and threw them to the earth. And the dragon stood before the woman who was ready to give birth, to devour her Child as soon as it was born.

This verse tells us what Satan does. The Dragon turned against God in Heaven and was thrown out of it. He drew a third of the angels of Heaven to his fold and led them to their destruction along with his own. He was thus driven out from the presence of God. But even while on this earth, he still tries to stop the work of God's gospel by persecuting those who believe in it.

Verse 5: She bore a male Child who was to rule all nations with a rod of iron. And her Child was caught up to God and His throne.

This tells us that God's Church, because it is martyred by believing in Jesus Christ, will be resurrected with Christ and be raptured to the Kingdom of Heaven.

Verse 6: Then the woman fled into the wilderness, where she has a place prepared by God, that they should feed her there one thousand two hundred and sixty days.

This verse tells us that God would feed His people for three and a half years in this world. God's Church will be fed and protected by God for 1,260 days before the advent of the full-scale tribulation, and when the time comes, it will fight against the Antichrist and be martyred.

Verses 7-8: And war broke out in heaven: Michael and his

angels fought with the dragon; and the dragon and his angels fought, but they did not prevail, nor was a place found for them in heaven any longer.

This refers to Satan being completely driven out of Heaven.

Before coming to this world, Satan will be thrown out of Heaven completely. The Devil will no longer be able to stay Heaven. Satan, who has the power over the air, sits on both the air and the earth and rules over them now. As he would thus be completely thrown out of Heaven, on this earth he would persecute the saints even more when the last days come. But Satan will then be cast out and totally bound in the bottomless pit and hell prepared by God.

Verse 9: So the great dragon was cast out, that serpent of old, called the Devil and Satan, who deceives the whole world; he was cast to the earth, and his angels were cast out with him.

In the end times, Satan, as he is cast out from Heaven and thrown down to this earth, will persecute and kill the saints for the last time. Many saints will then be martyred at his hands.

Verse 10: Then I heard a loud voice saying in heaven, "Now salvation, and strength, and the kingdom of our God, and the power of His Christ have come, for the accuser of our brethren, who accused them before our God day and night, has been cast down."

Satan would no longer be found in the Kingdom of Heaven. When the end times pass by, he will not be able to remain in Heaven anymore. This is why Revelation 21:27 tells us that neither evildoers nor liars are found in Heaven.

Verse 11: "And they overcame him by the blood of the

Lamb and by the word of their testimony, and they did not love their lives to the death."

When the end times come, the saints will be martyred to defend their faith. Whosoever is a saint will achieve the victory of faith through his/her martyrdom of faith in the end times. The martyrs who believe in the Lord, in other words, will overcome in their fight against the self.

Verse 12: "Therefore rejoice, O heavens, and you who dwell in them! Woe to the inhabitants of the earth and the sea! For the devil has come down to you, having great wrath, because he knows that he has a short time."

As Satan, thrown out of Heaven, temporarily has power over the world, he will torment and persecute the saints terribly when he comes down to this earth. But for the saints who would be martyred and lifted up to the air, only joy will await them. After the rapture, God will pour down the plagues of the seven bowls on all the earth and the sea.

Verse 13: Now when the dragon saw that he had been cast to the earth, he persecuted the woman who gave birth to the male Child.

This refers to the persecution of the saints to come during the time of the Great Tribulation. The saints and the servant of God will die at this time as they are martyred, but this would in fact be the achievement of their victory of faith. There will no longer be any more death, suffering, or curse for them. All that remains for them would be to praise God and be glorified forever in Heaven.

Verse 14: But the woman was given two wings of a great eagle, that she might fly into the wilderness to her place, where

she is nourished for a time and times and half a time, from the
presence of the serpent.

The Bible tells us that the rapture will happen after the first three and a half years of the Great Tribulation pass by. This Word says that God will give the saints His special protection and nourishment in the midst of the natural plagues of the Great Tribulation. God will nourish those of us who keep our faith so that we may fight against and overcome Satan with this faith.

That we are now living for the gospel of the water and the Spirit is our nourishment, and so is our preaching of this gospel. Even until the plagues of the seven trumpets descend on this earth, we will continue to live our lives by preaching the gospel. Why? Because if we do not preach this gospel until the very last moment of our martyrdom, too many souls will be lost to hell. There is no other time but now.

Verses 15-17: So the serpent spewed water out of his
mouth like a flood after the woman, that he might cause her to
be carried away by the flood. But the earth helped the woman,
and the earth opened its mouth and swallowed up the flood
which the dragon had spewed out of his mouth. And the dragon
was enraged with the woman, and he went to make war with
the rest of her offspring, who keep the commandments of God
and have the testimony of Jesus Christ.

Before, Satan killed the saints by persecuting them and making them move away from the gospel. But nowadays, as the gospel has been widely spread through various ways, he tries to kill the saints by pouring down sin and drowning them in its flow. Satan has thus tried to bring death to many saints by pouring the river of sin and making them drink from its water, but those who have not been born again have drunk all of the water of this river of sin instead. As saints have survived and have not been killed even with this effort, Satan will come up with another method to kill them off completely, as shown in chapter 13. ⊠

Embrace Your Martyrdom With Bold Faith

< Revelation 12:1-17 >

Chapter 12 shows us how God's Church will face its tribulations of the end times. Verse 1 says, *"Now a great sign appeared in heaven: a woman clothed with the sun, with the moon under her feet, and on her head a garland of twelve stars."* The "woman clothed with the sun" here refers to God's Church on the earth, and the phrase "with the moon under her feet" means that God's Church is still under the rule of the world. This tells us that God's Church on this world, and the saints who belong to it, will glorify God by being martyred.

The phrase, "on her head a garland of twelve stars," shows that the Church will fight against Satan in the end times and be martyred by faith. As the Word of God tells us, God's Church will indeed triumph. Though Satan will, to destroy our faith, threaten us in all kinds of ways, make us suffer, harm us, and eventually even demand our lives, we will still defend our faith and be martyred righteously. This is the victory in faith.

In the Early Church period, many saints that preceded us were also martyred. This martyrdom comes not by our own strength, but by the Holy Spirit who dwells in our hearts.

From the phrase, "a woman clothed with the sun," the "woman" here refers to God's Church, and that she is "clothed with the sun" means that the Church would be heavily persecuted. Even in the midst of the fearful tribulations and plagues of the end times, the saints will defend their faith stoutly and never surrender to Satan. Why? Because the Holy Spirit in their hearts would make them stand and fight against Satan, and would give them the faith that never surrenders to any threat or persecution even at the risk of their lives.

Also, because those who have placed their hope in the Kingdom of Heaven believe in the Word of God that tells them that the plagues of the seven trumpets would soon end and be followed by the plagues of the seven bowls that would wipe out the earth, they never capitulate before Satan.

Those who know and believe that a better world does not await them if they were to surrender to Satan can never bow before him. The plagues of the seven bowls that would be poured on the Antichrist and his followers will devour them restlessly and mercilessly. The saints who know all about such plagues, 100 percent of them, will never throw away their faith because of the threats, for the Holy Spirit will work in their hearts. The Holy Spirit who dwells in us will give us the strength to stand against Satan, overcome him, and be martyred.

When the plague of the fourth trumpet passes by and the plagues of the fifth and the sixth trumpets come, "martyrdom" will come to us. Those who defend their faith and are martyred are only those who are born again by the water and the Spirit. When the plagues of the seven trumpets descend, the Antichrist will have authority over the world temporarily permitted by God.

Knowing that his authority would last only for a short while, Satan's servant, the Antichrist, will persecute those who serve Jesus Christ as their Lord, so that he may take as many people as possible with him to hell. But those who have passed all their sins onto Jesus through His baptism will not surrender to the Antichrist' persecution, but stoutly defend the gospel given by Jesus Christ and be martyred.

As such, martyrdom is the evidence of faith. Those who have this evidence will have the Millennial Kingdom and the New Heaven and Earth prepared by the Lord. This applies to all those who believe in the gospel of the water and the Spirit scattered throughout the whole world. The Bible tells us that almost all the born-again saints will be martyred during these end times.

But those who, in order to avoid martyrdom, abandon their faith of the water and the Spirit, stand on the Antichrist's side, and serve and worship him as God will be killed by the plagues of the seven bowls and at the hands of the Antichrist himself. Their death would never constitute their martyrdom, but only a hopeless death in vain. When Satan and the Antichrist are cast out to hell, these people will together fall into it.

Betraying Jesus Christ to avoid martyrdom and lessen the tribulations' hardships even by a little will be a foolish thing to do. When the plagues of the seven trumpets end and those who have defended their faith are martyred, the plagues of the seven bowls will soon ravage throughout this earth, leaving few survivors. What are clear is that those who have received the remission of sin will most certainly be martyred, and that for us not to betray our Lord at this moment of martyrdom, we must prepare our faith now by believing with the proper knowledge of the end times and the correct understanding of the Word.

We have received the remission of our sins, and when we are martyred, we will experience a joy heretofore unknown to us, as God would strengthen us. Let our faith be clearly set in our hearts that you and I are fated to be martyred for the Lord. When this moment of martyrdom passes by, God will most certainly give us our resurrection and rapture, allow us to be glorified in the Millennial Kingdom, give us His eternal New

Heaven and Earth and make us reign, and permit us to forever live in wealth—if we steadfastly believe in all these, our suffering itself will be transformed into our joy.

The Apostle Paul said, *"For I consider that the sufferings of this present time are not worthy to be compared with the glory which shall be revealed in us" (Romans 8:18).* While serving the gospel, Paul had suffered greatly, beaten to near death on more than several occasions. But by believing that this suffering was for the glory of God, Paul's pain became his tremendous joy. And according to the historical records and folklore, almost all the apostles, including Paul, were martyred. Peter is said to have been crucified on the Vatican Hill upside down. And the Early Church leaders, including Polycarp, and many other saints sang praises to God even as they were burnt to death on stake. Such things would not have been possible had God not strengthened His saints.

Even as there were such faithful saints in this time, there also were those who betrayed their faith. Origen, a theologian who is highly regarded by today's theologians, was someone who heard the gospel directly from the apostles. Yet when the time for his martyrdom came, he escaped it, as his life was spared even as his fellow saints were martyred. This would not have been possible had he not denied everything that Jesus had done for him. Origen was thus representative of those who denied the divinity of Jesus. But despite his betrayal, today's theologians place him very high among the most renowned theologians.

Why did Origen escape martyrdom while the other saints embraced it? It was not because Origen's willpower was weak while that of the other martyred saints was strong. The saints who were martyred while praising God did so because they believed in what Paul had spoken of—that is, in *"that the sufferings of this present time are not worthy to be compared with the glory which shall be revealed in us.*" They could bear their present suffering, in other words, because they believed in God's Word of promise that He shall resurrect and rapture them, and give them His Millennial Kingdom.

We must realize clearly that martyrdom will come to us. Those who live their lives of faith with a clear knowledge of this fact are different from the rest. Those who believe that the picture of the martyred saints of the Early Church period is their own picture can have a life of faith that is strong, dignified and bold, for all the Word of the Bible would then be their own story. They always live with the faith that can embrace martyrdom—that is, they live by always believing that after their martyrdom, God would give them their resurrection and rapture, and the New Heaven and Earth that He planned and prepared for them beforehand.

Those who believe in this can always live a bold life of faith, for they know that their faith prepares them for their end, when they would be able to die while praising God. And because this is not just a simple matter of doctrine, but of actual faith, those who do not fully believe in this Word and the gospel will be the first to sell us out to the Antichrist. This is why, once you and I realize that we are to be martyred, our brothers and sisters in God's Church, who have the same faith as ours and will be together with us forever, are so important to us. The servants of God, His people, and His Church—all these are precious to us as well.

The saints of the Early Church period had a faith that was even more earnest and definite than that of us who now live in the end times. They believed in their martyrdom, in their following resurrection and rapture, and in the Millennial Kingdom and the New Heaven and Earth. This is why they lived their lives of faith as if they were actually living in the time of the Great Tribulation, as if the Lord's return were imminent. So when we who live in the age of the impending arrival of the era of the Tribulation read about them, their stories appeal to us as realistic and vivid, for they, too, knew and believed in all the Word of God on the Tribulation, and their martyrdom, resurrection and rapture.

Because we actually live our lives with the end times nearing us right before our own eyes, we must prepare our faith of martyrdom tightly in our hearts. Satan will challenge whoever believes in Christ's water and blood, trying to bring down their faith. To not surrender to this challenge from Satan, we must bind the gospel of the water and the Spirit to our hearts, reexamine its grasp once more with our hope for the New Heaven and Earth, and make sure that this faith of ours is not loosened until the very moment of our martyrdom.

The reason why the saints of the Early Church period defended their faith desperately is because they had also known and believed in all the Word of the Scripture on the Tribulation, and their martyrdom, resurrection and rapture. You and I, too, will be martyred. I'll die, and so will you—we will all die to defend our faith. Perhaps I'll be the first to be dragged and killed. This in itself may appear as a terrifying prospect, but in the end, there is nothing to be feared, for the logical conclusion of avoiding martyrdom would be to deny our faith, something that we absolutely cannot do.

After all, God is to be glorified through our martyrdom, and He has set this as our fate. So this is something that we must go through at least once. Since we can neither avoid nor escape from going through it, let us instead run to it in full strength and leap over it boldly. We have the King's authority that no one else has, and we also have our hope of eternal blessings. As such, we can always pray to God to strengthen us, and give even more glory to Him. By believing without fearing our martyrdom, we will receive an ever greater joy. This is a great glory for God, and a great blessing for us.

God wrote the Book of Revelation to speak to us about the saints' martyrdom, resurrection and rapture, the Millennial Kingdom, and the New Heaven and Earth. As such, knowing Revelation is the same as having a definite faith in this declining world. The road to the New Heaven and Earth written in Revelation cannot be traveled on without the gospel of the water and the Spirit. And this faith cannot be confirmed without going through martyrdom. I hope and pray, therefore, that you would bind your faith to your heart tightly, believing that you would not betray the gospel but be martyred when the time comes, and look ahead with your faith. Your life of faith will then change drastically from this very moment.

We will not die in vain, caught in the traps of Satan. Following the work of the Holy Spirit in our hearts, we will die to defend our faith. This is the very martyrdom. The day of our martyrdom will surely come. But we do not fear it, for we know that though our bodies would be killed by Satan, God would soon make us live again in our new, glorious bodies. We also know that our martyrdom will shortly be followed by our resurrection and rapture, and that all that awaits us from then on is the blessing of reigning in the Millennial Kingdom and our eternal kingship in Heaven.

Long ago, the Roman Emperor Nero set fire to Rome to rebuild the city. When the Roman citizens became furious at this, he blamed the incendiary fire upon Christians and massacred them indiscriminately. Likewise, when natural disasters strike the world during the Great Tribulation, the Antichrist will blame us the saints for all the plagues, accuse us falsely, and kill us.

So, we must pray to God, from now on, to give us the faith of martyrdom, the faith with which we can die. If we do not abandon our faith and are martyred, the glory of God will appear. But if we abandon our faith, surrender to the Antichrist, and accept him as God, we will be thrown into the eternal fire. If we pray to God for the faith with which we can overcome the Antichrist, in other words, our Lord will give us strength and power, but if do not set our hearts steadfastly and betray our faith, He will only have hell to give us.

Let me tell you a small story from the Korean War. The North Korean troops came to a certain church in the southern countryside, where a deacon named Chudal Bae was taking care of it. Seeing that the churchyard was dirty, an invading soldier told the deacon to clean it up. But this deacon refused to do so, saying that he had to keep the Lord's day holy. The soldiers, getting impatient, threatened to kill him right before the whole congregation if he did not clean up the yard. But the deacon continued to refuse, saying that he had to defend his faith, and was eventually killed. Later on, some Christians have called his death martyrdom, but this is not martyrdom. Why? Because martyrdom is dying for the righteous work—that is, to reveal the glory of God. Dying for one's stubbornness under the pretext of God is far from constituting martyrdom.

Could we throw away the love of salvation that God has given us? Because of our blemishes and sins, Jesus Christ took upon all our sins on Himself with His baptism and was crucified to death. If we cannot render our full devotion to this love of our Lord to death, far less can we throw away the gospel that gives us the New Heaven and Earth for the sake of the flesh that would simply disappear with our death. We were born into this world fated to be saved, to preach the gospel of salvation to everyone on this earth, and to die while preaching. Do not forget that the fate of the saints who have received the remission of sin, that is, our own fate is to live by faith and be martyred to overcome Satan's challenge of faith for the sake of the glory that God will bestow on us.

We have so many shortcomings and are so full of blemishes that we cannot give glory to God with anything. To such people as us, God has given the opportunity to give a great glory to the Lord, and this is none other than martyrdom. Do not avoid it. Let us believe in God who will lessen the time of the Tribulation if we ask Him, and by holding onto our hope for the inheritance of the New Heaven and Earth, let us overcome our transient suffering that will quickly end. Let us live by believing that the Lord will not allow too great a suffering to those who have faithfully lived for Him, nor permit them anything that would make them betray their faith, but that He will protect them and bestow them with even more abundant grace.

Realizing that we are to be martyred, we need the experience of facing hardship, persevering through suffering, and laboring for the Lord. Through such things, we will grow our faith through the experience of walking with the Lord, and when the end times come, we will be able to face our martyrdom with the strength given by the Lord. If we remain without having any experience of suffering for the Lord, of devotion to Him, or of labor and sacrifice for Him, fear will overwhelm us when the time of our martyrdom comes with the arrival of the Great Tribulation. Only those who have suffered and overcome pain before can beat their suffering once again.

I pray to God that your life of faith would be that of suffering for the Lord and of victory over it, and that when the moment of martyrdom arrives, you, too, would be among the faithful who can remind their hearts and confess with their lips that all these things are their own glory permitted to them through the blessing and grace of God.

If you desperately want to take the Kingdom of Heaven with your faith, the New Heaven and Earth will surely be yours. God desires all men to be saved and to come to the knowledge of the truth (1 Timothy 2:4). ✉

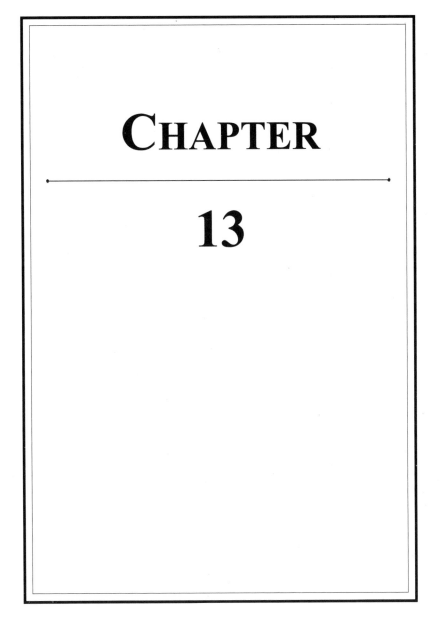

CHAPTER

13

The Emergence of the Antichrist

< Revelation 13:1-18 >

"Then I stood on the sand of the sea. And I saw a beast rising up out of the sea, having seven heads and ten horns, and on his horns ten crowns, and on his heads a blasphemous name. Now the beast which I saw was like a leopard, his feet were like the feet of a bear, and his mouth like the mouth of a lion. The dragon gave him his power, his throne, and great authority. And I saw one of his heads as if it had been mortally wounded, and his deadly wound was healed. And all the world marveled and followed the beast. So they worshiped the dragon who gave authority to the beast; and they worshiped the beast, saying, 'Who is like the beast? Who is able to make war with him?' And he was given a mouth speaking great things and blasphemies, and he was given authority to continue for forty-two months. Then he opened his mouth in blasphemy against God, to blaspheme His name, His tabernacle, and those who dwell in heaven. It was granted to him to make war with the saints and to overcome them. And authority was given him over every tribe, tongue, and nation. All who dwell on the earth will worship him, whose names have not been written in the Book of Life of the Lamb slain from the foundation of the world. If anyone has an ear, let him hear. He who leads into captivity shall go into captivity; he who kills with the sword must be killed with the sword. Here is the patience and the faith of the saints. Then I saw another beast coming up out of the earth, and he had two horns like a lamb and spoke like a dragon. And he exercises all the authority of the first beast in his presence, and causes the earth and those who dwell in it to worship the first beast, whose deadly wound was healed. He performs great signs, so that he even makes fire come down from heaven on the earth in the sight of men. And he deceives those who dwell on the earth by those signs which he was granted to do in the sight of the beast, telling those who dwell on the earth to make an image to the beast who was wounded by the sword and lived. He was granted power to give breath to the image of the beast, that the image of the beast should both speak and cause as many as would not worship the image of the beast to be killed. He causes all, both small and great, rich and poor, free and slave, to receive a mark on their right hand or on their foreheads, and that no one may buy or sell except one who has the mark or the name of the beast, or the number of his name. Here is wisdom. Let him who has understanding calculate the number of the beast, for it is the number of a man: His number is 666."

Exegesis

Verse 1: Then I stood on the sand of the sea. And I saw a beast rising up out of the sea, having seven heads and ten horns, and on his horns ten crowns, and on his heads a blasphemous name.

The Apostle John saw a beast rising up out of the sea. Through this Beast that John saw, God shows us what the Antichrist will do when he emerges on this earth. God showed John this Beast with seven heads and ten horns not to tell us that a beast in this shape will actually appear and be active in the world, but to tell us that someone with the authority and power of this Beast will appear, persecute the saints, and make martyrs out of them.

Does this then mean that everything that appears in Revelation is only symbolic? Not at all! Just to reveal the appearance and works of the Antichrist in the end times, God could not but speak through such visions. This is the wisdom and power with which God alone can speak. Through the Word of Revelation 13, we must be able to see the vivid picture of the end times.

What John saw first was the shape of a beast that came out of the sea. The Beast's seven heads and ten horns here refer to the power of the Antichrist to come out to this world. The phrase, *"on his horns ten crowns, and on his heads a blasphemous name,"* means that the Antichrist will gather together the nations of the world and stand against God. It also tells us that he will rule over all the kings of the world. The ten crowns refer to their victory, and the blasphemous name on the Beast's head refers to their pride.

In the future, the world will be ruled by a united body of nations, based on a governing system that pursues the common interests of the states thus unified. This integrated superpower, a huge supranational entity, will extend its sovereignty and rule over all the nations of the world, and it will eventually do the works of the Antichrist when he finally makes his appearance on this earth. He is God's enemy, the one who works clothed with the power of Satan, and a servant of the Devil.

Verse 2: Now the beast which I saw was like a leopard, his feet were like the feet of a bear, and his mouth like the mouth of a lion. The dragon gave him his power, his throne, and great authority.

This Word tells us what the Antichrist will do to the saints and the people of the world with his appearance. The Antichrist to come will do such cruel things to the saints because he would have received from Satan the authority and power to do these things. This shows us just how viciously the Antichrist will treat the saints when he makes his appearance, indicating what kind of suffering the saints would endure from the Antichrist with their martyrdom.

This Word shows us how ferocious the Antichrist is. The phrase, *"his feet were like the feet of a bear,"* indicates how destructive his power is. The "Dragon" here was originally an angel created by God, who had challenged Him for His throne. The Beast that appears in this chapter refers to the one who received authority from the Dragon and who does the works of standing against God and His saints.

Satan, an angel driven out of Heaven, will give his power and authority to the one who would stand against God, and lead him to his death by making him fight against God and His saints. The Antichrist, clothed in Satan's power, will viciously oppress the people of God and all the mankind in the future.

Verse 3: And I saw one of his heads as if it had been mortally wounded, and his deadly wound was healed. And all the world marveled and followed the beast.

This verse tells us that the Antichrist will emerge as one of the seven kings. The Antichrist is called as the Beast because he will do beastly things to the saints.

Here, the enemy of God and the saints will appear as the one who is able to solve even the problem of death in the end times. As such, many people of the end times believe him to be capable of solving all the problems that plagues the earth. But he is the enemy of God. Though he will make the worldly people surrender to him, he will be destroyed in the end for standing against God and His saints.

Verse 4: So they worshiped the dragon who gave authority to the beast; and they worshiped the beast, saying, "Who is like the beast? Who is able to make war with him?"

This tells us that the Dragon will give all his power to the one who does beastly things, whom he would have turned into his servant. Because of this, all the people of this world would think of Dragon as a god, tremble in fear, and worship him. Because at this time no king on this earth would have the kind of power that the Beast wields, no one would be able to stop him from proclaiming himself as a god and his deification.

As the Dragon gives the Beast great power, everyone would respect the Dragon and the Beast and worship the latter as their god. When the Antichrist possessing such great power appears, those who love the darkness more than the light will follow him, worship him as their god, and raise him high.

Verse 5: And he was given a mouth speaking great things and blasphemies, and he was given authority to continue for forty-two months.

The Beast will receive from the Dragon his prideful heart and his authority to speak prideful words for three years and six months (42 months). The Beast would thus receive the authority to harm the saints and the people of this world for these three and a half years.

The Beast, who is the Antichrist, will receive the authority to utter words that stand against God and to blaspheme His Church for three and a half years. All the sinners will thus end up surrendering to this Beast, and ultimately fall into their destruction together with the Beast.

Verse 6: Then he opened his mouth in blasphemy against God, to blaspheme His name, His tabernacle, and those who dwell in heaven.

The Beast, having received authority from the Dragon, will blaspheme God, all His angels and saints for three years and six months, cursing and defying them. All these things would be done according to what the Dragon tells him to do. Here, we must realize and believe that this act of Satan—that is, giving the Beast his authority to blaspheme God for three and a half years—would be made possible only by the permission of God.

Essentially, the Antichrist exists to blaspheme God and His people. Having received authority from the Dragon, the Antichrist will blaspheme the name of God and His people for the first three and a half years of the Great Tribulation.

Verse 7: It was granted to him to make war with the saints and to overcome them. And authority was given him over every tribe, tongue, and nation.

The Beast will receive the authority to kill the saints from the Dragon and make martyrs out of the saints. And he will also rule over the whole world, having been granted the authority to subject everyone in this world under his reign.

The Antichrist will kill the saints, for the only way for him to reign this world would be to fight against and overcome the saints. The wirepuller of the Antichrist is the Devil, a fallen angel in his essence who wants to be worshiped like God. And by killing the saints he will be adored as such by those who are not born again. In this time of the Tribulation, all the saints will be persecuted and martyred by the Antichrist.

Verse 8: All who dwell on the earth will worship him, whose names have not been written in the Book of Life of the Lamb slain from the foundation of the world.

When the Antichrist conquers this earth, everyone except those who have been born again by believing in the gospel of the water and the Spirit—that is, all those who otherwise have not been born again—will worship him as their god. But the Antichrist will be worshiped only by the sinners whose names have not been written in the Book of Life.

Verse 9: If anyone has an ear, let him hear.

This tells us that whosoever belongs to the people of God must prepare his/her faith to be martyred, for all these things will be fulfilled exactly as written in the Scripture.

Verse 10: He who leads into captivity shall go into captivity; he who kills with the sword must be killed with the sword. Here is the patience and the faith of the saints.

God says here that He will bring the same death and tribulations to those who kill the born-again saints in the end times. The saints will be killed by the Antichrist and his followers as the first three and a half years of the Tribulation pass by. But to all those who would thus have killed the saints, God will pay back with even greater tribulations and sufferings. As such, all the saints must unite their hearts, overcome this difficult Tribulation with their faith in the Word of the Lord, and give glory to God by embracing their martyrdom.

Verse 11: Then I saw another beast coming up out of the earth, and he had two horns like a lamb and spoke like a dragon.

Here we see not the first Beast, but the second beast. The

second beast, too, thinks and speaks like the Dragon. Not only does he think that he is like the Dragon, but basing his acts on this belief, he persecutes the saints even more viciously. This beast is the prophet of the Antichrist.

Verse 12: And he exercises all the authority of the first beast in his presence, and causes the earth and those who dwell in it to worship the first beast, whose deadly wound was healed.

The second beast, granted power by the first Beast, would worship the first Beast and make everyone who still remains on this earth worship him also. His work would be idolizing the first Beast and making everyone worship him like God. Because of this work, the first Beast and he would become the objects of all the people's worship like God. This is his essence, and the true self of Satan.

Verse 13: He performs great signs, so that he even makes fire come down from heaven on the earth in the sight of men.

As Satan would perform great miracles on this earth in the sight of men, he would be able to deceive many people. He would even have the power to make fire come down from heaven on the earth.

Verse 14: And he deceives those who dwell on the earth by those signs which he was granted to do in the sight of the beast, telling those who dwell on the earth to make an image to the beast who was wounded by the sword and lived.

But Satan will soon reveal his true colors. What he wants to do is to steal from the people's hearts their faith in God and have them worship him instead. To achieve this, he will perform many miracles before men and kill the people of God.

To fulfill his final purpose—that is, to become like God—he will then try to climb into God's place. He thus makes an image to the first Beast and makes people worship it like God.

Verse 15: He was granted power to give breath to the image of the beast, that the image of the beast should both speak and cause as many as would not worship the image of the beast to be killed.

As the biggest obstacle to deifying himself would be the people of God, Satan would do his utmost to get rid of them. He will thus murder all those who do not worship the image of the Beast, no matter how many they may be. But the saints will not surrender to this Beast. As such, countless saints would willingly embrace their martyrdom for their faith at this time, looking toward their afterlife. As the Antichrist would have brought great sufferings to the saints, God would have prepared for him the plagues of the seven bowls and the punishment of the eternally burning hell.

Verse 16-17: He causes all, both small and great, rich and poor, free and slave, to receive a mark on their right hand or on their foreheads, and that no one may buy or sell except one who has the mark or the name of the beast, or the number of his name.

At the peak of the Tribulation, the Antichrist will require all to receive a mark on their right hands or their foreheads, in order to ensure that everyone comes under his control. This mark is the mark of the Beast. To make everyone his servant, the Antichrist will coerce the people to receive his mark.

Holding people's lives as his collateral, the Antichrist then proceeds with his political schemes. He thus makes it impossible for anyone who does not have his mark of the Beast, the proof of his/her allegiance to him, to buy or sell anything in anyway. This mark is the name of the Beast, or his number. When the Beast comes to the world in the future, everyone will be required to receive his mark, made of his name or its number. We must therefore remind ourselves of God's warning that all those who receive this mark will be thrown into the lake of fire and brimstone.

Verse 18: Here is wisdom. Let him who has understanding calculate the number of the beast, for it is the number of a man: His number is 666.

The number of the Beast is 666. This means, in short, that the Beast himself is God. Is there a number that indicates that "a man is God?" A number bearing such meaning is the number of the Antichrist. As such, the saints cannot receive this mark, for only the Triune God is the true God for us. The saints must overcome Satan with their faith in the Lord and give glory to God. This is the best faith and worship with which the saints can give all glory to the Lord. Let us win with our faith.

Explanation of the Key Terms

The topic of chapter 13 is the appearance of the Antichrist and Satan. With their appearance, the saints will engage in a spiritual battle, in which they would have no choice but be martyred by the Antichrist. The Antichrist is a servant of Satan, the very one who would persecute the saints and have them be martyred.

Living in the present era, all the Christians and non-Christians of the world alike must know the Word of

Revelation. Chapter 13 of Revelation prophesizes that a time will come when Satan would idolize the Antichrist like God. Satan will give great authority to one of the politically powerful leaders of the world and make him stand against God and His saints. In particular, the Antichrist will idolize himself as God and confront Him.

Everyone, including the people of God, will suffer greatly from the tribulations and persecutions brought by the beastly Antichrist. The main passages shows us that the Antichrist's image, having received Satan's breath of life, would speak as if it were alive, as well as have the authority to harm the people. Those who are not born again would thus surrender to him and become his servants. All those who do not worship the idolized image of Satan, on the other hand, would be killed, no matter how many they may be. Satan also makes all to receive his mark or his number on their right hands or foreheads.

We must all prepare our faith in advance, and fight against and overcome Satan with our faith in the future by understanding and believing in the meaning of this Word revealed in Revelation 13 beforehand. Today's people of God must give glory to the Lord by learning from and believing in this Word of Revelation, and thus standing firmly against the Antichrist and overcoming him in victory.

The Origin of Hell

We must first know why there must be hell and why it came to its existence. Hell is a place prepared for Satan. The Bible tells us that he was not Satan from the beginning, but one of the many angels created by God. But by challenging God with his pride, this angel became Satan for the price of his sin, and hell is the place that God created to confine him. God made hell to give Satan and his followers the punishment reserved for those stand against Him.

Isaiah 14:12-15 explains how this angel ended up turning into Satan: *"How you are fallen from heaven, O Lucifer, son of the morning! How you are cut down to the ground, You who weakened the nations! For you have said in your heart: 'I will ascend into heaven, I will exalt my throne above the stars of God; I will also sit on the mount of the congregation On the farthest sides of the north; I will ascend above the heights of the clouds, I will be like the Most High.' Yet you shall be brought down to Sheol, To the lowest depths of the Pit."*

This angel who stood against God in Heaven coveted the throne of God. Seeing that only God was above him, he sought to drive Him out and sit on His throne, and as a result of this failed rebellion, he himself was driven out of Heaven by God and ended up becoming Satan. The Bible also refers to the angels who followed Satan in this rebellion as demons.

To render His just punishment to the creatures that had turned against Him, God made this place called "hell." Though Satan may seem to challenge God endlessly and blaspheme His works, when the gospel of the water and the Spirit is preached to all, he will eventually be bound in the bottomless pit for a thousand years.

Because Satan would fundamentally not repent his sin of turning against God, he would continue to try to raise himself high as God, and end up receiving the fearful punishment of hell for eternity. Until his very end, Satan will continue to stand against God and the righteous by making the people idolize him. The Bible calls this fallen angel, who blasphemes God and His saints, Satan or the Devil, and the Dragon or the serpent of old (Revelation 12:9).

666, the Number of the Beast

God will finally bind Satan in his prison. But before he is confined to hell, Satan will make the people receive the mark of 666, his name and number, on their right hands or foreheads. He will forbid everyone who does not have this mark from buying or selling anything.

The number 7 is the number of perfection, which implies God. On the other hand, the number 6 implies man, for God created man on the sixth day according to His own image and His likeness. The number of the Beast here, 666, reveals the pride of man trying to become like the Triune God. In not too distant future, the time will come to this world when the people would receive this mark of 666.

Revelation 13:1 tells us that seven kings will emerge out of ten nations. Of them, the one who has great power, and given authority from Satan, will subject this world under his rule. Performing great miracles such as healing his mortal wounds and bringing down fire from the sky, he will make all the people of the world follow him.

In other words, as Satan makes people follow him more than they follow God, many people end up worshipping him as God. As heroes emerge in trouble times, the Antichrist, having received great authority from Satan, will seek to be followed after as God by everyone by resolving the difficult politico-economic problems that the world would then be facing. Eventually, Satan will reveal his true colors by trying to challenge God directly in the end times.

As we can see from the Book of Daniel, the Great Tribulation will turn extremely harsh when it reaches the end of its first half. This first half, lasting for three and a half years, is the period of horrendous plagues and Satan's powerful reign.

But when these first three and a half years are over, what follows will be an even greater tornado of tribulations. At this time, Satan will be given authority to do his works among the people of the world, killing everyone who does not listen to him, deceiving them with his miracles that bring down fire from the sky, idolizing himself, and making them do the works of blasphemy against God.

At the same time, the Antichrist, having received all authority from Satan, will blaspheme the saints and kill all the saints who do not obey him. As verses 7-8 tell us, *"It was granted to him to make war with the saints and to overcome them. And authority was given him over every tribe, tongue, and nation. All who dwell on the earth will worship him, whose names have not been written in the Book of Life of the Lamb slain from the foundation of the world."* There are, however, those who refuse to worship the Beast at this time, and these are none other than the born-again people of God whose names have been written in the Book of Life of the Lamb.

The Event of Martyrdom

Martyrdom is an event that arises when the saints who have been born again by believing in the gospel of the water and the Spirit defend their faith in the Lord by rejecting the mark of Satan. Put differently, the Great Tribulation will get into its full-blown stage as its first half-period of three and a half years come to close. At this time, the righteous' faith must get ready for their martyrdom.

However, those who, though believing in Jesus as their Savior, have not believed in the gospel of the water and the Spirit, and thus have not received the remission of their sins and still have sin in their hearts, will end up siding with Satan and eventually surrender to him. Because the Christians who believe in Jesus but are not born again have no Holy Spirit in their hearts, when push comes to shove, they will capitulate to Satan, receive his mark on their right hands or foreheads, and worship him as God in the end.

We must know clearly that those who do not worship Satan at this time would be only those who have received the remission of their sins. We must also realize that God has clearly told us that He will throw, along with Satan, all those who surrender to the Beast into the lake of fire and brimstone.

Verses 9-10 tell us, *"If anyone has an ear, let him hear. He who leads into captivity shall go into captivity; he who kills with the sword must be killed with the sword. Here is the patience and the faith of the saints."* At this time, the Antichrist and his followers will bring great persecution to the righteous, selling them out and putting them to death with their swords. What we must definitely realize here, however, is that God will most certainly avenge us on our enemies who persecute and kill the righteous.

As such, the saints must go through their persecution and death by believing in God's promises. Were God not to bring His vengeance to our enemies, how could we ever close our eyes in our frustrated sense of justice? But as God has promises us to avenge us on our enemies who harm us, our death would not be in vain. God will most certainly avenge on those who torment and repress the righteous, and guide the righteous to their resurrection, rapture, and the marriage supper of the Lamb, making them reign with the Lord for a thousand years and live with Him for eternity. We all believe in this and hope for it. Our Lord therefore is the best God who will fulfill all our hopes. ⊠

The Appearance of the Antichrist

< Revelation 13:1-18 >

Based on the main passage, I will now discuss the appearance of the Antichrist and the martyrdom of the saints. From chapter 13 we see a beast coming up out of the sea. This Beast, which has ten horns and seven heads, is none other than the Antichrist. The passage tells us that on the Beast's horns were ten crowns, and on his heads a blasphemous name. We are also told that this Beast was like a leopard, with his feet like the feet of a bear, and his mouth like the mouth of a lion. In addition, the Dragon gave him his power, his throne, and great authority. One of his heads was mortally wounded, but this deadly wound was miraculously healed.

Marveled by this, the whole world began to follow the Beast, and as he was given authority by the Dragon, they worshiped both the Dragon and the Beast, saying, "Who is like the beast? Who is able to make war with him?" The passage also tells us that the Beast was given a mouth speaking great things and blasphemies, and authority to continue his works for 42 months.

The Beast Rising up out of the Sea

What the Apostle John saw was the emergence of the Antichrist amongst the rulers of this world appearing in the end times. This Antichrist was the Beast coming up out of the sea, a monster with ten horns and seven heads.

We must first find out whether or not this Beast is the real Beast that will actually appear in the world. There are two main things of the Beast that interest us: first, whether or not this Beast will actually make his appearance in this world and kill many people; and second, whether or not this Beast refers to the tyrannical Antichrist who would emerge from the rulers of the world. These are some of the issues that draw the most interest from the people. Those who know about these issues may say that they are easy to understand, but for those who are ignorant of them, it is quite natural to be puzzled over the question of whether or not such a Beast will indeed appear in the end times' world and rule over the people.

What God speaks to us in chapter 13 is about the future appearance of a king in this world who would be ruled by Satan. The phrase, "a beast rising up out of the sea," means that a king among the seven kings of the world will become the Antichrist. The passage also tells us that ten nations will unite around the Antichrist and rule over the thoroughly destroyed world.

The mortal wound of one of the Beast's heads and its healing, on the other hand, tells us that one of the seven kings would be mortally wounded, but would also be healed of his deadly wound. This king would be medically pronounced as dead, but miraculously be resuscitated to life, and then act like the Dragon. The Dragon here refers to Satan. Like the Dragon, the Beast would have all authority to destroy and harm people. When the end times come, such a beastly man will make his appearance in this world and massacre people, as monstrous as the Godzilla in the movie.

With the appearance of the servant of Satan, the world

will start to dash toward its destruction. The method by which Satan has chosen to work in the last era is to take his atrocities to the people through his servant. This is the same principle as God saving sinners from their sins through His saints.

We need to pinpoint exactly what this passage means for us. As one of the Beast's heads were wounded in the passage, a ruler of this world, resuscitated from his deadly wound, will receive authority from the Dragon and be honored by the people as if he were God. This is why, we must remember, the people proclaimed, *"Who is like the beast? Who is able to make war with him?"*

This Antichrist that appears in the present passage will be respected by all the people under the dominion of Satan and stand against God. It means that a powerful leader will emerge in the last world and rule over it. This leader would be one of the rulers of the world's nations. Having received the spirit of the Antichrist from Satan, he will emerge as a powerful leader. The world will then come under the rule of this leader and be reigned by him. The world will be united into a single state in the future. The advanced nations of the present times will cooperate among each other and extend their rule over the whole world by fronting the powerful ruler.

In Europe, we now have the European Union, and in Asia and Americas as well, there are organizations that are seeking further integration of individual states into a single political body. When such organizations develop further, united supranational states will appear, and a very powerful leader will emerge from such integrated states. This leader will play the role of the Antichrist who stands against God. He would be a charismatic leader with power to reign over and repress the whole world as he pleases.

- Why? Because by receiving great ability and authority

from the Dragon, Satan, his wisdom would be different from that of the ordinary people, and his thoughts would also be different from that of the latter. His wisdom and power would reach the sky. What he says would be fulfilled without any problem, and no one could dare to covet his place. This period of his reign is the era of the pale horse written in Revelation 6.

The era of the pale horse will most certainly come in the near future, and the world will then belong to the Antichrist for a while. But those who do not know this truth actually want to see a powerful leader like the Antichrist to appear. The saints, however, know this truth and will be awake in this era, and so when this time comes, they will be able to resist and fight against the Antichrist, and be martyred to defend their faith.

Not many people nowadays fully respect the leaders of their own countries. Regardless of which country they live in, people in general have some kind of discontent with their political leaders. People throughout the whole world wait for a strong and capable leader. Why? Because they want a leader who can solve all the problems that are mounting in this world, from food shortage to environmental degradation, religious problems, economic stagnation, racial tension, and so on. When a world leader, armed with great wisdom and power, is able to solve all the problems, everyone in the world would honor him like God and be glad to be ruled by him. This leader, the Antichrist who has the whole world in his hand, will take care of everything.

We all want a political leader whom we can respect in all aspects, but such a wish is too great to be met, for this kind of leader can neither arise nor come into existence in actuality. But as the Antichrist to come solves this world's many political and economic problems, he would become the kind of leader whom everyone wishes for, the one who can bring political and economic stability to the world.

When the era of the black horse passes by and the era of the pale horse begins, because of the plagues of the seven trumpets, the ruined world will seek for a strong and able leader. Powerless leaders of small countries cannot solve global problems. As such, people will look for an absolute leader. The Antichrist will appear at this time, speaking and acting like God. Because he would have been healed from his mortal wounds, people would be marveled by him. As he would live again and work as a ruler with great power, courage, determination and wisdom, people throughout the whole world would think of him as God.

As such, even the people of Israel would believe him to be their long-awaited Messiah. But the Israelites will soon realize that he is a liar and that Jesus Christ is their true Messiah, and many of them will thus be saved. The Antichrist will hear people saying, *"Who can possibly ever stand against him?"* All those who do not obey him, without any exception, will then be killed.

When the era of the pale horse comes, the entire world will not only suffer greatly from the natural plagues, ravaged by the fire that burns down a third of its forests and choked by heavy smog, but the people of the world will also unite to come under a single ruler to serve him as their king. The one who solves all these problems will be raised by them high above as God.

All these things are but among what God has planned. For these things to come to this world, there must first be drastic global environmental changes, and a consensus among the opinion-leaders of each nation on the need for a centralized governing authority. Such a consensus that seeks after this kind of ruler is now being forged in today's era of the black horse.

The world now wants a very strong leader. As the leaders of each nation are unable to dispel the discontent of their own people individually, the mankind is now looking for a strong leader who can solve all the problems that they are facing.

If you take a closer look at what is happening in this world, you would realize that all these things are very much possible to be actualized. The prophesized leader will be extremely ferocious, a man of absolute power and great abilities, as shown by his description as having feet that are like the feet of a bear, a mouth like the mouth of a lion, and a face like the face of a leopard.

This man, receiving authority from the Dragon, will blaspheme God, his angels in Heaven, and His saints. And he will fight against the saints and overcome them. The Antichrist will kill the saints in his fight against them, demanding them to renounce their faith. Because the saints would not give up their faith at this time, they will all be martyred. And as the Antichrist would have authority over the entire world, he will freely kill and destroy all those who do not listen to his commands.

Verse 8 tells us, *"All who dwell on the earth will worship him, whose names have not been written in the Book of Life of the Lamb slain from the foundation of the world."* Because the Antichrist would reign as the absolute ruler in this time, everyone who does not obey him will be killed at his command. However, for all the saints, such a time would be the time of their martyrdom.

From verse 8 above quoted, the word "worship" here means to honor and serve the one who is absolute. In the end times, the Antichrist will be worshiped by the people on this earth like God, receiving far greater honor than what any king had ever received before. Yet a group of people will not worship this leader. They are none other than the "born-again Christians." They will not recognize the Antichrist as God, and as such, they will not worship him and instead be killed to defend their faith.

Another Beast Coming out of the Earth

The Antichrist also has his false prophet. This false prophet is the one who would raise the Antichrist high, as well as threaten and kill those who do not obey the Beast. Revelation 13:11 says, *"Then I saw another beast coming up out of the earth, and he had two horns like a lamb and spoke like a dragon."* The second beast that appears here is the servant of the first Beast—that is, of the Antichrist. Like the Antichrist, he will also stand against God and kill the people of the world and the righteous.

Receiving authority from the Dragon, he will foster the people to worship the Antichrist who came before him as God. Because he, too, would have received authority from the Dragon, he will do what the Dragon wants him to do. He will not only make the people worship the Antichrist who came before him and kill all those who do not obey him, but he will also perform miracles, such as bringing down fire from the sky, and even act like the Antichrist. He will deify and idolize the Beast, who would have been mortally wounded but revived from this wound, before everyone.

Who, then, would do all these things? It is the prophet of the Antichrist. His work is to make an image of the Antichrist that came before him and have the people raise this Antichrist high above as God. To do so, he will breathe life into this image of the Antichrist to make it speak, and kill all those who do not worship this idol of the Beast regardless of their number. Because the saints would be martyred by refusing to worship the idol, a countless number of martyrs will come out at this time.

Everyone in the world who has not been born again, on the other hand, will tremble before their death and end up becoming slaves to death. As such, they will all worship the Antichrist as God. The conscientious intellectuals may arise in a rebellion against the dictator, but they will be quickly put down, killed by the fire that comes out of the mouths of the false prophet and the Antichrist.

This false prophet, having built the idol, would say, "Everyone must receive the mark of his name or number!" He would then make it his policy to forbid anyone who does not have this mark of the Beast from making any kind of trade, so that everyone would indeed receive this mark of the name of the Beast. Verse 18 says, *"Here is wisdom. Let him who has understanding calculate the number of the beast, for it is the number of a man: His number is 666."*

This is rather straightforward. Though we think the number 666 as a complicated thing, it simply means the name of the Antichrist, or his number. To receive the mark of the Beast means to receive the mark of his name on either the forehead or the right hand. It is to imprint this ruler's name into one's body, numerated into a number and digitalizing into a bar code.

This mark would be needed everywhere whenever one tries to buy anything. Even when you get on the bus, you would need this digital number imprinted in your body, and without it you would be restricted. Today's era is this very digital age. It is an age of numbers. As everything is translated into numbers, what were once extremely complicated have now become extremely simple. In such an era would appear this mark of the Beast.

The Antichrist will make an idol out of himself and demand that people worship him like God. The time will actually come when people would thus be required to call the Antichrist as their "God," praise him and call upon his name in honor, and receive his name on their right hands or foreheads. When such things happen, the saints will all be martyred. The Antichrist will demand the saints to receive his mark and worship him, saying, "So you believe in Jesus? You believe Him as your God? Throw Him away! Bow before this image and call me God instead! Believe in me as the one who is absolute! If you don't, you will surely die!"

The Antichrist will demand a single faith from the entire world. And he will demand everyone to worship him as God. Those who do not admit that he is God at this time will all be killed. The Antichrist will publicly execute the saints who stand against him.

All those whose names are not written in the Book of Life of the Lamb will receive his mark and worship him. When we receive the remission of sin into our hearts, the Holy Spirit dwells in us, and our names are written in the Book of Life in the Kingdom of Heaven. Because our names are written in the Book of Life and because the Holy Spirit has sealed our hearts, we will all be lifted up as the children of God when He calls us.

Could we ever abandon Jesus Christ who has saved us, and declare to the image of the Beast that it is now our God and Savior? Of course not! No matter how insufficient we have been before Him, our Lord came to this earth in the flesh of a man, cleansed away all our sins by taking them upon Himself with His baptism, and saved us by being judged vicariously on the Cross.

Also, because our Lord has already told us about all these things to come beforehand, we the saints can never betray our faith during this time of the Antichrist. Although the time of the Tribulation will come to us and be followed by our death, we still believe that our Lord will make us live in His Kingdom of Heaven by resurrecting and rapturing us shortly after our martyrdom.

Because we believe that after our rapture God will destroy this world by pouring down His plagues of the seven bowls, and that after this we will descend on the earth and reign over it for a thousand years, we can never kneel before the idol. This is why the servants and saints of God would willingly give up their lives.

The false prophet will then try to convince us otherwise. He will try to buy us over by saying, "Look, chaos is running rampant in this world right now. When everyone, including all the intellectuals and scholars, believe in and follow our supreme leader as God, how can you still go on refusing to believe in this absolute king of ours?" But if we know and believe in the Word of God always, we will triumph in the end by embracing our martyrdom.

In Revelation 14 appear the 144,000 saints who praise God in Heaven. This tells us of the saints' resurrection and rapture following their martyrdom. From elsewhere in the Bible, such as what Paul told us of the second coming of Christ or what other servants of God had prophesized in the Old Testament, we can also find out about the rapture, with which the saints will be lifted up to the air and join the marriage supper of the Lamb with the Lord. To this marriage supper will enter the saints.

When the saints have thus entered into the marriage supper of the Lamb in Heaven, the plagues of the seven bowls will be poured on this earth, completely laying it to waste. After this, the earth is renewed, and the saints will then descend onto it with the Lord and reign in the Kingdom of Christ for a thousand years to come. When we know all these facts, could we really call the Antichrist as God, even if he throws in all kinds of appeasement and enticements to make us bow before his image, worship him as God, and abandon our faith in the true God? Of course not!

As it is written in the Bible, *"faith is the substance of things hoped for, the evidence of things not seen (Hebrews 11:1),"* the prophets believe in what God has told them beforehand about the things to come. The servants and people of God who believe in the Word are all priests and prophets. By making us preach the gospel of the remission of sin to everyone throughout the whole world, God leads many souls to receive their remission of sin. As our Lord has saved us regardless of how insufficient we are before Him, God has made us His people, and until this very moment, He has loved, guided, and blessed us unchangingly.

The Lord has not only given us the peace of our spirits, but He has also made us place our hope in the Kingdom of Heaven by giving us the Holy Spirit. As such, when we hear the Antichrist telling us to worship him as God, we cannot help but resist him deep from our hearts.

We may at first be startled by the unfolding events when we suddenly realize that the time that God spoke of has finally arrived, but we the saints will soon regain our composure and begin resisting the Antichrist. "So you think you are the real God? Did you create the universe? Did you create the mankind? Are you really the lord of the people's souls?" These are the words with which we will fight against the Antichrist.

When the Antichrist kills the saints and the servants of

God at this time, we, too, would die. There can never be a change of our God to us. Faith does not come by coercion. Nor does faith appear or disappear by the logic of force. Far from it, the true faith in fact has even greater power to overcome coercion. The saints will therefore be martyred, and the Antichrist will end up losing to the saints.

When the Antichrist makes idols in his own image and demands the saints to worship him as God, the saints and the servants of God would shout to him, "Are you God's servant or Satan's servant? Do you know the gospel of the water and the Spirit? Do you know and believe that Jesus Christ is God? When Jesus Christ returns to this earth, He will throw people like you into the deepest end of hell! Do you understand, you son of Satan?" The Antichrist and his prophet would then kill the saints, and the saints would joyfully embrace their martyrdom for God.

Verse 10 tells us that *"he who kills with the sword must be killed with the sword."* This means that if the Antichrist kills the saints, God, too, will throw him and his followers to the bottomless pit, as well as kill them on this earth. When those who stand against God torment the saints, they, too, will face even greater torments from God.

As such, we must stand against the Antichrist with our perseverance of faith. The duration of the saints' persecution at this time will altogether last for only three and a half years. But God may reduce the saints' persecution and tribulations, shortening their duration to just a few months or a couple of weeks. Though the saints would be martyred, they will live again. They will be resurrected and raptured, and they will be blessed to reign with Jesus Christ in the Millennial Kingdom.

When the Millennial Kingdom comes, the beauty of the nature will reach its height, and the saints will reign with the

Lord in their holy bodies transformed from their old flesh. They will then live happily with the Lord in the New Heaven and Earth forever. How could we, who know and believe in all these things, not persevere through the short-lasting sufferings that will come to us for our faith in Jesus?

No matter how harsh the tribulations of this time are, innumerable saints will nevertheless be martyred, and so there is no reason why we, too, would not embrace our martyrdom as well. As all of these things are true, we will never surrender to the Tribulation that lasts only a short while in this world. In a further example, even if the world were to turn into a paradise for a hundred or a thousand years, we just cannot surrender to the Antichrist. All these things are not far away from us, but will come to us in a very near time.

We must therefore preach the gospel of the water and the Spirit now, when the world is at peace. To prepare for this time of the Great Tribulation, we are diligently spreading the gospel of the water and the Spirit now. In a year's time, the gospel that we are preaching will do the most wondrous works. Nationally and internationally, marvelous works of the gospel will come. People may take the gospel of the water and the Spirit lightly at first, but many who do not know the Word of Revelation will seek and hear it and return to the gospel of the water and the Spirit, because they would be very interested in the Word of Revelation and would not be able to take it lightly.

Revelation 13 is the chapter of the saints' martyrdom. When the time of martyrdom comes, the saints will be killed by sword or shot to death. Many saints will thus be killed at the hand of the Antichrist. But we can face our death without any fear, for it would be the death of our flesh, not of our faith itself. Filled by our faith and the Holy Spirit, we will shout out the indescribable words of courage.

You have nothing to fear, even if you are not good at speaking or are timid. Just think of the old saints of the Early Church period. The saints of that time did not surrender to the forces of Satan because they were killed not alone but together, and because they were also filled by the Holy Spirit. Just remember that Jesus already told us, *"But when they deliver you up, do not worry about how or what you should speak. For it will be given to you in that hour what you should speak; for it is not you who speak, but the Spirit of your Father who speaks in you" (Matthew 10:19-20).* To receive the Kingdom of God, could we not, as the people of God, bear our death? We can all bear it.

This world will be ruined completely by God's plagues of the seven trumpets, when an absolute tyrant called the Antichrist will reign for a while. How then could we exchange the eternal Heaven for anything on this world, no matter how nice it might be? When the world would have turned into an impossible place to live, where the rivers would have turned into wormwood, the sea into blood, and the nature laid to waste, far less could we surrender to the beastly man who would try to make us betray our faith.

From the very day of our martyrdom, the only world that awaits those who still remain on this earth would be the kind where unidentified epidemics would be raging fiercely and crops would cease to produce harvests, as they wither away or are wiped out by hail. In such a world, even putting aside the matter of faith, no one would want to live any longer.

The Book of Revelations shows us the things to come in the future. When today's era of the black horse moves only a little bit further, the era of the pale horse will actually arrive. Our Lord, in other words, will return soon. What I am saying is not that you should give up all your possessions since the

Lord's return is imminent. Rather, what I am saying is that we should continue to serve our Lord until the very day of the Antichrist's appearance, as faithfully and unchangingly then as now.

If you are, by any chance, troubled or depressed now, you should no longer worry. When you and I realize that we are to become martyrs, our hearts will turn peaceful and calm. Since we are to become martyrs, in other words, what greed would we have left in us? If there is one desire left in us, it would be to preach this gospel to everyone throughout the entire world, so that many saints will rise up in the end times, be saved and martyred by believing in this gospel, and thereby receive the New Heaven and Earth. I also hope that all the saints would make the Kingdom of Christ theirs with their faith, having been nourished by believing in this truth, and thus willingly go through all these things that await them in the time of the Antichrist.

God has given us His blessing of martyrdom. Not just anyone can be martyred, and not just anyone can live for the Lord. I am only grateful to God for giving us such a blessing, and I am only happy for the fact that I would die for faith. Because we have neither hope nor any lingering attachment to this world, martyrdom is a great happiness for us.

All that we have to do is hope for the Millennial Kingdom and Heaven that God has prepared for us, live our lives by uniting our efforts to preach the gospel throughout the whole world until the day of the Lord's return, receive Him in joy when He returns, and just to the place where we have hoped for. Believe in this Word, for these are the things that will indeed come.

We cannot receive the mark of the Antichrist, for we are the people of the Kingdom of Heaven. Because receiving the mark would be a matter of personal choice, it would not be done by physical force, but by the acceptance of heart.

Even our children, if the gospel is found in their hearts, would embrace their martyrdom even more boldly than the grown-ups, for they, too, would have the Holy Spirit dwelling in them. As the grown-ups confess that Jesus is their Savior, if the Holy Spirit is found in the children's hearts, they, too, will most certainly confess that Jesus is their Savior and God. The Bible tells us not to think of what to say when we are dragged before the Antichrist, for the Holy Spirit will fill our hearts with the words that we can speak with.

God's children may also fear as they are spiritually young and weak, but the Holy Spirit in them does not fear. They will be martyred by the power of the Holy Spirit dwelling in them. Because they, too, belong to God, He will receive their souls, permit them to have their bodies be killed, and also reward them to reign in a better world.

God would have filled the hearts of those who have been born again by the water and the Spirit with His Words to speak with. Because only the souls that have been chosen and received by God can be martyred, God cannot but prepare their faith for His name's sake. Just by the fact that we have the Holy Spirit dwelling in our hearts because we have believed in the gospel of the water and the Spirit, we will all receive the reward of the Millennial Kingdom and the glory of the New Heaven and Earth.

In the end times, we will all experience the fullness of the Holy Spirit in our hearts. As we have been fated to become martyrs, when we are thus martyred according to God's plan, we will all go through our martyrdom while praising, worshiping, and glorifying Him in His presence. Because we believe in God, we follow Him only by our faith that shouts out

"Amen!" Because we know that we are to be martyred, our greed of the flesh naturally sheds away from us, making our souls very pure.

Being martyred, which is God's will for us, is to receive a great blessing and be glorified greatly. As the saints have their hope to dwell forever in the New Heaven and Earth, they will fight against the Antichrist and defend the gospel of the water and the Spirit in their hearts until the end. In this time of the Great Tribulation, all the saints, recognizing Jesus Christ as their God and believing in their perfect salvation given by Him, will embrace their martyrdom before God.

I thank the Lord who has given us this blessing of martyrdom. ✉

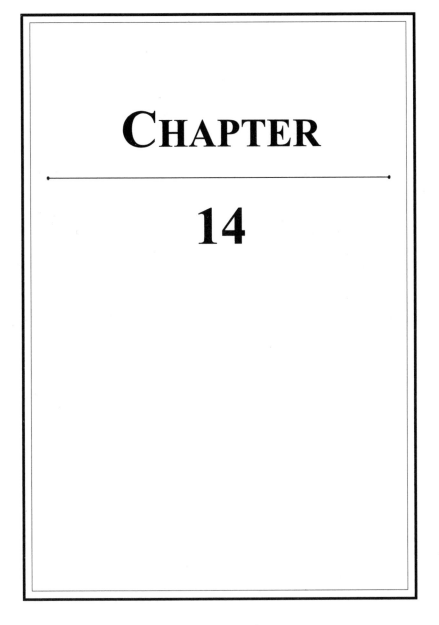

CHAPTER

14

The Praise of
The Resurrected and
Raptured Martyrs

< Revelation 14:1-20 >
"Then I looked, and behold, a Lamb standing on
Mount Zion, and with Him one hundred and forty-four
thousand, having His Father's name written on their
foreheads. And I heard a voice from heaven, like the voice
of many waters, and like the voice of loud thunder. And I
heard the sound of harpists playing their harps. They sang
as it were a new song before the throne, before the four
living creatures, and the elders; and no one could learn that
song except the hundred and forty-four thousand who were
redeemed from the earth. These are the ones who were not
defiled with women, for they are virgins. These are the ones
who follow the Lamb wherever He goes. These were
redeemed from among men, being firstfruits to God and to
the Lamb. And in their mouth was found no deceit, for they
are without fault before the throne of God. Then I saw
another angel flying in the midst of heaven, having the
everlasting gospel to preach to those who dwell on the
earth—to every nation, tribe, tongue, and people—saying
with a loud voice, 'Fear God and give glory to Him, for the
hour of His judgment has come; and worship Him who
made heaven and earth, the sea and springs of water.' And
another angel followed, saying, 'Babylon is fallen, is fallen,
that great city, because she has made all nations drink of

the wine of the wrath of her fornication.' Then a third angel followed them, saying with a loud voice, 'If anyone worships the beast and his image, and receives his mark on his forehead or on his hand, he himself shall also drink of the wine of the wrath of God, which is poured out full strength into the cup of His indignation. He shall be tormented with fire and brimstone in the presence of the holy angels and in the presence of the Lamb. And the smoke of their torment ascends forever and ever; and they have no rest day or night, who worship the beast and his image, and whoever receives the mark of his name.' Here is the patience of the saints; here are those who keep the commandments of God and the faith of Jesus. Then I heard a voice from heaven saying to me, 'Write: 'Blessed are the dead who die in the Lord from now on.'' 'Yes,' says the Spirit, 'that they may rest from their labors, and their works follow them.' Then I looked, and behold, a white cloud, and on the cloud sat One like the Son of Man, having on His head a golden crown, and in His hand a sharp sickle. And another angel came out of the temple, crying with a loud voice to Him who sat on the cloud, 'Thrust in Your sickle and reap, for the time has come for You to reap, for the harvest of the earth is ripe.' So He who sat on the cloud thrust in His sickle on the earth, and the earth was reaped. Then another angel came out of the temple which is in heaven, he also having a sharp sickle. And another angel came out from the altar, who had power over fire, and he cried with a loud cry to him who had the sharp sickle, saying, 'Thrust in your sharp sickle and gather the clusters of the vine of the earth, for her grapes are fully ripe.' So the angel thrust his sickle into the earth and gathered the vine of the earth, and threw it into the great winepress of the

wrath of God. And the winepress was trampled outside the city, and blood came out of the winepress, up to the horses' bridles, for one thousand six hundred furlongs."

Exegesis

Verse 1: Then I looked, and behold, a Lamb standing on Mount Zion, and with Him one hundred and forty-four thousand, having His Father's name written on their foreheads.

This is about the born-again saints, who were resurrected and raptured after their martyrdom by the Antichrist, praising the Lord in Heaven. The saints who were martyred by the Antichrist and the saints who were asleep would now be in Heaven, praising the Lord with a new song. In verse 4 we see that 144,000 sang this new song. You might wonder, then, whether the raptured would amount to only 144,000 people. But number 14 here means that all things have changed (Matthew 1:17).

We must realize that after the martyrdom and rapture of the saints, the Lord will change this present world into a whole new world. Instead of this world, our Lord will build a world in which He will live with His people. This is the will of the Creator.

Those who praise the Lord in Heaven are those who have become saints by believing in the gospel of the water and the Spirit given by Christ while on this earth. As such, on their foreheads are written the names of the Lamb and of the Father, for they now belong to Christ.

Verse 2: And I heard a voice from heaven, like the voice of many waters, and like the voice of loud thunder. And I heard the sound of harpists playing their harps.

The saints in Heaven are those who were martyred to defend their salvation given by the Lord and their faith in the fact that the Lord alone is their God, and who were thereafter resurrected. Because their bodies were resurrected and they were raptured by the Lord's power, they are praising Him in Heaven for His salvation and His blessing of giving them authority. The sound of their praise is as beautiful as the sound of flowing currents, and as majestic as thunders. All of them have been saved eternally from their sins through the redemption of their sins by believing, while on this earth, in the gospel of the water and the Spirit given by the Lord.

Verse 3: They sang as it were a new song before the throne, before the four living creatures, and the elders; and no one could learn that song except the hundred and forty-four thousand who were redeemed from the earth.

The 144,000 people here refer to the raptured saints. In the Bible, the number 14 means a new change. Those who can praise the Lord with a new song in Heaven are those who have been transformed while on this earth by receiving the remission of sin and being born again through their faith in the gospel of the water and the Spirit. This is why the Lord says here that they were 144,000.

Apart from them, there is no one else who can praise the Lord for His blessing of redemption through the gospel of the water and the Spirit. Our Lord is thus being praised by those whose sins have been forgiven by believing in the gospel of the water and the Spirit and who have received the Holy Spirit as their gift.

Verse 4: These are the ones who were not defiled with

women, for they are virgins. These are the ones who follow the Lamb wherever He goes. These were redeemed from among men, being firstfruits to God and to the Lamb.

The saints are the ones who have not defiled their faith with any worldly power or religions. There are many people in this world who easily change their faith. But for those who have become saints by believing in the Lord's baptism and His blood on the Cross, and by thus receiving the remission of their sins, their faith can never be changed for anything in this world.

The saints who ascend into Heaven and praise the Lord are the ones who have unchangingly kept the gospel of the water and the Spirit given by the Lord and defended their faith. As such, the ones who can praise the Lord in the Kingdom of Heaven are those who are raptured by the Lord for their faith in the gospel of the water and the Spirit.

In the middle of verse 4 is written, *"These are the ones who follow the Lamb wherever He goes."* You must realize that those who have been cleansed of their entire sins all at once through their faith in the gospel of the water and the Spirit must, after thus being born again, follow the Lord wherever He leads them. Because they have received the remission of their sins, in their hearts is found the willingness to follow the Lord in joy wherever He leads them. In the end times, they therefore would be praising the Lord in Heaven, having been martyred by the Antichrist with their faith, and resurrected and raptured by the Lord.

It is also written, *"These were redeemed from among men, being firstfruits to God and to the Lamb."* Of the countless people living in this world, only a handful have been saved from all their sins by believing in the gospel of the water and the Spirit given by the Lord. This is why our Lord says in Jeremiah 3:14, *"I will take you, one from a city and two from a family, and I will bring you to Zion."* Those who have met the gospel of the water and the Spirit and received the remission of their sins are this few.

Because they belong to the Lamb, they would be the ones who receive the firstfruits of resurrection, who are raptured by the Lord's power, and who praise Christ forever, all as promised by the Lord. On this earth, too, they are the ones who follow the Lord wherever He leads them. All these are by the grace and power of God.

Verse 5: And in their mouth was found no deceit, for they are without fault before the throne of God.

Those who have been born again by believing in the gospel of the water and the Spirit can preach this true gospel with their mouths. While there are many people today who are preaching the gospel in their own way, it is also true that only a handful of them are actually preaching the true gospel of the water and the Spirit.

Those who preach only Jesus' blood on the Cross are not preaching the gospel of the water and the Spirit given by the Lord. Why? Because no other gospel but the gospel of the water and the Spirit alone is the true gospel of the Bible. As all the sins in the hearts of the righteous have been taken away by the Word of the true gospel, they can preach this gospel with their mouths with full conviction.

Verse 6-7: Then I saw another angel flying in the midst of heaven, having the everlasting gospel to preach to those who dwell on the earth—to every nation, tribe, tongue, and people—saying with a loud voice, "Fear God and give glory to Him, for the hour of His judgment has come; and worship Him who made heaven and earth, the sea and springs of water."

The born-again saints must continue to proclaim the gospel of the water and the Spirit on this earth. This work of preaching the gospel of the water and the Spirit, therefore, must continue on this earth until the very day of the saints' rapture.

Only those who believe in the gospel of the water and the Spirit would be martyred by the Antichrist to defend their faith, and they alone would thus be lifted up to the Kingdom of Heaven. Everyone must fear God, believe in the gospel of the water and the Spirit, and thereby receive their remission of sin and the Holy Spirit as their gift. If today's Christians are unable to believe in the gospel of the water and the Spirit given by the Lord in thankfulness, their faith in Jesus would be all in vain.

The One who created the whole universe and all things in it is none other than Jesus Christ. As such, the mankind must recognize Jesus Christ as their God who created them and gave them their salvation with His forgiveness of their sins, and thus worship Him accordingly, for by His hands were all things made and are completed. By believing in His gospel of the water and the Spirit in their hearts, all the people can be forgiven of their entire sins and receive the blessing of having the Holy Spirit as their gift.

This world must now prepare to receive the judgment that Jesus Christ would render on those who stand against God. We must, of course, also prepare our faith that would soon be raptured by the Lord, for the day of the judgment of God is near us. The way to prepare for the rapture is to believe in the Word of the gospel of the water and the Spirit given by the Lord. Why? Because only by believing in His gospel of the water and the Spirit, one can receive the Holy Spirit, and, when the last days come, they would be clothed in the glory of being lifted up to the air by the Lord in their rapture.

As soon as possible, all the sinners must therefore believe

in Jesus Christ as the God of creation and salvation, and worship Him accordingly. They must accept the gospel of the water and the Spirit into their hearts, and thus receive the grace of His redemption and the Holy Spirit as their gift. Those who worship God receive into their hearts the gospel of the water and the Spirit given by the Lord and do not reject it, for this is how they can worship God.

Verse 8: And another angel followed, saying, "Babylon is fallen, is fallen, that great city, because she has made all nations drink of the wine of the wrath of her fornication."
This world will disappear by the fearful judgment of Jesus Christ. Because its religions are made of what are fundamentally false teachings, it will be destroyed by God. These worldly religions have made people follow the world more than God Himself, and used them as the instruments to stand against God. This world will thus be destroyed, because its people have left God and lusted after such worldly religions.
That they have followed the worldly religions means that they have followed the false gods, the demons. God will therefore destroy this world in His wrath. Everything in this world and all its false religions will be brought down by God, and shall drink of the wine of the wrath of God. As such, those who stand against God, as well as the demons that live like parasites attached to the worldly religions, will all fall down by the plagues of God and be thrown into eternal hell.

Verse 9-10: Then a third angel followed them, saying with a loud voice, "If anyone worships the beast and his image, and receives his mark on his forehead or on his hand, he himself shall also drink of the wine of the wrath of God, which is poured out full strength into the cup of His indignation. He shall be tormented with fire and brimstone in the presence of the holy angels and in the presence of the Lamb. "

God warns everyone here, saying that if anyone worships the Beast and his image, or receives his mark on the right hand or the forehead, he/she will receive the punishment of hell. Working through many people, Satan will coerce the whole mankind to worship the idol made after the image of the Antichrist, but those who are born again will fight against the Antichrist and be martyred to defend their faith. The born-again saints must, to defend their faith, thus stand against the Antichrist and be martyred.

If anyone, surrendering to the Antichrist, bows down before his image and receives the mark of his name or number, he/she will garner the wrath of God that would throw him/her into the eternal lake of fire and brimstone. When the time of the Tribulation comes, the saints must pray to God, defend their faith in the Lord, and place their hope in His Kingdom. And by believing in Jesus Christ, they must stand against the Antichrist and defend their faith, join in their martyrdom, resurrection, and rapture, and thus receive the eternal blessing of dwelling with the Lord in His Kingdom.

Verse 11: And the smoke of their torment ascends forever and ever; and they have no rest day or night, who worship the beast and his image, and whoever receives the mark of his name.

Those who worship Satan as God will be given His plagues and the torment of eternally restless hell. Whoever surrenders to the Antichrist in the end times and worship his image as God will be tormented in the lake of fire and brimstone filled by the wrath of God. We must all believe that anyone who follows the Beast and his image, and anyone who receives the mark of the Beast, will have no rest day and night.

Verse 12: Here is the patience of the saints; here are those who keep the commandments of God and the faith of Jesus.

As the saints believe in all the wealth, glory, and blessing that the Lord has promised them, they must persevere through in patience. They must persevere through the time of the Tribulation, too. The promise that the Lord has made to the saints of the end times is that He would bestow on them the blessing of living with Him after their martyrdom, as, together with their resurrection by the power of the Lord, they are lifted up to Heaven.

The saints thus persevere because they believe in this blessing that would allow them to enter the marriage supper of the Lamb with the Lord, reign with Him for a thousand years, and always live with Him in the Kingdom of Heaven. When the end times come, the saints therefore need to be martyred to defend their faith. They must persevere through all the tribulations of the time in patience.

The saints who are now living in the present era must, when the Antichrist demands them to betray their faith with his threats, pressures and enticements, nevertheless embrace their martyrdom, believing in the Lord's promises. Why? Because shortly thereafter, all the blessing of our Lord would be fulfilled just as He promised us. All the saints can receive their rewards only by keeping their faith in the Word of God and in the Lord. Therefore, keep your faith in the Word of the Lord. God will welcome the saints who have thus defended their faith in His Word and in Jesus Christ into His whole new world.

There is a plenty of reasons as to why the saints who serve the Lord's gospel must persevere through all the difficulties of the time of the Tribulation in patience. For a better in the future, there is a need to bear with the present suffering in patience.

Romans 5:3-4 tell us, *"And not only that, but we also glory in tribulations, knowing that tribulation produces perseverance; and perseverance, character; and character, hope."* The saints who can persevere through the Great Tribulation by believing in the Lord will live a life of blessings, receiving their resurrection and rapture from Him and reigning in His Kingdom. As such, we must all persevere through the Tribulation with our faith. By keeping their faith in the Lord, the saints can truly persevere through the Great Tribulation of the end times. The saints believe in all the things that the Lord would fulfill for them in both this world and Heaven.

Verse 13: Then I heard a voice from heaven saying to me, "Write: 'Blessed are the dead who die in the Lord from now on.'" "Yes," says the Spirit, "that they may rest from their labors, and their works follow them."

The verse says here, *"Blessed are the dead who die in the Lord from now on."* Why? Because when the time of the Tribulation comes—that is, when the Antichrist rules over the world—every sinner then living on this earth would all be destroyed. The saints must therefore look to the coming Kingdom of Christ, defend their faith, and embrace their martyrdom of faith. Those who are martyred to give glory to the Lord are blessed, and as such, they must embrace their martyrdom to defend their faith.

The Lord will then take care of such saints, allowing their resurrection and rapture to lift them up to His Kingdom. All the labors of the saints on this earth would then end, and they will instead live enjoying their rewards given by the Lord. At this time, all the saints will have the joy of reigning with the Lord and of eternal life, and the wealth and glory of the His

Kingdom will be theirs forever.

This is why those who are martyred in the end times to defend their faith are so blessed, for they will live with the Lord in all the wealth and glory of His Millennial Kingdom and the His eternal Kingdom of Heaven forever. To those who do not surrender to the Beast and defend their faith in the Lord, God will give the blessing of reigning with the Lord forever.

Verse 14: Then I looked, and behold, a white cloud, and on the cloud sat One like the Son of Man, having on His head a golden crown, and in His hand a sharp sickle.

This verse tells us that the Lord will return to rapture the saints. Because the Lord is the Master of the saints, He will resurrect the saints who will have been martyred to defend their faith and lift them up to the Kingdom of God in rapture. In the time of the Great Tribulation, the rapture will most certainly come to the saints.

Verse 15: And another angel came out of the temple, crying with a loud voice to Him who sat on the cloud, "Thrust in Your sickle and reap, for the time has come for You to reap, for the harvest of the earth is ripe."

This Word refers to the completion of the saints' rapture by the Lord. Time-wise, the rapture will happen after the martyrdom of the saints. The Lord will allow the rapture to the saints who are asleep then, together with the saints who are martyred. The completion of the saints' faith is found in their salvation, martyrdom, resurrection, rapture, and eternal life. The time of the saints' rapture is after their martyrdom with the persecution of the Antichrist, and is simultaneous to their resurrection.

Verse 16: So He who sat on the cloud thrust in His sickle on the earth, and the earth was reaped.

This verse, too, refers to the saints' rapture. Rapture means the lifting of the saints up to the air. Does this then mean that the saints would be lifted up to the air, and then descend down to the earth with the Lord? But of course! After the saints are raptured, our Lord will destroy the earth, the sea, and all that is in them by pouring the plagues of the seven bowls, and after thus destroying the world, He will descend on to this earth together with the raptured saints.

Then, the Lord and His saints will reign on this earth for a thousand years, and when the marriage supper of the Lamb is over, they will ascend into the eternal Kingdom of Heaven. When the saints join the Lord in the marriage supper of the Lamb, the Lord would have already renewed the whole world and all things in it.

After their rapture, the saints will stay in the air with the Lord for a while, and when the plagues of the seven bowls are all over, they will come down to the renewed earth to reign with Him for a thousand years. They will then enter into the Kingdom of God with the Lord, and live with Him forever.

Verse 17: Then another angel came out of the temple which is in heaven, he also having a sharp sickle.

The angel that appears here is the angel of judgment. This angel will bring down great plagues on the people of the world who have stood against God, and throw them into the eternal fire. His duty is to throw and bind, together with the Antichrist and his servants, all the sinners of the world who have not been born again yet into the bottomless pit.

Verse 18: And another angel came out from the altar, who

had power over fire, and he cried with a loud cry to him who had the sharp sickle, saying, "Thrust in your sharp sickle and gather the clusters of the vine of the earth, for her grapes are fully ripe."

This Word tells us that the time has now come for the sinners to be judged by God for their sin of standing against Him. In God's times are the hours of His plans' implementation. To give the sinners His judgment of fire, God will gather together all the sinners and all those who had stood against God, and punish them accordingly.

Verse 19: So the angel thrust his sickle into the earth and gathered the vine of the earth, and threw it into the great winepress of the wrath of God.

This Word shows us that after the rapture of the saints, the Antichrist and the sinners would suffer greatly under the plagues of the seven bowls. On this earth, too, God will bring His wrath to the sinners by unleashing His fearful plagues on them, and then follow this with the punishment of hell. The plagues that God would thus pour on these sinners, the Antichrist and his followers are His righteous wrath. This is God's providence for the sinners who stand against Him.

Verse 20: And the winepress was trampled outside the city, and blood came out of the winepress, up to the horses' bridles, for one thousand six hundred furlongs.

The verse here tells us just how harsh the punishment of the wrath of God and its suffering would be to those who still remain on this earth, both men and living creatures, brought by the plagues of the seven bowls poured on them. It also tells us that these plagues will ravage throughout the entire world. When the saints are martyred, resurrected, and raptured, from this moment and on, the wrath of the plagues of the seven bowls will be brought down altogether, and thus ending everything.

No one except the saints in Heaven and the angels who have stood on God's side will escape from these fearful plagues. For those who stand against God, on the other hand, only the punishment of hell would wait. In contrast, by then the born-again saints would find themselves in the feast of the marriage supper with the Lord in the air, thanking and praising Him for His salvation. From then on, the saints will live with the Lord forever in His eternal blessings. ⊠

How Should the Saints React to the Appearance of the Antichrist?

< Revelation 14:1-20 >

To overcome the Antichrist when he appears in the near future, the saints must prepare themselves to be martyred with their faith in the Lord. To do so, they must know well about the wicked schemes the Antichrist would bring on this earth. Only then can the saints stand against him and overcome him with faith. Stan will try to destroy Christians' faith by making people receive the mark of his name or number.

The reason why he tries to destroy the faith of Christians is because by standing against God and bringing down the faith of the righteous, he seeks to prevent people from receiving the remission of their sins through the gospel of the water and the Spirit. The Antichrist will turn people into his servants and make them stand against God. For this, the Antichrist and his followers who still remain on this world receive great punishments and plagues.

The righteous must live their lives of faith with a clear understanding of the plagues of the seven bowls that God would pour on their enemies. As God says in Deuteronomy 32:35, *"Vengeance is Mine, and recompense,"* He will avenge His children's death on them. As such, we must defend our faith and live a life of victory, rather than being overwhelmed by our anger and doing its fruitless works. Believing in the fact that God would destroy all those who still remain on this earth after their martyrdom, the saints must fight against the Antichrist.

The Word of Truth That Must Never Be Forgotten

What all those who have received the remission of their sins must remember is that only the sinless saints will all be resurrected and raptured shortly after being martyred by the Antichrist. When the day of the Antichrist's appearance and the saints' martyrdom comes, we must never forget that every promise of God will all be fulfilled.

From verse 14 and on, the Word of God in chapter 14 teaches us that the rapture will most certainly come to the saints, and that the time of this rapture is right after their martyrdom.

We must not forget that our resurrection and rapture will come after Satan makes people receive his mark. For the righteous who are martyred by the Antichrist, the blessings of the first resurrection and rapture await them. The righteous will embrace their holy martyrdom to defend their faith at this time, for they will refuse to receive the mark of Satan. The martyred righteous will therefore receive their rewards according to their labor on this earth, and the glory of God will be added to them.

Do not be mournful, nor angered, when you see that the fellow saints or servants close to you are martyred to defend their faith. On the contrary, all the saints must in fact thank God and give glory to Him for allowing them to be martyred to defend their faith, for shortly thereafter the martyrs would be resurrected in holy bodies and raptured by the Lord.

What Are the Plagues of the Seven Bowls Prepared for Those Who Stand against God?

Verse 19 says, *"So the angel thrust his sickle into the earth and gathered the vine of the earth, and threw it into the great winepress of the wrath of God."* Those who had always stood against His love are destined to receive from God His fearful plagues after the martyrdom of the saints, for they had, while on this earth, refused to accept into their hearts the gospel of the water and the Spirit given by the Lord, and instead stood against it. These are the ones who have become God's enemies by not believing in the salvation of Jesus Christ, who came by His blood and water to save them from sin. They must receive not only the plagues of the seven bowls poured by God, but they must also receive the plague of the fearful punishment of hell forever.

These are the seven plagues that God would bring to those who are not raptured by the Lord. After the martyrdom of the saints, God will mercilessly pour down these plagues of the seven bowls that He had prepared to those who, not having participated in the rapture, still remain on this earth as Satan's slaves and continue to blaspheme against the glory of God.

Why, then, would God make the righteous be martyred? Because were the righteous to remain on this earth with those who are not born again, He would not be able to pour down the plagues of the seven bowls when their time comes. And because God loves the righteous, He allows them to be martyred so that they may join in His glory. This is why God would have the righteous be martyred before unleashing the plagues of the seven bowls. And after resurrecting and rapturing the martyred righteous, He will freely pour down these plagues on the earth. These plagues of the seven bowls are the last plagues that God would to bring to the mankind on this earth.

The Millennial Kingdom and the Saints' Authority

The age of the Millennial Kingdom will begin when the Lord, together with His saints, descends to this earth again. Matthew 5:5 tells us, *"Blessed are the meek, For they shall inherit the earth."* When the Lord returns to this earth with the saints, the Word of Psalms 37:29, that "the righteous shall inherit the land," will all be fulfilled.

When the Lord thus descends on this earth with all the saints, He will give them the authority to make this earth theirs. At this time, He will give them authority to reign over ten cities, and another five more cities. The Lord will renew this earth and everything on it when He returns, and make the saints reign with Him over it for a thousand years from then on.

What, then, is the hope that the righteous of this era must live with? They must live hoping for the day when the Kingdom of Christ is built on this earth. When the Lord's Kingdom comes to this earth, the peace, joy, and blessings that flow from His reign will finally being on it. Living under the Lord's reign, we shall lack nothing, but live only in His overflowing abundance and perfection.

When the Kingdom of the Lord comes to this earth, all the hopes and dreams of the righteous will be fulfilled. After living on this earth for a thousand years, the righteous will then enter the eternal Kingdom of Heaven, but those who had stood against God, in contrast, will be thrown into the lake of eternal fire and brimstone, suffering forever and having no rest day and night.

The righteous must therefore live in hope, waiting for the day of the Lord. All the righteous must not forget that martyrdom, resurrection, rapture, and eternal life all belong to them. Keep in your heart this Word of truth and hope that you have heard so far and hold on to it in steadfastness.

Until the day of the Lord's return, the righteous will live preaching the gospel of the water and the Spirit and placing their hope in the Kingdom of Heaven. The righteous have the authority to live forever in the Kingdom of God, and the authority to preach the gospel of the water and the Spirit on this earth.

What Must the Saints Who Live in This Dark Age Do?

It is quite clear that this age is an age of darkness, and that it is becoming ever more difficult to live in it. As such, we must preach the gospel of the water and the Spirit to the sinners and nurture them. Throughout the whole world, the righteous must spread the love of God and the remission of their sins coming through the gospel of the water and the Spirit given by Jesus Christ. This is what the righteous must do now.

If they were to lose this present opportunity, it will never come back to them again. Because the end of this world is not too far away, we must preach the gospel of the water and the Spirit all the more, and nurture the lost souls with the hope of the Kingdom of God. This is the good thing that the righteous ought to do.

In the present world, there are many who, even as they do not have the Word of the gospel of the water and the Spirit, claim to believe in Jesus and live their lives serving the Lord.

But those who lead their religious lives without the real truth are all false prophets. These liars are the deceivers who only exploit the material possessions of the believers in the name of Jesus.

We therefore pity those who try to live their lives of faith while deceived by these false prophets. Living their lives of faith without the gospel of the water and the Spirit, these nominal Christians still remain as sinners and continue to live under the curse of the Law of God, even as they claim to believe in Jesus. They are living in sin always, ignorant of the fact that if they were just to believe in the gospel of the water and the Spirit, all the sins in their hearts would simply disappear and make them as white as snow, and the Holy Spirit would be given to them as their gift.

But in contrast, the servants of God who believe in and preach the gospel of the water and the Spirit live in peace. The servants of God and His people rejoice in the gospel of the water and the Spirit. They testify: "By taking the sins of the world upon Himself all at once with His baptism from John, and by being judged for these sins on the Cross, the Lord Jesus has made all the sins of the world disappear. When I believed in this salvation of atonement, all my sins that had weighed me down heavily have also disappeared. I have now become righteous."

With such testimonies, the saints in God's Church are giving glory to God. Those who have this faith can finally have their hope for Heaven.

The First Resurrection Is an Event Reserved for the Saints

In just a short while, the Lord will soon return to this earth. In not too distant future, someone who would become the Antichrist will appear and imprint the right hands or the foreheads of many people with his mark. When this time comes, you should realize that the second coming of the Lord, as well as the saints' martyrdom, resurrection, and rapture, are all near you. When such a day and hour arrive, you should realize that it is a day of joy for the saints, but for the sinners who are not born again, a day of their judgment of sin.

All the saints will be resurrected after their martyrdom, and then join the marriage supper of the Lamb with the Lord. When you and I are martyred in this time, our bodies will soon be resurrected and raptured. It does not matter what might have happened to the bodies of the saints who had gone before us—whether or not their bodies have already turned into dust, or they no long have any form left in them, poses no problem. When this time comes, the saints will be resurrected not in the weak bodies of the present, but in perfect bodies. The righteous will be resurrected in holy bodies at this time, and live with the Lord forever.

Even when difficult times await us, when the Antichrist will emerge and persecute us, we must defend our faith in Jesus Christ by believing in the Word of God that we have now listened to. Also, we must not forget that because you and I have believed in the gospel of the water and the Spirit, we will all participate in the martyrdom of the saints, their first resurrection, and their rapture.

Now, you must not fall away from your faith in this truth, and live a life that fights against and overcomes the Antichrist.

Until this day comes, we must be together with those who were saved before us by believing in the truth, hold on to the Word of God, and follow the Lord in faith.

Even Now, There Are Many Liars Who Are Deceiving People

Even now, a countless number of people, as servants of Satan, are teaching false faith. In particular, there are many liars who advocate and teach the doctrine of pre-tribulation rapture to their congregations, trying to convince them that they have nothing to do with the Great Tribulation of seven years.

The Bible, in contrast, clearly testifies to us that the saints' martyrdom and rapture would come slightly past the first three and a half years of the Tribulation. Let us not be deceived by such liars. Let us instead know and believe that when the first three and a half years of the seven-year period of the Great Tribulation passes by us, we would all be martyred, and shortly thereafter be resurrected and raptured simultaneously.

You must therefore stay away from the false prophets who teach that they would have nothing to do with the Great Tribulation of seven years. The true saints believe that their martyrdom, resurrection and rapture, and the marriage supper of the Lamb would all come slightly past the first three and a half years of the Tribulation.

Then, How Should We All Live Now?

By now, you should have realized that if anyone believes

in the Lord as the Savior—that is, the Lord who came to this world, carried the sins of the world with His baptism from John, bled on the Cross, and rose again from the dead—the Holy Spirit would come to the heart of this believer as his/her gift.

You must listen to with your ears and believe with your heart what the Holy Spirit says to you through God's Church, and dwell in your faith in God. All the saints must live their lives of faith led by God's Church. By oneself, no one can preach the gospel of the water and the Spirit, neither keep it, nor serve it. This is why God's Church is so important even for the saints who have already been born again.

God has thus established His Church and His servants on this earth, and through them He is feeding His lambs. In particular, the works of God become even more precious and important as the end times come nearer to us, and as such, I pray and hope that you would live a faithful life filled by the Holy Spirit. As the end times get nearer, the righteous must labor even harder to come together, to pray, to comfort, hold, and help each other, and to live for the Lord, united into a single heart and a single purpose.

God has allowed martyrdom, resurrection, rapture, and eternal life to the saints. Let us all live the kind of life that fights against and overcomes the Antichrist, and then confidently stand before God. Hallelujah! ✉

CHAPTER

15

The Saints Who Praise the Lord's Marvelous Works In the Air

< Revelation 15:1-8 >

"Then I saw another sign in heaven, great and marvelous: seven angels having the seven last plagues, for in them the wrath of God is complete. And I saw something like a sea of glass mingled with fire, and those who have the victory over the beast, over his image and over his mark and over the number of his name, standing on the sea of glass, having harps of God. They sing the song of Moses, the servant of God, and the song of the Lamb, saying:

'Great and marvelous are Your works,

Lord God Almighty!

Just and true are Your ways,

O King of the saints!

Who shall not fear You, O Lord, and glorify Your name?

For You alone are holy.

For all nations shall come and worship before You,

For Your judgments have been manifested.'

After these things I looked, and behold, the temple of the tabernacle of the testimony in heaven was opened. And out of the temple came the seven angels having the seven plagues, clothed in pure bright linen, and having their chests girded with golden bands. Then one of the four living creatures gave to the seven angels seven golden bowls full of

the wrath of God who lives forever and ever. The temple was filled with smoke from the glory of God and from His power, and no one was able to enter the temple till the seven plagues of the seven angels were completed."

Exegesis

Verse 1: Then I saw another sign in heaven, great and marvelous: seven angels having the seven last plagues, for in them the wrath of God is complete.

Chapter 15 tells us of the end of the world brought by the plagues of the seven bowls poured by the seven angels. What is this *"another sign in heaven, great and marvelous,"* that the Apostle John saw? It is the wondrous scene of the saints standing on the sea of glass and praising the Lord's works.

Verse 2: And I saw something like a sea of glass mingled with fire, and those who have the victory over the beast, over his image and over his mark and over the number of his name, standing on the sea of glass, having harps of God.

The phrase *"something like a sea of glass mingled with fire"* here tells us that the moaning of suffering on this earth would reach its height as God pours the plagues of the seven bowls on it, and that the saints, on the other hand, would be praising the Lord in the air. The plagues of the seven bowls poured on this earth by God are brought to avenge the saints on their enemies.

At this time, the saints, having participated in their resurrection and rapture by God, would be standing on this sea of glass mingled with fire to praise His works. The saints who are resurrected and raptured by being martyred on this earth through the power of the Lord will forever praise Him for His salvation and power. The praising saints are those who would have achieved the victory of faith by overcoming the Antichrist with the kind of faith that rejects him, his image, and the mark of his name or the number of his name.

Verse 3: They sing the song of Moses, the servant of God, and the song of the Lamb, saying: "Great and marvelous are Your works, Lord God Almighty! Just and true are Your ways, O King of the saints!"

The saints standing on the sea of glass are singing the song of Moses and the song of the Lamb. And its lyrics are: *"Great and marvelous are Your works, Lord God Almighty! Just and true are Your ways, O King of the saints!"* The lyrics of this song, just as they are written, praise God for the fact that with His almighty power there is nothing that He cannot do. It is also written here that "great and marvelous are [His] works."

The word "marvelous" here means "something so great that words cannot express it." It is simply wonderful and marvelous, in other words, that our Lord God has saved, through the gospel of the water and the Spirit, all the saints of both the Old Testament and the New Testament from all their sins, make them sinless, and allow these saints, who are saved through their faith, to praise the Lord in the air by resurrecting them from their death of the flesh and lifting them up to the air. These saints are praising the Lord God for being their Savior, their Lord, and the Almighty.

Do you really believe that the Lord God has created the universe and all things in it, including you and me, and that He is indeed our Lord? Only those who believe in this truth can become believers in the gospel of the water and the Spirit given by the Lord. Those who have this faith are the ones who have the truest faith. Christians must know and believe that Jesus is the Creator who made the whole universe and everything in it. And they must praise and worship the Lord God by knowing and believing in His works. *"Great and marvelous are Your works, Lord God Almighty!"* This praise of faith shows the true faith of the truly born-again saints who sing the song of Moses and the song of the Lamb.

Do you believe that the Lord Jesus is God Almighty? Those who believe that Jesus is God Himself who created the whole universe also believe that the Lord came to this earth in the flesh of a man, that at the age of 30 He was baptized by John to take upon the sins of the mankind all at once, and that He bled and died on the Cross and rose from the dead again. Through their faith they receive the remission of sin and become saints. Those who know this truth, and have the true faith in it, can indeed be described as the people of great faith.

The passage here says that the raptured saints praised God in the air, saying, *"Great and marvelous are Your works."* They were praising the Lord God, in other words, for creating the universe and the mankind, for saving the sinners on this earth by cleansing away all their sins all at once with the Lord's baptism received from John, and for giving them the right to become the children of God—all through the gospel of the water and the Spirit given by the Lord. That the saints can take part in their martyrdom for Christ, their resurrection and rapture, and eternal life—all these are blessings bestowed by God.

All the saints must give to God their praises that reveal all His glory for all the righteous works that the Lord has done for the sinners—that is, for making all sins disappear, as well as for all other works that He had done while on this earth. The saints sing the song of Moses and the song of the Lamb in the air. They praise the Lord singing how great and marvelous is what the Almighty Lord God has done for the sinners and to His enemies.

Indeed, what the Lord has done for the saints and to all those who stand against Him is not only wonderful to us, but it is even marvelous. The purpose of God in creating this world was to make the mankind His people. As such, all His works that He has done for the mankind appear before us as wonderful and marvelous. We give glory to God by believing in all that He has done for us, and we praise Him by believing in all His works.

That God created man after His own images is also marvelous. That He gave His Law to everyone, and that He worked through the Virgin Mary to send Jesus Christ to this earth are also wondrous before our eyes. But we believe, at the same time, that all these works were done as a means to save the sinners from their sins. Also marvelous is the fact that our Lord God had passed all the sins of the world onto the body of Jesus Christ, all at once, by having Him receive baptism from John, so that He could make every sin of the mankind disappear completely and perfectly.

For those who believe in the gospel of the water and the Spirit, that the Lord God has thus given them the eternal remission of sin and His Holy Spirit is also wonderful and marvelous. And that He has made His saved saints preach the gospel of the water and the Spirit throughout the entire world is another wonderful blessing, something that is, once again, marvelous to us. The fact that our Lord God would allow martyrdom to the saints, permit them to be resurrected and raptured, and have them live in glory forever in Heaven—all these works are also wonderful blessings.

Having planned all these things, God will fulfill them all

accordingly when the time comes—these works of the Lord that make the saints glorify and praise God are turned into great blessings in our hearts. We also thank the Lord for and are blessed by the fact that He would avenge Himself on His opponents with His almighty power through the plagues of the seven bowls.

Because all the works of the Lord God appear before the saints' eyes as something far beyond their limits, they praise Him. They therefore praise the Lord for His omnipotence, for His marvelous works and power. Our Lord God is worthy to receive all praise from not only every mankind, but also from every creation in the universe. Hallelujah!

Those who have known, experienced, and witnessed with their own eyes what our Lord God has done for them cannot help but praise Him for His almighty power, His perfect wisdom, His righteousness, His eternally unchanging just judgment, and His everlasting and unchanging love. The Lord has allowed the saints to praise Him forever for His marvelous works.

As such, the saints praise the Lord God eternally for all the works that He has done for them, for His goodness and greatness. Our Lord God is worthy to receive praise from all things in the universe, for all His works are made possible only by His almighty power. Hallelujah! I praise the Lord for His power and His everlasting, unchanging and blessed love!

Verse 4: "Who shall not fear You, O Lord, and glorify Your name? For You alone are holy. For all nations shall come and worship before You, For Your judgments have been manifested."

The saints in the air sing the praise of the Lord's works with their mouths. *"Who shall not fear You, O Lord, and glorify Your name?"* This is a praise filled by conviction and faith, proclaiming in confidence that no one can ever stand against the glory of the Lord God, and that no one can ever dare to stop Him from receiving praise. Who can stand before the name of the Lord without trembling in fear? There is no one and nothing in this world, in the whole universe and the entire eternal domains, that can stand against and overcome our Lord God, for Jesus is King of kings and Almighty God.

All things in this world and the saints cannot help but tremble in fear before the name of Jesus Christ, the almighty power of the Lord God, and His truth. Because the power of the Lord God is infinitely great, and because He is true and perfect, all the creatures give thanks, glory and praise before His name. Everyone must have a heart that fears God. And all things in the universe must praise the name of our Lord. Why? Because our Lord is holy, and He has delivered all mankind from all their unrighteousness.

Because the plagues of the seven bowls that the Lord would pour on the Antichrist, his followers and religionists living on this earth will manifest His righteousness, we cannot help but praise Him. Because the Lord's righteous justice is revealed through the great plagues of the seven bowls, our Lord God is worthy to receive glory, praise and worship from all the living creatures, angels, and saints in the air.

Who can dare to not fear the name of the Lord Jesus Christ? Our Lord is not a creature, but the Lord Almighty God. By pouring the fearful plagues of the seven bowls to all those who stand against Him, the Lord God makes it simply unavoidable that all His creations would praise Him before His majesty and power.

"For all nations shall come and worship before You, For Your judgments have been manifested." We must realize,

therefore, that no one who stands against and blasphemes the name of the Lord can ever live happily.

Only kneeling before the name of the Lord, and believing in, thanking and praising Him for His supremacy, His omnipotence, His mercy, and His great salvation and love are the kind of worship that is worthy of His name. All the creations must therefore believe in what the Lord has done while on this earth, and praise and worship Him. Our Lord is worthy to receive praise from all people and all nations. Amen. Hallelujah!

Verse 5: After these things I looked, and behold, the temple of the tabernacle of the testimony in heaven was opened.

This verse tells us that when the plagues of the seven bowls that our Lord God would pour on this earth end, God would give the saints His house of Heaven. All these things will be fulfilled by the Lord God. What is this tabernacle of the testimony then? It is the house of God that is like the tabernacle of this earth. The phrase, *"the temple of the tabernacle of the testimony in heaven was opened,"* means that the era of the Kingdom of the Lord God would open from then on.

With the opening of the door of the temple of the tabernacle of the testimony, the final plagues and the Kingdom of the Lord God will be brought to this earth. Without knowing the gospel of the water and the Spirit, no faith will be admitted before God. As such, we must know and believe in this gospel of truth, and realize and believe also that the time for us to go to and live in the Kingdom of Christ is now nearing us.

Verse 6: And out of the temple came the seven angels having the seven plagues, clothed in pure bright linen, and having their chests girded with golden bands.

This Word shows us that when God pours the plagues of the seven bowls on this earth, He will work through the angels who believe in the essential justice and fairness of these seven plagues. It tells us, in other words, that the servants of God can become qualified to serve the Lord as His servants only when they always believe in His righteousness and place their complete trust in His goodness.

Only when they believe that the Lord's works are always right, God's servants can do such works of the Lord. The saints can thus be used as the precious servants of God only when they are always clothed in the righteousness of the Lord, put on the hope of salvation as a helmet, defend their faith, and live a life that glorifies the Lord.

Verse 7: Then one of the four living creatures gave to the seven angels seven golden bowls full of the wrath of God who lives forever and ever.

This tells us that when God works through His servants, He makes them work in an orderly manner, and that such works are also fulfilled in good order. The phrase, "one of the four living creatures," shows us that the Lord has His precious servants placed for His purposes, and that He works through them. The four living creatures that appear here are the four most precious servants of the Lord who always stand by Him, and who are the first to serve His purposes. We must realize the supremacy of God and His omnipotence, and we must also believe that He works through His servants.

Verse 8: The temple was filled with smoke from the glory of God and from His power, and no one was able to enter the temple till the seven plagues of the seven angels were completed.

Before the Lord God completes His judgment of this earth, no one can enter His Kingdom. This tells us just how perfect God's holiness is. It also tells us that He is not a God who takes pleasure in wickedness (Psalm 5:4). We must therefore remember that if anyone wants to enter the Kingdom of God, he/she must believe in the gospel of the water and the Spirit that the Lord has given to the mankind. Our Lord God allows only those who believe in this gospel of the water and the Spirit to enter His Kingdom.

To the saints who have received the remission of sin, God has given the blessing of living forever in His Kingdom after destroying His enemies by pouring the plagues of the seven bowls. All the works of God reach far beyond the imagination of man, revealing His greatness and supremacy. By judging His enemies, God manifests His omnipotence. Were God not to have the power to punish His enemies for their sin of standing against Him, He would not be able to receive praise from all.

But as God has more than enough power to punish those who stand against Him, the Lord God will bring His judgment on His enemies and condemn them with the eternal punishment of hell.

Our Lord God is more than worthy to be praised forever by every people of every nation. God will thus complete His judgment on the enemies for all their sins and open His Kingdom. Amen. We thank our Lord God for His great power, His glory and holiness. Hallelujah! ⊠

The Division Point of Eternal Destiny

< Revelation 15:1-8 >

Chapter 15 describes the plagues of the seven bowls, which would be poured right after the saints' rapture on those who, as God's enemies, have stood against Him. The number "seven" that appears in common in Revelation, such as the seven seals, the seven trumpets and the seven bowls, signifies God's perfection and His almighty power. Jesus Christ is the omniscient and omnipotent God. That Jesus is the omniscient and omnipotent God to us means that our Lord is God Almighty for whom nothing is impossible. Our Lord is God Himself who has planned all things and who has the power to fulfill them all.

The saints, as such, must praise the Lord for His omniscient and omnipotent majesty and power revealed through the plagues of the seven bowls that He would pour on this world. We thank our Lord for the fact that such judgment is made possible by His omniscience and omnipotence. That the Lord would take His avenge on His enemies with the plagues of the seven bowls and the eternal suffering of hell is, for the saints, something that they can only be grateful and is most appropriate. The saints thus cannot help but praise the Lord. Hallelujah!

The plagues of the seven bowls will arrive after the saints are raptured at slightly past the first three and a half years of the seven-year period of the Great Tribulation. Because of these plagues of the seven bowls, the hearts of the enemies of God will be dejected, and as they find out that our Lord is God Almighty, they will fear Him.

The *"sign in heaven, great and marvelous"* stated in verse 1 refers to the last plagues that will be poured on this world— that is, the plagues of the seven bowls. What the phrase "great and marvelous" tells us, on the other hand, are three-fold: first, through the Word of prophecy, the saints already know all about the plagues that will come to this world; second, the saints will be exempted from the plagues of the seven bowls; and third, the power of these plagues of the seven bowls brought by the Lord will be worldwide and fatally destructive.

On the other hands, the redeemed and raptured saints will sing "the song of Moses, the servant of God, and the song of the Lamb" in the air. The background to this song, as can be seen in Exodus 15:1-8, is the song of Israelites, who praised the Lord for His power and authority after crossing the Red Sea led by Moses. They could not help but praise the Lord for saving them with His power and authority from the desperate situation of being pursued by the Egyptian army.

Likewise, the saints of the New Testament cannot help but praise the Lord for their eternal salvation, which came through the remission of sin fulfilled by the baptism that Jesus received from John and His blood on the Cross. When the end times come, the people of God will once again praise the Lord, thanking Him for their martyrdom, resurrection, rapture and eternal life, all made possible through Jesus Christ who delivered them from their enemies, and all their sins.

In addition, the important distinction of this song is that it praises the Lord's omnipotence, majesty, and righteousness. The martyrs cannot help but praise the Lord for His power, the grace of their salvation from sin, and the blessing of eternal life.

"The temple of the tabernacle of the testimony" in verse 5 refers to the tabernacle that God allowed to the Israelites when they left Egypt so as to give them the blessing of accompanying the Lord.

The "linen" in verse 6 refers to the righteousness of God. It tells us that the angels would be clothed in God's righteousness and receive from Him the authority to render the kind of judgment that no enemy can ever reject.

Verse 8 says, *"The temple was filled with smoke from the glory of God and from His power, and no one was able to enter the temple till the seven plagues of the seven angels were completed."* We can discover three meanings here. First, it shows just how complete God's wrath on His enemies is.

Second, it tells us that no one can enter into the Lord's Temple without believing in the baptism of Jesus Christ and His blood, for God's salvation of the sinners is so perfect.

Third, it shows that no human goodness can ever enable anyone to avoid the righteous judgment of God, and that only by believing in the baptism of Jesus Christ and His blood on the Cross can one escape from the wrath of God poured on the sinners.

The saints must therefore hold steadfast to the gospel and preach it to the last moment. And those who have not yet received the remission of their sins must realize that they are bound to face the righteous judgment of God, and they must return, as soon as possible, to the gospel of the water and the Spirit given by the Lord. The passage shows us that, as the judgment that God would bring on His enemies with the plagues of the seven bowls is perfect before all eyes to see, no one would ever be able to stop it until this judgment of sin is all completed.

Chapter 15 of Revelation shows us that the Antichrist,

Satan, demons, and all those who stand against and do not believe in the gospel of the water and the Spirit, which has been made available to us by the love of Christ, are the enemies of our Lord. I praise and thank the Lord for bringing His plagues to these enemies of God to judge them. It is only appropriate for the saints to praise the Lord with the song of Moses, the servant of God, and the song of the Lamb.

No one can stop our praise of the Lord's righteousness, power, majesty, and truth. I praise the Lord for giving us such blessings. Hallelujah! ✉

CHAPTER

16

The Beginning of the Plagues of The Seven Bowls

< Revelation 16:1-21 >

"Then I heard a loud voice from the temple saying to the seven angels, 'Go and pour out the bowls of the wrath of God on the earth.' So the first went and poured out his bowl upon the earth, and a foul and loathsome sore came upon the men who had the mark of the beast and those who worshiped his image. Then the second angel poured out his bowl on the sea, and it became blood as of a dead man; and every living creature in the sea died. Then the third angel poured out his bowl on the rivers and springs of water, and they became blood. And I heard the angel of the waters saying:

'You are righteous, O Lord,
The One who is and who was and who is to be,
Because You have judged these things.
For they have shed the blood of saints and prophets,
And You have given them blood to drink.
For it is their just due.'

And I heard another from the altar saying, 'Even so, Lord God Almighty, true and righteous are Your judgments.'

Then the fourth angel poured out his bowl on the sun, and power was given to him to scorch men with fire. And men were scorched with great heat, and they blasphemed the name of God who has power over these plagues; and they did not repent and give Him glory. Then the fifth angel poured out his bowl on the throne of the beast, and his kingdom became full of darkness; and they gnawed their tongues because of the pain. They blasphemed the God of heaven because of their pains and their sores, and did not repent of their deeds. Then the sixth angel poured out his bowl on the great river Euphrates, and its water was dried up, so that the way of the kings from the east might be prepared. And I saw three unclean spirits like frogs coming out of the mouth of the dragon, out of the mouth of the beast, and out of the mouth of the false prophet. For they are spirits of demons, performing signs, which go out to the kings of the earth and of the whole world, to gather them to the battle of that great day of God Almighty. 'Behold, I am coming as a thief. Blessed is he who watches, and keeps his garments, lest he walk naked and they see his shame.' And they gathered them together to the place called in Hebrew, Armageddon. Then the seventh angel poured out his bowl into the air, and a loud voice came out of the temple of heaven, from the throne, saying, 'It is done!' And there were noises and thunderings and lightnings; and there was a great earthquake, such a mighty and great earthquake as had not occurred since men were on the earth. Now the great city was divided into three parts, and the cities of the nations fell. And great Babylon was remembered before God, to give her the cup of the wine of the fierceness of His wrath. Then every island fled away, and the mountains were not found. And great hail from heaven fell upon men, each hailstone about the weight of a talent. Men blasphemed God because of the plague of the hail, since that plague was exceedingly great."

Exegesis

Verse 1: Then I heard a loud voice from the temple saying to the seven angels, "Go and pour out the bowls of the wrath of God on the earth."

With the plagues of the seven bowls of wrath, God will bring His wrath upon the servants of the Antichrist and his people who are still living on this earth. All the creatures and men will be swept up by the storm of God's wrath, exploding after so many years of His patience, and they will suffer from the great plagues that will ravage through for the remaining years of the Great Tribulation. At this time, this world will be reduced to ashes as it is broken apart, smashed to pieces, and destroyed into oblivion.

Revelation 16 is the chapter where the plagues of the seven bowls are poured. Those who, until this final moment, have neither known nor believed in the gospel that bears the testimony of salvation, which would have allowed them to be lifted up to the air by the Lord—that is, the gospel of the water and the Spirit—will all be destroyed by these plagues.

Verse 2: So the first went and poured out his bowl upon the earth, and a foul and loathsome sore came upon the men who had the mark of the beast and those who worshiped his image.

The plague of the foul and loathsome sore that God would pour through His angel will descend on those who have received the mark of the Beast. This plague of sore is an incurable skin disease that would fester on the skins of the inflicted, whose infection would also spread around beyond the festering skins. How great would the suffering be, when the inflicted are to be tormented by this plague of the foul and loathsome sore until their death? But God will not only pour down the plague of sore on all those who received the mark of the Beast, but He will also pour down six more plagues on their heads afterward. As such, all must find the way to escape from these plagues in the gospel of the water and the Spirit, and avoid these fearful plagues by believing in this gospel right now, at this very moment.

Our Lord says that He will pour down six more plagues on those who worship the Beast and his image. What is the sin that God hates the most? This sin is making images after something or someone other than God, deifying them, and surrendering to them. We must therefore know exactly who our Lord God and Jesus Christ are, and believe in and worship Christ Jesus. Nothing and no one in this whole universe, other than the Lord God Himself, can ever be our God.

If you really want to avoid the plague of sore and the additional six plagues, learn about and believe in the gospel of the water and the Spirit given by the Lord. A countless number of people who have stood against God in their everyday lives, and who have refused to believe in the gospel of the water and the Spirit, will all suffer from these plagues until they are ultimately destroyed.

Verse 3: Then the second angel poured out his bowl on the sea, and it became blood as of a dead man; and every living creature in the sea died.

The second plague is where the sea turns into the blood of the dead. God will kill off all the creatures in the sea with this plague. From this plague of the second bowl poured by God, the sea will rot away and all its creatures will no longer be able to live in it. No man will therefore be able to eat the sea's harvests when God brings this second plague. Through the second plague, God will make it manifest that He is alive, and that He is the Lord over all life.

This second plague is God's judgment rendered on all the people of the world who, rather than worshipping the Lord God for His creations, instead bowed to the image of the Beast, God's enemy, and shed the blood of the saints. This second plague is also most appropriate. God shows us that He will thus take away the richness of nature from those who do not thank the Lord for all its creatures made by God.

Verses 4-7: Then the third angel poured out his bowl on the rivers and springs of water, and they became blood. And I heard the angel of the waters saying: "You are righteous, O Lord, The One who is and who was and who is to be, Because You have judged these things. For they have shed the blood of saints and prophets, And You have given them blood to drink. For it is their just due." And I heard another from the altar saying, "Even so, Lord God Almighty, true and righteous are Your judgments."

The third plague that would turn the rivers and springs of water into blood is indeed one of the most terrible plagues. This plague, coming as the punishment for the sins of all those who do not believe in God, will turn springs into blood and make it impossible for them to live on this earth. God will turn all the springs and rivers on this earth into blood. This plague, too, is the judgment rendered on the people of the world as the price and punishment of their standing against God, who had given them water, the root of all life.

The reason why God would bring this plague on those who had stood against Him is because they had murdered His saints and prophets while on this earth. They are the ones who had not only refused to believe in God as God, but also stood against Him in union with the Antichrist.

Overwhelmed by the power of the Antichrist, those who stand against God's love in this world will persecute and murder God's most beloved saints and His servants. Those who do not believe now in the gospel of the water and the Spirit, which our Lord has given us to deliver the people of this world from sin, will murder many saints and prophets of the end times and shed their blood. God will therefore pour His third plague on this world where His enemies are living, turn its water, the root of all life, into blood, and thus destroy them.

This is the just judgment of God, and for it the saints in the air will all rejoice. Why? Because with His righteous judgment rendered on the enemies who had killed the saints, God would avenge the saints' death on them. As such, the saints and servants of God must not fear, but instead defend their faith in the Lord God, and look toward God's promise and His power when they face their martyrdom.

Verses 8-9: Then the fourth angel poured out his bowl on the sun, and power was given to him to scorch men with fire. And men were scorched with great heat, and they blasphemed the name of God who has power over these plagues; and they did not repent and give Him glory.

As the fourth angel pours out the bowl of the fourth plague on the sun, people would be burnt to death from its scorching heat. God will bring the plague of the sun's scorching heat to those who have stood against Him. Because this earth orbits around the sun precisely, if the earth were to deviate from this orbit and get closer to the sun even by the smallest distance, its inhabitants would all be burnt to death. As such, when this fourth plague is poured, people still living on this earth will all suffer from burning.

Yet they would still not repent of their sin of standing against God. Why? Because by standing against the gospel of the water and the Spirit, they had already been destined to destruction. As soon as possible, therefore, everyone must now prepare their faith that can allow them to escape from the wrath of God. This faith is to believe in the gospel of the water and the Spirit as one's salvation. Everyone must therefore believe in the truth of the water and the Spirit.

Verses 10-11: Then the fifth angel poured out his bowl on the throne of the beast, and his kingdom became full of darkness; and they gnawed their tongues because of the pain. They blasphemed the God of heaven because of their pains and their sores, and did not repent of their deeds.

The plague of the fifth bowl is one that brings darkness and pain. God will pour out this bowl of the fifth plague on the throne of the Antichrist and bring the plague of darkness and pain. From this plague, people will gnaw their tongues because of its pain and suffering. God will make sure to avenge the saints' sufferings on them with twice as great pain.

God will make them suffer, in other words, just as much as they had made the saints suffer before. And yet they would still blaspheme God and not repent, even as they suffer from their sores. As such, they are to receive the eternal punishment of hell burning with fire and brimstone.

Verse 12: Then the sixth angel poured out his bowl on the great river Euphrates, and its water was dried up, so that the way of the kings from the east might be prepared.

The plague of the sixth bowl poured by God is the plague of famine that would dry up the Euphrates River. The mankind will face its greatest suffering from this plague. The plague of famine is the most frightening plague for everyone's life. This plague, which will be poured on those who had rejected the gospel of the water and the Spirit given by the Lord, shows us just how great the punishment is for those who had rejected God's love and stood against Him. Later on, God's army of Heaven and Satan's army of this earth will wage the final war on this battlefield. Satan and his followers, however, will be seized upon and destroyed by God.

Verse 13: And I saw three unclean spirits like frogs coming out of the mouth of the dragon, out of the mouth of the beast, and out of the mouth of the false prophet.

This verse shows us that the works of all unclean spirits and demons originate from the mouths of Satan, His Beast, and the false prophets. The works of demons will prevail throughout the world when its end nears. The demons will deceive the people and lead them to their destruction by performing miracles and signs through Satan, the false prophets, and the Antichrist. The world of the end times will thus become a world of demons. But their world will all be brought to its end with the plagues of the seven bowls poured by Jesus Christ and His second coming.

Verse 14: For they are spirits of demons, performing signs, which go out to the kings of the earth and of the whole world, to gather them to the battle of that great day of God Almighty.

The spirits of demons will incite the hearts of all the kings of the entire world to gather together in one place to battle against God. In the world of the end times, everyone's heart will be ruled by the spirits of demons, and he/she will thus be turned into Satan's servant doing the Devil's works.

Verse 15: "Behold, I am coming as a thief. Blessed is he who watches, and keeps his garments, lest he walk naked and they see his shame."

The Lord will come to this world like a thief, and those who defend their faith and preach the His gospel until the pouring of the plagues of the seven bowls are greatly blessed. Our Lord tells the saints living in the end times' world that they must live by their faith in the gospel of the water and the Spirit given by Him and defend this faith until their last day. Those who defend their faith in the Lord before the pouring of His plagues of the seven bowls will receive great rewards from Him. Our Lord will surely come again to find those on whom He would bestow His blessings.

Verse 16: And they gathered them together to the place called in Hebrew, Armageddon.

The Bible prophesizes that the final war between Satan and God will be waged on a place called Armageddon. But because God is omnipotent, He will triumph over Satan and throw the Beast into the lake of fire and brimstone. We must realize that Satan has always been a deceiver, and we must keep our faith in the Lord in steadfastness until the day we stand before God.

Verses 17-21: Then the seventh angel poured out his bowl into the air, and a loud voice came out of the temple of heaven, from the throne, saying, "It is done!" And there were noises and thunderings and lightnings; and there was a great earthquake, such a mighty and great earthquake as had not occurred since men were on the earth. Now the great city was divided into three parts, and the cities of the nations fell. And great Babylon was remembered before God, to give her the cup of the wine of the fierceness of His wrath. Then every island fled away, and the mountains were not found. And great hail from heaven fell upon men, each hailstone about the weight of a talent. Men blasphemed God because of the plague of the hail, since that plague was exceedingly great.

As God pours the plague of the seventh bowl into the air, thundering and lightening will ravage the sky, while a great earthquake and great hail, the likes of which have never been seen before, will strike this earth. With these disasters, the first world will disappear without a trace. After this, the saints will live in glory with Jesus Christ on this renewed earth for a thousand years to come.

When the thousand years pass by and the time to fulfill God's promise of the New Heaven and Earth for the saints comes, God will make the first world disappear and give the saints the second heaven and earth. The saints will then reign with God in this New Heaven and Earth forever. The saints must believe that they are to live in Christ's Kingdom of one thousand years and then live forever in glory in His New Heaven and Earth. They must live in this hope, waiting for the Lord's return. ✉

All That You Have to Do Before the Pouring of Seven Bowels Is...

< Revelation 16:1-21 >

Of the plagues of the seven bowls, the first plague is that of sore, the second plague is that of the sea turning into blood, and the third is that of fresh water turning into blood. The fourth plague is the one where people are burnt to death from the sun's heat.

The main passage tells us, *"Then the fourth angel poured out his bowl on the sun, and power was given to him to scorch men with fire. And men were scorched with great heat."* This tells us that God will move the sun nearer to the earth and burn its life forms to death. When God permits this to happen, no one will be able to escape from the scorching heat of the sun, even if one were to dig a deep cave beneath the ground and hide there. Nor by turning on high-efficiency air conditioners prepared for this plague would they be able to stop God's plague. All of them will have no choice but to die.

We can just imagine what will happen to them when the time of this plague comes—their skin will peel off; their inner flesh will literally be cooked red, crumbling and rotting away. Everyone will then die from skin cancer.

And yet, even as they are burnt to death from the sun's scorching heat, people will still not repent of their sins. God's plague is amazing, but so are these people who refuse to repent even as they undergo this plague. As they refuse to repent, the plagues of God will continue on.

The main passage says, *"Then the fifth angel poured out his bowl on the throne of the beast, and his kingdom became full of darkness; and they gnawed their tongues because of the pain. They blasphemed the God of heaven because of their pains and their sores, and did not repent of their deeds."* When we look at today's world, do we not see a countless number of people who should be judged by God right now? But because God is holding His wrath in patience, they are not judged yet. However, if they were to die without having believed in the gospel of the water and the Spirit given by Jesus Christ, they will be brought to life again by God in undying bodies, and face eternal suffering in the forever-burning fire of hell.

When this happens, people will want to die, as their suffering would be too great to tolerate. But the suffering of hell lasts forever. The time will come when those who are to be judged by God will desire to die, but death will flee from them, for God would prevent them from dying so that He could judge them forever.

The sixth plague is of the war of Armageddon. And the seventh is the last and finishing plague of a great earthquake and great hail.

Verses 17-21 tell us, *"Then the seventh angel poured out his bowl into the air, and a loud voice came out of the temple of heaven, from the throne, saying, "It is done!" And there were noises and thunderings and lightnings; and there was a great earthquake, such a mighty and great earthquake as had not occurred since men were on the earth. Now the great city was divided into three parts, and the cities of the nations fell. And great Babylon was remembered before God, to give her the cup of the wine of the fierceness of His wrath. Then every island fled away, and the mountains were not found. And great hail from heaven fell upon men, each hailstone about the weight of a talent. Men blasphemed God because of the plague of the hail, since that plague was exceedingly great."*

The above passage tells us that as God pours the seventh bowl, a great earthquake would strike the planet, the whole world would split into three, and the buildings still standing on this earth would all be brought down, leaving not a single one of them left intact. As this world is subjected under the fierce wrath of God, all the islands and mountains would disappear.

Would the Himalayan Mountains still be standing when this happens? Of course not! All the high mountains will disappear right before the eyes of the alive. Every mountain in this world will simply evaporate away without a trace. The passage also tells us that huge hailstones, each weighing as much as 100 pounds (45 kg), will fall upon this earth. Would there be anyone who could survive through these earthquakes and hails?

Revelation 18 tells us that the wrath of God is brought upon those who had not believed in Him and who had ignored His Word. Some people in this world claim, as if they were divine, "I will never be subjected under the wrath of God, nor would I ever be judged by Him." However, God's judgment is brought upon precisely this kind of people who are full of their own pride and arrogance. We must believe that this world will disappear when it is struck by the plagues of the seven bowls poured by God.

We Must Have Faith in the Word of God

God tells us that He will make this world disappear. This

world therefore will not last forever. As such, all those who are facing its nearing end must believe in this truth even more firmly and pursue their spiritual faith. All the people of this world must therefore be awakened from their spiritual sleep. I don't know with what kind of faith you might have lived your life so far, but now is the time for you to concentrate your attention on what will be going on in the end times, and to wake up and to believe. You must therefore have the exact knowledge of the plagues prophesized in Revelation, and you must be alert.

Our Lord has told us that this earth will soon be come under the plagues of the seven bowls of God. As such, we must wait for the Lord while continuing to preach the gospel, even if people do not receive it well.

The fate of this world is now at risk. Today's world is exposed to all kinds of danger, from the threat of war to precarious weather, environmental degradation, multiplying social conflicts, and all kinds of diseases. God therefore told us that the present era is like the time of Noah. If present time is like Noah's time, it only means that this world has now entered into its last days. The sign of the end times is that people would be interested only in the things of the flesh, such as eating, drinking, marrying, and other such petty affairs. They therefore deserve to be judged by God. In Noah's time, too, such people did not listen to what Noah had told them, and so they were all destroyed, except for Noah and his family of eight. The world to come would be like this as well.

Almost all the things that God has promised have been fulfilled as they were recorded in the Bible. Of these, about 5 percent still remains to be fulfilled, but the rest of them have all been fulfilled already. The Word of salvation and of the redemption promised by the Lord has also been all fulfilled. In the Word of God, only the judgment reserved for those who do not believe in the gospel of the water and the Spirit remains. And for the born-again saints, only the Millennial Kingdom and the New Heaven and Earth, where the righteous shall enter and live in, await them.

God is merciful, and He stands on the side of the righteous. However, to those who deserve His wrath, God will most surely bring His wrath to bear upon them, while on those who deserve His mercy, He will most surely bestow His mercy.

When will these plagues happen? The plagues of the seven bowls will come after the saints' martyrdom, as the mark of 666 is thrust upon this world and is resisted by the saints. After the plagues will come the first resurrection, the Millennial Kingdom, and the final judgment of Jesus sitting on the great white throne. This will be followed by the opening of the eternal Kingdom of Heaven. Through the Bible, we must attain the knowledge of God's providence.

Do you believe in the fact that Jesus rose from the dead again? Do you believe that the Lord has made all the sins of the mankind disappear through His baptism and blood? Our Lord took away all the sins of the mankind with His water and blood, rose from the dead again in three days, and is now sitting on the right side of the Father's throne. As such, the sins of those who believe in Jesus Christ have clearly disappeared, and as Christ rose from the dead again, so will they be resurrected.

The saints will therefore be glorified with the Lord, but while on this earth, they will also face many sufferings for the Lord. But the sufferings of this present time are not worthy to be compared to the glory that awaits them, for this glory is the only thing that awaits the born-again saints. The saints therefore have nothing to worry about the future. All that the righteous have to do is live the rest of their lives for the gospel and by their faith. We must dedicate ourselves to the work of saving souls, and not follow the world.

Let's Devote the Rest of Our Lives to God

I am worried that there might be someone among us who would betray the gospel. Whoever betrays the gospel of the water and the Spirit will deny the Lord Himself in the end. Though we are weak, if we believe in and follow the gospel of the water and the Spirit accomplished by the Lord, we will all be able to live by faith. The saints cannot live only by their own wisdom and strength. If they were to do so, they would end up betraying their faith and facing their own destruction. To avoid this, we must live by faith.

Why would our Lord allow the mankind to receive the mark of 666? This is to separate the grain from the chaff. Before allowing the saints to be raptured, the first thing that God must do is to clearly separate the grain from the chaff.

There are spiritual battles to be fought by the saints. As such, the saints must not avoid fighting against God's enemies. If they hesitate to fight against Satan, they might receive a fatal blow from Satan instead. Therefore, all the saints must and can fight spiritual battles even for themselves. All the spiritual battles fought by the saints are justifiable. To follow God, every saint must fight and overcome Satan and his servants.

The saints must fight for the Kingdom of God. They must also be persecuted for God's Kingdom, and be hated by the people of the world. That the saints are given the opportunity to fight for the Lord is a good thing in itself. If this opportunity to fight for God was given to you, you should thank Him for it. Such a fight is a good fight, for it is a fight for the righteousness of God.

God helps the righteous. There are not so many days left in our lives, and my hope and prayer are that we would all live our remaining lives fighting the spiritual battles and doing the spiritual works until we stand before the Lord. No matter what the people of this world say to us, we should fight the spiritual battles, bear the spiritual fruits, and offer these fruits before our Lord. When the day of our Lord's return comes, let us all stand before Him confidently. When this day comes, the Lord will wipe away our tears and let us live in a place where we will no longer cry, nor suffer pain ever again, nor find sin any longer.

Let us all live by faith, and by this faith let us all enter the Kingdom of God. ⊠

CHAPTER

17

The Judgment of the Harlot Who Sits on Many Waters

< Revelation 17:1-18 >

"Then one of the seven angels who had the seven bowls came and talked with me, saying to me, 'Come, I will show you the judgment of the great harlot who sits on many waters, with whom the kings of the earth committed fornication, and the inhabitants of the earth were made drunk with the wine of her fornication.' So he carried me away in the Spirit into the wilderness. And I saw a woman sitting on a scarlet beast which was full of names of blasphemy, having seven heads and ten horns. The woman was arrayed in purple and scarlet, and adorned with gold and precious stones and pearls, having in her hand a golden cup full of abominations and the filthiness of her fornication. And on her forehead a name was written:

MYSTERY, BABYLON THE GREAT, THE MOTHER OF HARLOTS AND OF THE ABOMINATIONS OF THE EARTH.

I saw the woman, drunk with the blood of the saints and with the blood of the martyrs of Jesus. And when I saw her, I marveled with great amazement. But the angel said to me, 'Why did you marvel? I will tell you the mystery of the woman and of the beast that carries her, which has the seven heads and the ten horns. The beast that you saw was, and is not, and will ascend out of the bottomless pit and go to perdition. And those who dwell on the earth will marvel, whose names are not written in the Book of Life from the foundation of the world, when they see the beast that was, and is not, and yet is. Here is the mind which has wisdom: The seven heads are seven mountains on which the woman sits. There are also seven kings. Five have fallen, one is, and the other has not yet come. And when he comes, he must continue a short time. The beast that was, and is not, is himself also the eighth, and is of the seven, and is going to perdition. The ten horns which you saw are ten kings who have received no kingdom as yet, but they receive authority for one hour as kings with the beast. These are of one mind, and they will give their power and authority to the beast. These will make war with the Lamb, and the Lamb will overcome them, for He is Lord of lords and King of kings; and those who are with Him are called, chosen, and faithful.' Then he said to me, 'The waters which you saw, where the harlot sits, are peoples, multitudes, nations, and tongues. And the ten horns which you saw on the beast, these will hate the harlot, make her desolate and naked, eat her flesh and burn her with fire. For God has put it into their hearts to fulfill His purpose, to be of one mind, and to give their kingdom to the beast, until the words of God are fulfilled. And the woman whom you saw is that great city which reigns over the kings of the earth.'"

Exegesis

Verse 1: Then one of the seven angels who had the seven bowls came and talked with me, saying to me, "Come, I will show you the judgment of the great harlot who sits on many waters,"

Knowing who the harlot, the woman, and the Beast of the main passage are is essential to interpret and understand chapter 17. The "harlot" in verse 1 refers to the world's religions, while the "woman" refers to the world. The "Beast," on the other hand, refers to the Antichrist. The "many waters" refers to the teachings of the Devil. The phrase, *"I will show you the judgment of the great harlot who sits on many waters,"* tells us that God would judge the world's religions that sit on the many teachings of Satan.

Verse 2: "with whom the kings of the earth committed fornication, and the inhabitants of the earth were made drunk with the wine of her fornication."

The "fornication" refers to loving this world and its things more than loving God Himself. Making images after the things of the world, and worshipping and loving them like God are in fact all acts of fornication.

The phrase above, *"with whom the kings of the earth committed fornication,"* means that the leader of this world have lived their lives drunk in the worldly religions, and that all the worldly people have also lived drunk with such sins that the worldly religions provide.

Verse 3: So he carried me away in the Spirit into the wilderness. And I saw a woman sitting on a scarlet beast which was full of names of blasphemy, having seven heads and ten horns.

The phrase, *"woman sitting on a scarlet beast,"* tells us that the people of this world would unite their hearts with that of the Antichrist to persecute and murder the saints. It shows us that the worldly people will end up turning into the servants of

God's enemy, doing the works of the Antichrist at his bidding. The Beast is the Antichrist who stands against God. The Antichrist rules over many kings, and he also reigns over the many nations of the world.

But being arrogant, the Antichrist will not hesitate to blaspheme God and to utter prideful words. He will blaspheme God by uttering arrogant words, claiming that he himself is God or Jesus Christ, and he will raise himself up high like God. His power will therefore reach and reign over all the kings of the world and all its nations.

From the phrase, *"having seven heads and ten horns,"* the "seven heads" here refer to the seven kings of the world, and the "ten horns" refer to the nations of the world.

Verse 4: The woman was arrayed in purple and scarlet, and adorned with gold and precious stones and pearls, having in her hand a golden cup full of abominations and the filthiness of her fornication.

By the phrase, *"the woman was arrayed in purple and scarlet, and adorned with gold and precious stones and pearls,"* the passage tells us that the worldly religions, scheming with the Antichrist, would think of him as their king. As such, they would consider it only proper that all those who stand against them should be sentenced to death, and would in fact implement their thoughts through their acts against the saints.

And to decorate this world as an eternal kingdom of happiness, they would adorn themselves beautifully with the world's gold, precious stones and pearls. But their faith is most interested solely in how much pleasures of the flesh they can have while living in this world. Because when God looks at the people of this world He would see a world filled by their filthy sins, they will all appear as abominations before Him.

Verse 5: And on her forehead a name was written: MYSTERY, BABYLON THE GREAT, THE MOTHER OF HARLOTS AND OF THE ABOMINATIONS OF THE EARTH.
Though the religious people of the world would try to adorn themselves as a queen, they will be revealed as a harlot in fact. On the one hand, her name, *"Babylon the Great,"* shows us the prideful, idolatrous, and oppressive character of the harlot, while the word *"mother,"* on the other hand, shows us that all the forces of the Antichrist in history have originated from none other than the world itself, and that the world is the root of all kinds of idolatry and corruption.

Though this world is adorned with glittering and beautiful jewels, the Antichrist who stands against God and works in the hearts of these people of the world will work as their mother. As such, our Lord God has decided to destroy them all with His great plagues of the seven bowls.

Verse 6: I saw the woman, drunk with the blood of the saints and with the blood of the martyrs of Jesus. And when I saw her, I marveled with great amazement.
The "saints" refer to the people of faith throughout the entire Church history who have believed in the gospel of the water and the Spirit given by Jesus Christ. *The phrase "the martyrs of Jesus"* refers to those among the saints who have testified the truth that Jesus is the Son of God and their Savior, and who specially have been martyred to defend their faith.

This verse emphasizes that the ones who would persecute and kill the saints are none other than the religious people of this world. They will do such evilness as the vanguard force of the Antichrist.

John says here that when he saw the woman, he "marveled with great amazement." This world is indeed a curious world. The saints have done nothing to harm it, and yet this world schemes with the Antichrist and kills many saints. How could this world not be anything but strange? These things will surely be brought to bear upon the saints by the people of this world. Because this world is under the control of the Antichrist, its people, as his servants, would seize the saints and kill them.

They therefore will indeed appear very alien to us. When we look at the worldly people, do they not in fact appear as somewhat strange? When people are made after the image of God, how could they become the Antichrist's servants and murder people—not just any people, but the countless people who believe in God? It is because this world is the servant of Satan.

Verse 7: But the angel said to me, "Why did you marvel? I will tell you the mystery of the woman and of the beast that carries her, which has the seven heads and the ten horns."

The "woman" here refers to the people of this world. This verse tells us that the Beast, called the Antichrist, will reign over all the kings of the world and its nations, and through them he will do his works of standing against God, of persecuting the saints, and of murdering them. The *"mystery of the beast"* refers to the identity of the Antichrist, moving at the command of Satan. And he will turn the nations of this world into his own.

The people of this world, scheming with the Antichrist, will end up as Satan's instruments in massacring a great number of the Lord's people. This world and the Antichrist are the instruments of Satan, hidden from our eyes for now. But when the first three and a half years of the Great Tribulation pass by, they will rise up and kill the saints.

One may then wonder how this would be possible, when this world has so many conscientious, learned, and smart people, from politicians to educators to philosophers and PhDs. But because the world would conspire with the Antichrist, all these things, including the massacre of the saints, would become feasible. As such, that this world would surrender to the Antichrist and murder the saints is the key to solving the mystery of the Antichrist.

Verse 8: "The beast that you saw was, and is not, and will ascend out of the bottomless pit and go to perdition. And those who dwell on the earth will marvel, whose names are not written in the Book of Life from the foundation of the world, when they see the beast that was, and is not, and yet is."

This verse tells us that the Antichrist was found among the kings of the old ages, and that though he is not in this world now, he will come out to the world in the future. It tells us that the people of this world would be greatly amazed when they see the Antichrist emerging and killing the saints.

The Antichrist would carry out his purposes by participating in the new politics of this world. He would continue to remain mysterious to the people of this world and yet be spotlighted as amazing. Because he would take upon the many political, economic, ideological, and religious problems of this world and solve them all with his ability, many people would think of him and follow him as Christ Jesus who would come again at the end times. He would therefore remain as amazement before the eyes of the people of the world.

Verse 9: "Here is the mind which has wisdom: The seven

heads are seven mountains on which the woman sits."
This verse tells us that the Antichrist would institute his own laws to rule over the people of the world and turn these laws into his governing body to carry out his purposes. The reason why the people of the world would unite together is to come under the rule of Satan by receiving the mark of the Antichrist, and to stand against God and His saints, placing their trust in the power of the laws made by the Antichrist.

Verse 10: "There are also seven kings. Five have fallen, one is, and the other has not yet come. And when he comes, he must continue a short time."
This verse tells us that the kings who stand against God will continue to come out of this world, just as such kings had risen before. When the time of the final Great Tribulation comes, a leader of this world will rise as the Antichrist and massacre the saints. But the persecution of this world leader, who would become the Antichrist, will last for only a short while permitted by God.

Verse 11: "The beast that was, and is not, is himself also the eighth, and is of the seven, and is going to perdition."
This tells us that the Antichrist coming to this world will rise as the last of the kings of the world. When the Antichrist emerges out of the kings of the world, many people of the world will follow him, as he would, having received the spirit of the Dragon, exercise power like God and perform signs and miracles. The servants of God and the saints will also be killed by the Antichrist, but all these things will last only a short while permitted by God. After such things come to pass, the Antichrist will be bound in the bottomless pit, and then be thrown into the fiery hell, never to be released from it.

Verse 12: "The ten horns which you saw are ten kings who have received no kingdom as yet, but they receive authority for one hour as kings with the beast."

This verse tells us that ten nations will unite their power to rule over the whole world. These ten nations, having thus united, will come to wield their power over the world with the Antichrist for a short while. But the verse also tells us that these kings of the world have not yet received the kingdom ruled by the Antichrist. In the near future, however, these kings of the world will reign with the Beast as the kings of darkness for a while. But their reign will last only briefly, and as such, they will reign over the dominion of darkness only for this short period of time.

Verse 13: "These are of one mind, and they will give their power and authority to the beast."

When the time comes, the kings of this world will transfer all their power and authority to the Antichrist. At this time, God's Church, its saints, and His servants will be greatly persecuted by the Antichrist and be martyred. But the Antichrist himself will be destroyed by the power and authority of Jesus Christ and the sword of the Word of His mouth.

Verse 14: "These will make war with the Lamb, and the Lamb will overcome them, for He is Lord of lords and King of kings; and those who are with Him are called, chosen, and faithful."

Though Satan will seek to wage war against Jesus Christ, he will be no match for Him. The saints, too, will overcome him in their struggle against him. The Lord will give the saints the strength to fight against and overcome the Antichrist with their faith. As such, the saints will not fear their struggle against the Antichrist, but live the end times in peace and tranquility by believing in their Lord God. They will then overcome their enemies with their faith in the Lord.

This victory of the saints means that they would defend their faith and be martyred. When this time comes, the saints will overcome Satan and the Antichrist by embracing their martyrdom with their faith in Jesus Christ and their hope for the Kingdom of Heaven, participate in their resurrection and rapture, receive the new Kingdom of Christ, and thereafter live forever in glory.

Verse 15: Then he said to me, "The waters which you saw, where the harlot sits, are peoples, multitudes, nations, and tongues."

The worldly religions have deceived and ruled over the people of all nations with its teachings of Satan. This verse tells us that the satanic teachings working in the midst of the worldly religions have penetrated all the nations and tongues of the world, and that their influence has reached such a great extent as to bring destruction to the people's souls.

Verse 16: "And the ten horns which you saw on the beast, these will hate the harlot, make her desolate and naked, eat her flesh and burn her with fire."

The verse here tells us that the nations of this world will unite with the Antichrist to kill and destroy its religious people. It tells us, in other words, that the people of this world and the Antichrist will hate and abuse the religious people, and exterminate all the religions of the world from its face. Though the world's religious people had killed the saints before with the support of the Antichrist, they themselves are now to be destroyed by Satan and the secular people. Satan, in the end, had only used the world's religions just to deify himself as God.

Verse 17: "For God has put it into their hearts to fulfill His purpose, to be of one mind, and to give their kingdom to the beast, until the words of God are fulfilled."
This tells us that the people of this world would give their kingdom and power to Satan. As such, they would become the Antichrist's people as they receive his mark voluntarily, take pride in being his servants, and also murder those who refuse to receive his mark. However, their persecution of the saints would be allowed only for the duration of time that the Word of God has permitted. During this allowed period, the Antichrist will pour out all the evilness of his heart and freely stand against God and His saints.

Verse 18: "And the woman whom you saw is that great city which reigns over the kings of the earth."
God tells us here that this world will institute a new set of laws to rule and control over its kings, and that the kings of the world will be ruled within the bounds of these new laws. The supreme power of this world will reign over all the kings of the world, as if it were a person itself. The world, in other words, will make the laws that bind all the kings tightly, and become like a god ruling over them.

The *"great city"* refers to the political institution through which the Antichrist would reign. Everyone of this world will end up having to serve the ruling entity of the world, which God had given them, as if it were God Himself, and be reigned by it. Because men had become the servants of Satan, they would thus be destroyed.

Psalms 49:20 tells us, "A man who is in honor, yet does not understand, Is like the beasts that perish." As such, the people of this world must know beforehand what Satan's scheme is, believe now in the gospel of the water and the Spirit preached by the saints of this age, and thereby escape from the curse of turning into Satan's servants and instead live clothed in the blessing of the eternal Kingdom of God as His people. ⊠

Concentrate Our Attention On His Will

< Revelation 17:1-8 >

Revelation 17:1-5 states, *"Then one of the seven angels who had the seven bowls came and talked with me, saying to me, 'Come, I will show you the judgment of the great harlot who sits on many waters, with whom the kings of the earth committed fornication, and the inhabitants of the earth were made drunk with the wine of her fornication.' So he carried me away in the Spirit into the wilderness. And I saw a woman sitting on a scarlet beast which was full of names of blasphemy, having seven heads and ten horns. The woman was arrayed in purple and scarlet, and adorned with gold and precious stones and pearls, having in her hand a golden cup full of abominations and the filthiness of her fornication. And on her forehead a name was written:*
MYSTERY, BABYLON THE GREAT, THE MOTHER OF HARLOTS AND OF THE ABOMINATIONS OF THE EARTH."
The harlot in the above passage refers to the religious of this world, and it tells us that they have indulged in extravagant luxuries with the things of the world and the material abundance given by the Lord. They adorned themselves with all kinds of luxuries, with necklaces of gold and earrings of diamonds, and put on all kinds of fragment oil. The passage tells us that in her hand was a golden cup, and that it was full of abominations and filthiness of her fornication. This is what

God showed John.

What this passage tells us is that Satan contrives in people's souls and seeks to make them surrender to him by having them be drunk with the things of the world. All the kings of the world, too, have been made drunk with the things of the world by Satan. As such, everyone on this earth is made drunk with the wine of the world's fornication.

Satan achieves his goals when people become drunk with the tide of this world, its pleasures, and its material greed. The truth is that his goal is to prevent people from looking toward God. To do so, Satan makes their souls drunk with the material things of the world. We must realize this truth.

There is no one in this world who would not fall into the materialist trap. Everyone falls into materialism. The fashionable trends of this world are all manipulated and led by Satan. Everyone thinks that he/she has his/her unique style. But behind it lies a manipulator, and this manipulator is none other than Satan. This is why we must not live soaked in materialism, but instead live imbibing from His Word and doing the works of God.

The Word of Revelation that God reveals to us through the Apostle John is the truth. What, then, is God trying to tell us with this Word? Our Lord is telling us that we should not saturate ourselves with this world, but instead stand against it. He is telling us, the saints, in other words, to think of and believe in God with our hearts.

1 John 2:15 says, *"Do not love the world or the things in the world. If anyone loves the world, the love of the Father is not in him."* When our hearts love the material things of the world, God cannot dwell in our hearts. But when our hearts throws away the things of the world, God would then dwell in our hearts. We must not live our lives saturated in the material

things of the world. Only when we contemplate on the Word of our Lord and His purposes alone can we be led by His guidance.

We can change our minds at any time. When the things of the world try to enter into our hearts, we should always reject them. We can then drive away all the filthy things of the world from our hearts, and our hearts soon dissolve into the Lord's own heart. What does our Lord want from us? And what does He tell us to do? To make sure that such godly thoughts would spring up in our hearts, we must erase the worldly things from our hearts.

God has given us so many blessings, and we realize now that we should preach the gospel of the water and the Spirit to the people of the entire world for the rest of our remaining days. We therefore do not let down our guards, and come to concentrate our attention on His will. By thinking of spiritual works, we can drive out the things of the world found in our hearts.

We the saints must drive out the things of the world. Until the Lord comes again, we must live our Christian lives with faith. For the remainder of our lives, we must do what the Lord has entrusted us with until we stand before Him. And we must love the Lord, and live by faith, doing whatever works He permits us to do. ⊠

CHAPTER

18

The World of Babylon Is Fallen

< Revelation 18:1-24 >

"After these things I saw another angel coming down from heaven, having great authority, and the earth was illuminated with his glory. And he cried mightily with a loud voice, saying, 'Babylon the great is fallen, is fallen, and has become a dwelling place of demons, a prison for every foul spirit, and a cage for every unclean and hated bird! For all the nations have drunk of the wine of the wrath of her fornication, the kings of the earth have committed fornication with her, and the merchants of the earth have become rich through the abundance of her luxury.' And I heard another voice from heaven saying, 'Come out of her, my people, lest you share in her sins, and lest you receive of her plagues. For her sins have reached to heaven, and God has remembered her iniquities. Render to her just as she rendered to you, and repay her double according to her works; in the cup which she has mixed, mix double for her. In the measure that she glorified herself and lived luxuriously, in the same measure give her torment and sorrow; for she says in her heart, 'I sit as queen, and am no widow, and will not see sorrow.' Therefore her plagues will come in one day—death and mourning and famine. And she will be utterly burned with fire, for strong is the Lord God who judges her. The kings of the earth who committed fornication and lived luxuriously with her will weep and lament for her, when they see the smoke of her burning, standing at a distance for fear of her torment, saying, 'Alas, alas, that great city Babylon, that mighty city! For in one hour your judgment has come.' And the merchants of the earth will weep and mourn over her, for no one buys their merchandise anymore: merchandise of gold and silver, precious stones and pearls, fine linen and purple, silk and scarlet, every kind of citron wood, every kind of object of ivory, every kind of object of most precious wood, bronze, iron, and marble; and cinnamon and incense, fragrant oil and frankincense, wine and oil, fine flour and wheat, cattle and sheep, horses and chariots, and bodies and souls of men. The fruit that your soul longed for has gone from you, and all the things which are rich and splendid have gone from you, and you shall find them no more at all. The merchants of these things, who became rich by her, will stand at a distance for fear of her torment, weeping and wailing, and saying, 'Alas, alas, that great city that was clothed in fine linen, purple, and scarlet, and adorned with gold and precious stones and pearls! For in one hour such great riches came to nothing.' Every shipmaster, all who travel by ship, sailors, and as many as trade on the sea, stood at a distance and cried out when they saw the smoke of her burning, saying, 'What is like this great city?' They threw dust on their heads and cried out, weeping and wailing, and saying, 'Alas, alas, that great city, in which all who had ships on the sea became rich by her wealth! For in one hour she is made desolate.' Rejoice over her, O heaven, and you holy apostles and prophets, for God has avenged you on her!' Then a mighty angel took up a stone like a great millstone and threw it into the sea, saying, 'Thus with violence the great city Babylon shall be thrown down, and shall not be found anymore. The sound of harpists, musicians, flutists, and trumpeters shall not be heard in you anymore. No craftsman of any craft shall be found in you anymore, and the sound of a millstone shall not be heard in you anymore. The light of a lamp shall not shine in you anymore, and the voice of bridegroom and bride shall not be heard in you anymore. For your merchants were the great men of the earth, for by your sorcery all the nations were deceived. And in her was found the blood of prophets and saints, and of all who were slain on the earth.'"

Exegesis

Verse 1: After these things I saw another angel coming down from heaven, having great authority, and the earth was illuminated with his glory.

Through the servants whom God sent to this earth to do His works, people can hear the sermons of God's blessings and curses. To be freed from all their sins and unhappiness, therefore, all of you must receive into your hearts and believe in the Word of the spiritual blessings of Heaven preached by the servants of God.

Verse 2: And he cried mightily with a loud voice, saying, "Babylon the great is fallen, is fallen, and has become a dwelling place of demons, a prison for every foul spirit, and a cage for every unclean and hated bird!"

In the phrase *"Babylon the great is fallen,"* the word Babylon is used by the Bible to refer to the secular world. In the Old Testament, for instance, we find the story of the Tower of Babel, a tower built by the mankind seeking to defy God by garnering together their own strengths, which was then brought down by God for this reason. When the above passage says that Babylon the great is fallen, it is telling us that this world would be fallen. There are some people who might think, "This world is standing just fine now, and so how could it ever fall?" But God is telling us here that when the plagues of the seven bowls are poured one after another, He will bring down this world just as He had brought down the Tower of Babel.

What, then, is the reason why this world would be destroyed by God with the plagues of the seven bowls? It is because the people of this world would have united themselves with the Antichrist in murdering the born-again saints who believe in the gospel of the water and the Spirit, and it is because they would have thus stood against God to their very end. It is also because this world would have become "a dwelling place of demons."

Why would this be the case? Why, that is, would this world have become a dwelling place of demons? It is because when the end times come, many people would surrender to the Antichrist and turn into this evil one's servants by receiving the mark of Satan from him.

In the Scripture, Dragon is used to refer to Satan, and demons to the servants of the Dragon. Thus, when it says here that the world has become a dwelling place of demons, it means that the Antichrist, a servant of the Dragon, would fully occupy the world. The world of the end times will face the age of extreme tribulations when the plagues of the seven bowls are poured on it. This world will become a world of the Dragon, and demons will run rampant as if the whole world belonged to them. And this world will fall down rapidly, brought down by the final plagues of the seven bowls poured by God.

Verse 3: "For all the nations have drunk of the wine of the wrath of her fornication, the kings of the earth have committed fornication with her, and the merchants of the earth have become rich through the abundance of her luxury."

Just as the verse says here, literally *"all the nations"* on the earth have drunk of the wine of the wrath of the world's fornication. In other words, the people of this world have thought of this world as God, and believed in and followed it as such. They have loved the world more than God. This world has thus become a hotbed of sin, and its people have lived their lives drunk in sin.

The result, therefore, is the fall of the world brought down by sin. Because people have loved and followed the world like God, He will destroy them with His punishment of the plagues of the seven bowls. Everyone living in this world will ultimately be destroyed by these seven great plagues brought by God and be cast into hell.

God is giving us His clear warning that everyone who does not believe now in the gospel of the water and the Spirit given by the Lord will face the plagues of the seven bowls in the end. You must remember that if you do not believe in this gospel and continue to stand against God despite His warning, you will not only be punished by the plagues of the seven bowls, but you will also receive the eternal punishment of hell.

People must realize, therefore, that they have to believe in the gospel of the water and the Spirit now, in order to escape from God's great and terrible plagues, and they must return to the faith in the true gospel of the water and the Spirit as soon as possible.

Though many kings and merchants of the world have amassed great wealth with its material abundance, they will all end up weeping, lamenting, mourning and wailing when they see this world crumbling down with the great plagues brought by God.

So, we must all never forget that we have to preach the gospel of the water and the Spirit to everyone, and that we have to live our lives by looking toward the new millennium. We must lead everyone to the gospel of the water and the Spirit, so that every mankind may escape from the great plagues.

Verse 4: And I heard another voice from heaven saying, "Come out of her, my people, lest you share in her sins, and lest you receive of her plagues."

"Come out of her, my people, lest you share in her sins, and lest you receive of her plagues." This is the Word of God spoken to His saints. The saints must not, in other words, belong to the world of the end times and live their lives as its slaves. Even those who had already become saints before, if they fall into the sins of the world of the end times, they will not be able to avoid being judged by God with His fearful plagues. God is telling all the saints, in other words, to not garner His wrath by ending up as the slaves of the world.

Verse 5: "For her sins have reached to heaven, and God has remembered her iniquities."

God indeed remembers all the sins and deeds of this world and waits only for its judgment day. With the sudden appearance of the Antichrist one day, destruction will soon cover the entire world just as God has planned. Yet there are still some people who believe that this world would not be destroyed, but that it would last forever.

This world will not, however, last as they think, but be destroyed suddenly by the plagues of the seven trumpets and of the seven bowls brought by God. When the end times come, God will bring tribulations to everywhere in the world and destroy it. We must thus be diligent in our lives of faith to the very end, holding steadfast to our faith that the Kingdom of Jesus Christ will indeed come.

Before God commands His angels to pour the seven bowls on this earth, the sins of the world would have become so rampant and widespread that it more than deserves to receive God's judgment. God will therefore remember its sins, and hold its destruction no longer. Moreover, the Antichrist and the worldly people would be persecuting God's people, coercing the saints to deny their faith, and making martyrs out of them. When these things happen, this world will face the plagues of the seven bowls.

Verse 6: "Render to her just as she rendered to you, and repay her double according to her works; in the cup which she has mixed, mix double for her."

It is written here, *"Render to her just as she rendered to you."* To whom does this "she" here refer? This refers to this world, namely sinners living in it, the Antichrist, and Satan. It tells us that God will pay them back just as they had brought persecution, torment, tribulation and death to the saints.

Verse 6 also says, *"in the cup which she has mixed, mix double for her."* This is God's command given to His angels to punish all the false religions of the world that had led people to hell by spreading the Devil's lies. It means that God will bring His wrath and punishment on today's Christianity for its sin of giving false teachings, mixing the Word of God with the teachings of Satan, and thereby leading people to the Devil. Therefore, Christians who do not believed in the gospel of the water and the Spirit will receive the same punishment of sin as the secular people of the world.

Verse 7: "In the measure that she glorified herself and lived luxuriously, in the same measure give her torment and sorrow; for she says in her heart, 'I sit as queen, and am no widow, and will not see sorrow.'"

God says here to repay the sins of these prideful people with torment and sorrow. To all the religious people of the world who are not born again, and to the unbelieving, secular people of the world, God will ask after their sins and punish them.

Yet they remain prideful, saying to themselves, *"I sit as a queen, and am not widow, and will not see sorrow."* God will therefore bring to them the plagues of their destruction. With the great plagues brought by God, they will all suffer the sorrow of losing all their worldly possessions and their beloved ones, all at the same time.

Verse 8: "Therefore her plagues will come in one day— death and mourning and famine. And she will be utterly burned with fire, for strong is the Lord God who judges her."

With the advent of the seven plagues, the plagues of death, mourning and famine will come to this world in one day. The Antichrist and all his worldly followers will thus be punished to burn forever in hell.

Verse 9: "The kings of the earth who committed fornication and lived luxuriously with her will weep and lament for her, when they see the smoke of her burning,"

The people and kings of the world will witness with their own eyes their world being engulfed in fire and earthquakes and destroyed by the plagues of the seven bowls. The kings of the world will therefore weep and lament, wailing for their loss.

Verse 10: "standing at a distance for fear of her torment, saying, 'Alas, alas, that great city Babylon, that mighty city! For in one hour your judgment has come.'"

The people who had not believed that this world would fall will be struck by fear when they see the whole world actually crumbling down right before their eyes. On a world glittering so much with its beauty, God's judgment will descend in one day, and it will be fallen all at once.

Verse 11-13: "And the merchants of the earth will weep and mourn over her, for no one buys their merchandise anymore: merchandise of gold and silver, precious stones and pearls, fine linen and purple, silk and scarlet, every kind of citron wood, every kind of object of ivory, every kind of object of most precious wood, bronze, iron, and marble; and cinnamon and incense, fragrant oil and frankincense, wine and oil, fine flour and wheat, cattle and sheep, horses and chariots, and bodies and souls of men."

Who could buy or sell anything when the world's destruction is at hand? The merchants of the earth, too, will weep and mourn over the loss of their world. When God pours the plagues of the seven bowls, no one in the whole world would be buying anything. This world will never be reconstructed again, and only the Kingdom of Christ will be built on its ruins.

Here is a list of the extravagant merchandises that people have adorned themselves in luxury to this very day. But all these things will become useless in just one day, and no one will ever again seek after such worldly things. All these things are what the worldly religions trade in. The religions of the world have done everything imaginable for their love of money, not hesitating to sell even souls for a penny.

Verse 14-18: "The fruit that your soul longed for has gone from you, and all the things which are rich and splendid have gone from you, and you shall find them no more at all. The merchants of these things, who became rich by her, will stand at a distance for fear of her torment, weeping and wailing, and saying, 'Alas, alas, that great city that was clothed in fine linen, purple, and scarlet, and adorned with gold and precious stones and pearls! For in one hour such great riches came to nothing.' Every shipmaster, all who travel by ship, sailors, and as many as trade on the sea, stood at a distance and cried out when they saw the smoke of her burning, saying, 'What is like this great city?'"

People will therefore never be able to see any of their worldly possessions again.

The merchants who had become rich through this world will weep and wail as they see their world crumbling down. They will wail in desperation, for when the world falls, they, too, will fall with it, and all their amassed possessions will disappear in just a day.

When the religions built on the worldly wealth fall, the people of this world will find themselves lamenting, "alas, alas!" International traders and shipmasters crisscrossing the world will also wail. These people will cry out in desperation, "What civilization ever built by the mankind has been greater and better than that of today?"

Verse 19: "They threw dust on their heads and cried out, weeping and wailing, and saying, 'Alas, alas, that great city, in which all who had ships on the sea became rich by her wealth! For in one hour she is made desolate.'"

Seeing the world brought down by the plagues of the seven bowls, all those who had thought that this world would last forever will be wailing in great sorrow. Those who still remain in this world will be weeping and lamenting as they witness the whole world being destroyed all at once with the plagues of the seven bowls brought by God, but all their crying would be of no use, for by then this world and everything in it would have ended already. If they have the strength to cry then, they should be wailing now over their own fate, that they are bound to hell because of their sins, and they should believe in the gospel of the water and the Spirit to be delivered from their eternal destruction.

Verse 20: *"Rejoice over her, O heaven, and you holy apostles and prophets, for God has avenged you on her!"*
The raptured saints in the air will rejoice when the plagues of the seven bowls are brought, because with these plagues God would avenge them all. It is only right that God would thus pour the terrible, great plagues on His enemies.

Verse 21: *Then a mighty angel took up a stone like a great millstone and threw it into the sea, saying, "Thus with violence the great city Babylon shall be thrown down, and shall not be found anymore."*
God says here that this world will never be seen again, as a millstone is thrown into the sea. Our Lord will then renew the whole universe and all things in it, and fulfill His work of turning this earth into the Kingdom of Christ.

Verse 22: *"The sound of harpists, musicians, flutists, and trumpeters shall not be heard in you anymore. No craftsman of any craft shall be found in you anymore, and the sound of a millstone shall not be heard in you anymore."*
When the plagues of the seven bowls end, no sound of

music that people had heard in this world before will ever be heard again, nor will the sound of the hammering of craftsmen be heard.

Verse 23: "The light of a lamp shall not shine in you anymore, and the voice of bridegroom and bride shall not be heard in you anymore. For your merchants were the great men of the earth, for by your sorcery all the nations were deceived."

When the plagues of the seven bowls are completed, this world will never again see the light of a lamp, nor hear the voice of bridegroom and bride any longer. The deception of the sorcerers of the world will also end, for the world would have ended.

Verse 24: "And in her was found the blood of prophets and saints, and of all who were slain on the earth."

The reason why God would pour the great plagues of the seven bowls on this earth is because Satan's servants would have shed the blood of His prophets and saints. ✉

"Come Out of Her, My People, Lest You Receive of Her Plagues"

< Revelation 18:1-24 >

God tells us in chapter 18 that He would destroy the great city Babylon with His great plagues. Because by the end times this world would have turned too filthy and sinful before God's eyes, and because God would thus have no other choice but to destroy it despite having created it Himself, He will allow the great, apocalyptical plagues that would end the earth. This world will therefore be laid to ruins until it is completely brought down.

The actual reason why God would destroy the world is because He would have seen the blood of His prophets and saints. And because this world would have committed too many and too great sins with all the things that God had given it, it would have become too filthy for God to tolerate. The most beautiful planet that God has created is the planet earth. This is so because God Himself worked on this earth with keen interest, and because it is also the place where God's plans and His work of saving sinners in Jesus Christ have been fulfilled.

Nevertheless, God has already planned how He would destroy this world and how He would make the Kingdom of Christ come. When this world is filled with all kinds of filthiness, God will destroy it through His angels with the plagues of the seven bowls. He will then renew all things and have His saints reign in His new world.

The Fallen City of Babylon!

The kings of the earth have fornicated with the things of the world and lived in its luxury, while all the merchants, too busy selling and buying everything that God has given them, have lost God Himself in their pursuit of greed. God will destroy everything and all—buildings, religions, merchandises found within religion, people who have enriched themselves through religion, kings, politicians, people obsessed with material possessions, and more—all these will be brought down by God.

God will shake down every building on this earth and leave no building standing, and He will destroy all things, from people to forests and trees, with His fire. When everything in this world thus falls, people will lament and weep. In particular, God will make sure to destroy all those who had enriched themselves through religion. It is very important for us to know beforehand and believe in the fact that God will thus destroy this beautiful world that He had created Himself.

At this time, God will allow the born-again saints who had participated in the first resurrection of Jesus Christ to reign on this earth for a thousand years. With the Kingdom of the Lord, He will compensate the saints for serving the gospel of the water and the Spirit and for being martyred to defend their faith while on this earth. God will give them authority over ten cities, over five cities, and over two cities and let them reign for a thousand years, and after this, He will also give them the New Heaven and Earth to live forever.

Why, then, is God going to destroy the earth, the most

beautiful planet in the entire universe? It is only on this planet earth that fish can swim in rivers, wild animals can roam in the forests, and the mankind can live. But because God would no longer be able to tolerate a world where sin has become so rampant, He will lay this world to its complete ruins with His plagues. God has decided to destroy the world.

Everyone living on this earth, except those who have been saved, will be destroyed by the plagues of the seven bowls. Because all the righteous of the end times would be martyred, persecuted and oppressed by this world, God will trample on the world itself in return for its evil deeds. When this time comes, the religious leaders and merchants who had traded in people's souls will all be destroyed. God will not only kill all those who acted as religious leaders without having been born again, but He will also throw them, along with the Devil, into the lake of fire and brimstone.

God will most certainly destroy this world. As such, we much realize and believe beyond a trace of doubt that this world is to be destroyed. God will kill all the merchants who boast of all kinds of great things and traffic in people's souls with their religion. And yet, even as God's plagues are so imminent, people still remain arrogant in their confidence. Just take a look at the religious leaders of this earth. Are they not all prideful, as if they were doing the right thing before God? Would God really approve what such people do?

If God said that He would destroy this world for the sins of these people, then we must believe as such, for all things will come to pass exactly as God said that they would. And we must defend our faith. I am not saying this as just another one of those cult leaders who make up their own little doctrines and speak of the coming apocalypse, but I am saying this because we must believe in what God has told us in the Scripture —that is, the Living God will most certainly destroy this world with the great plagues of the seven bowls.

We Must Not Indulge Ourselves in This World That Will Soon Be Destroyed

As such, we must not be obsessed with accumulating the material possession of this world that is soon to be destroyed. We must be satisfied with what God has given us, and use and share them as God pleases. The material things of the world are needed only to serve God. We must live as the faithful servants who manage what God has given them for the preaching of the gospel. We must not be tangled up with the material things of the world, for we believe that God will destroy this world.

We must not fool ourselves thinking that the wealth and value of this world would last forever. Knowing that God will trample on all the religious leaders and their followers as well, we must live waiting for the day of the Lord's return. If not, we will end up falling into the world, a world that will shortly be destroyed. As such, to not fall into a world facing its own destruction, we must believe that this planet earth will indeed be destroyed.

God is alive at this very moment, and when the time comes, He will fulfill all that He has said. While it is true that even among the born-again there are those whose faith is yet to mature, we must nevertheless all believe without a doubt. And we must be all awake once again. We must never lose our hearts to this world that would soon be destroyed, but instead live our lives by placing our unfaltering and unshakable faith in the Word of God. Our hearts may at times weaken, but we must still live with strong faith.

That God will do all these things to this world is wonderful to us. Were God not to destroy this world and build the new Kingdom of Christ in its place, the righteous would be greatly disappointed. This is why God's plan is so wonderful, and why it gives hope to the righteous saints.

If the unbelievers were to remain in their arrogance and yet they live well in happiness while on this earth and even enter Heaven with us afterwards, it would be so unfair to us that God would never allow this to happen. God's promise, that He will judge and destroy all those who persecute the righteous, torment them with their lies, and shed the blood of the saints, is only just and right.

If there were to be no judgment of God for the sinners of this world, would it not be so unfair to the righteous who have lived all their lives for the sake of the Lord in perseverance despite facing all kinds of troubles and difficulties? It is therefore only right that God would judge this world. When this world becomes like the world of Noah's time, God will most certainly turn the whole world upside down and destroy it.

Because we believe in the Lord, we do not envy the people of the world at all. Because the Lord has said that He will judge this world and throw Satan, the Antichrist and his followers into the fire of hell, we can all persevere and wait.

This world is only a minute away from being destroyed, all in accordance to the prophecies of the Word of God. Throughout the earth, we have already seen many signs indicating the imminent arrival of the plagues of the end times.

Weather abnormalities such as the *El Niño* phenomenon and such new diseases as the Mad Cow Disease are rocking today's world. Incurable diseases that the mankind is powerless to tackle are engulfing the world, as are such large-scale, previously unimaginable disasters as great famines and devastatingly destructive earthquakes striking throughout the earth.

When all these things are happening, we must believe that God exists, and live our lives knowing that God will judge and bring down all those who had lived only for their lusts amassing their wealth while in this world. Sin has become so rampant in today's world. This world is too extravagant in its luxuries. People are too busy getting married, eating and drinking, and building their houses to pay any attention to their spiritual well-being. Today's world is a world where a man commits sexual sin with another man, and not a few women burn in their lust for one another (Roman 1:27).

Was the world not like this in Noah's time? You might know well of the etymology of the word 'sodomite.' When Sodom and Gomorra were destroyed, their culture had been just like that of today's world in which we now live. This world has become so filthy and sinful, to the extent that God would bring down fire and burn it to ashes, and it has turned into a world fully occupied by demons.

False Prophets Are to Be Put to Death

The false prophets always seek after material possessions and accumulate wealth illicitly, hiding behind the relative autonomy extended to their religious institutions. "If you believe in Jesus, you'll be rich, live well, and cure your disease"—you must realize that behind every such lie, the hidden purpose of material exploitation is always present.

In Korea, too, it's been a long time since Christianity has lost its fundamental faith and been corrupted, with all kinds of demonic forces running rampant in the name of Jesus. This is the reality of today's Christianity. But to the false prophets who measure faith with the material possessions of the world and commit sorceries with the Word of God, His fearful judgment of hell and the great plagues of the seven bowls are awaiting.

God tells us that both the ones who deceive the people and those who are deceived by the false prophets will alike be judged. We must not look toward this world and follow it. We must instead believe that because God is alive, those who, not believing in Jesus, stand against Him and persecute the righteous will all be judged and condemned to eternal death. And we must also believe that after thus judging the world, God will most certainly reward the saints for all their suffering and pain born for the sake of the name of Christ. ⊠

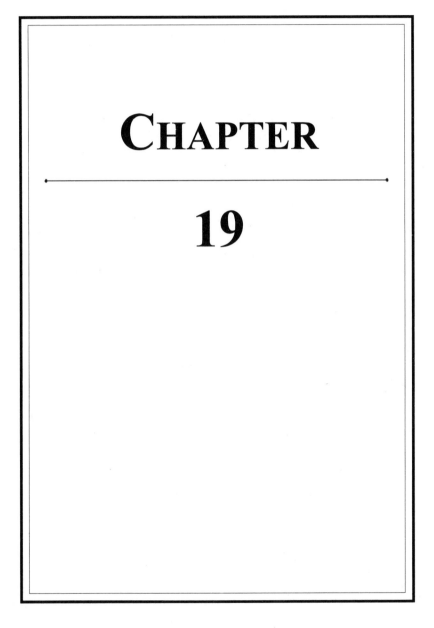

CHAPTER

19

The Kingdom to Be Reigned by The Omnipotent

< Revelation 19:1-21 >

"After these things I heard a loud voice of a great multitude in heaven, saying, 'Alleluia! Salvation and glory and honor and power belong to the Lord our God! For true and righteous are His judgments, because He has judged the great harlot who corrupted the earth with her fornication; and He has avenged on her the blood of His servants shed by her.' Again they said, 'Alleluia! Her smoke rises up forever and ever!' And the twenty-four elders and the four living creatures fell down and worshiped God who sat on the throne, saying, 'Amen! Alleluia!' Then a voice came from the throne, saying, 'Praise our God, all you His servants and those who fear Him, both small and great!' And I heard, as it were, the voice of a great multitude, as the sound of many waters and as the sound of mighty thunderings, saying, 'Alleluia! For the Lord God Omnipotent reigns! Let us be glad and rejoice and give Him glory, for the marriage of the Lamb has come, and His wife has made herself ready.' And to her it was granted to be arrayed in fine linen, clean and bright, for the fine linen is the righteous acts of the saints. Then he said to me, 'Write: 'Blessed are those who are called to the marriage supper of the Lamb!'" And he said to me, 'These are the true sayings of God.' And I fell at his feet to worship him. But he said to me, 'See that you do not do that! I am your fellow servant, and of your brethren who have the testimony of Jesus. Worship God! For the testimony of Jesus is the spirit of prophecy.' Now I saw heaven opened, and behold, a white horse. And He who sat on him was called Faithful and True, and in righteousness He judges and makes war. His eyes were like a flame of fire, and on His head were many crowns. He had a name written that no one knew except Himself. He was clothed with a robe dipped in blood, and His name is called The Word of God. And the armies in heaven, clothed in fine linen, white and clean, followed Him on white horses. Now out of His mouth goes a sharp sword, that with it He should strike the nations. And He Himself will rule them with a rod of iron. He Himself treads the winepress of the fierceness and wrath of Almighty God. And He has on His robe and on His thigh a name written: KING OF KINGS AND LORD OF LORDS.

Then I saw an angel standing in the sun; and he cried with a loud voice, saying to all the birds that fly in the midst of heaven, 'Come and gather together for the supper of the great God, that you may eat the flesh of kings, the flesh of captains, the flesh of mighty men, the flesh of horses and of those who sit on them, and the flesh of all people, free and slave, both small and great.' And I saw the beast, the kings of the earth, and their armies, gathered together to make war against Him who sat on the horse and against His army. Then the beast was captured, and with him the false prophet who worked signs in his presence, by which he deceived those who received the mark of the beast and those who worshiped his image. These two were cast alive into the lake of fire burning with brimstone. [21]And the rest were killed with the sword which proceeded from the

mouth of Him who sat on the horse. And all the birds were filled with their flesh."

Exegesis

Verse 1: After these things I heard a loud voice of a great multitude in heaven, saying, "Alleluia! Salvation and glory and honor and power belong to the Lord our God!"

The passage describes the saints praising the Lord God as their marriage day with the Lamb approaches. Our Lord God has given the saints their salvation and glory, so that they may praise Him for a good reason. The raptured saints in the air therefore continue to praise the Lord God, for so great is His grace of delivering them from all their sins and their inevitable condemnations.

The word *"alleluia"* or "hallelujah" is a compound word conjoining the Hebrew words of *"halal,"* meaning praise, and *"Yah,"* meaning "Jehovah"—its meaning, therefore, is "praise Jehovah." In particular, Psalms 113-118 of the Old Testament are called as the "Hallel of Egypt," and Psalms 146-150 are called as the "Psalms of Hallel."

These "Psalms of Hallel" are songs that had accompanied the joy and sorrow of the Jewish people, giving them strength in times of sadness and tribulations, and sung as songs of joy in times of salvation and victory. These songs were also sung whenever the praise of "hallelujah" can be sung only to God. The reason is because the Lord's judgment of the great plagues rendered on this world is true and righteous, and because salvation, power, and glory belong to only God.

Verse 2: "For true and righteous are His judgments,

because He has judged the great harlot who corrupted the earth with her fornication; and He has avenged on her the blood of His servants shed by her."

That the Lord God will avenge the saints by pouring the plagues of the seven bowls on all the religionists of the earth and all the unbelievers is the true and righteous judgment of God. Because the religionists of this world had murdered the sinless and righteous servants of God, they, in return, deserve to be condemned to eternal death by God.

Have the servants of God ever done anything on this earth to deserve to be killed by the worldly religionists? Of course not! Yet all the religionists of the world have united in their scheme to murder the children of the Lord God. As such, God's pouring of the plagues of the seven bowls on these murderers is just, which also manifests the righteousness of God.

Verse 3: Again they said, "Alleluia! Her smoke rises up forever and ever!"

The saints are praising the Lord God in the air because the day of their wedding with Jesus, who has become the Lamb, has approached.

"Her smoke rises forever and ever." This refers to the smoke coming out of this world destroyed and burnt by the great plagues of the seven bowls poured by God. It shows us that this world would never recover from its ruins because its destruction will be fatal and eternal.

Verse 4: And the twenty-four elders and the four living creatures fell down and worshiped God who sat on the throne, saying, "Amen! Alleluia!"

The fact that the marriage day of the saints with the Lord Jesus has approached is such a glorious event that the 24 elders and the four living creatures in Heaven worship and praise the Lord God sitting on His throne. This is why all the servants of God are praising the Lord God in the air.

Verse 5: Then a voice came from the throne, saying, "Praise our God, all you His servants and those who fear Him, both small and great!"

Because the Lamb's marriage day with the saints is such an unspeakably great joy for all His servants and the saints who have been saved by believing in the Lord God, the voice from the throne commands them all to praise God. The time has now come for the servants of God and all His saints to rejoice and praise the Lord.

Verse 6: And I heard, as it were, the voice of a great multitude, as the sound of many waters and as the sound of mighty thunderings, saying, "Alleluia! For the Lord God Omnipotent reigns!"

This verse tells us that as the time for the reign of the Lord God has approached, it now is time for His saints and the servants to receive their eternal peace, joy, and the blessings that flow like a river. This is why they are praising the Lord God. The saints are praising our God in the air even as the great plagues continue on this earth because the time has come for them to be reigned by the Lord God—that is, it is now time for God to glorify all His saints. The sound of the saints' praise at this time is like the sound of thunderings and of many waters. The marriage supper of the Lord's Kingdom thus begins with the beautiful praise of the saints.

Verse 7: "Let us be glad and rejoice and give Him glory, for the marriage of the Lamb has come, and His wife has made herself ready."

Now that the plagues of the seven bowls brought by God are ending, this verse tells us that the time has come for all the saints to be glad and rejoice. The saints are glad and rejoice here because the day has arrived for them to marry our Lord and live in His Kingdom. To live with the saints, our Lord God has prepared His New Heaven and Earth, the holy city and its gardens, and all glory and wealth, and He is only waiting for them. From this time and on, the saints are to reign with the Lord forever.

Verse 8: And to her it was granted to be arrayed in fine linen, clean and bright, for the fine linen is the righteous acts of the saints.

The Lord has given the saints new garments, which are made of fine linen. Anyone who lives serving the Lord God is clothed in these garments. God clothes the saints, in other words, in the garments of Heaven. These heavenly garments of fine linen are not wet with sweat. This tells us that the fact that we have become the Lamb's brides is not because of our man-made efforts and investments, but because of our faith in the gospel of the water and the Spirit given by the Lord God.

In distinctive contrast to the scarlet and purple garment worn by the Antichrist, this fine linen is the precious linen used to make garments for priests and kings. Free from sweat, the white, fine linen shows us that the ones who are clothed in God's grace and His righteousness have now become His people.

By the phrase, *"for the fine linen is the righteous acts of the saints,"* it is meant that the ones who became saints by the grace of salvation given by the Lord God gave glory to God with their martyrdom by the Antichrist and his followers in defense of their faith. "The righteous acts," in other words, refer not the righteousness of the Law, but to the saints' martyrdom in defense of their precious faith. Likewise, all the brides of Jesus Christ of the end times are the martyrs who, to defend the chastity of their faith in the Lord, had stood up to and fought against the Antichrist and his followers while on this earth.

To prepare for their faith of martyrdom, all the saints must be nourished for the first three and a half years of the Great Tribulation, for when these three and half years are over, they will indeed be martyred.

Verse 9: Then he said to me, "Write: 'Blessed are those who are called to the marriage supper of the Lamb!'" And he said to me, "These are the true sayings of God."

When the plagues of God are ended in this world, the Lord God will invite all the saints to the marriage supper of the Lamb (the Kingdom built and reigned by the Lord), and He will allow them to live in the Kingdom of Christ. Those who are invited to the marriage supper of the Lamb here are the blessed ones. Our God has told us that He will not fail to fulfill this Word of promise. The day will finally come when the saints are to marry the Lord. Our Lord will return to this earth to carry away His brides, who have been cleansed of all their sins by believing in the gospel of the water and the Spirit. And the Lord He will live with His brides forever and ever in His Kingdom.

The saints' union with the Lord is completed when they are raptured by Christ, at which time they are to receive endless glory and rewards in the Millennial Kingdom. Hallelujah! I praise and thank the Lord God who has made us His people.

Verse 10: And I fell at his feet to worship him. But he said to me, "See that you do not do that! I am your fellow servant, and of your brethren who have the testimony of Jesus. Worship God! For the testimony of Jesus is the spirit of prophecy."

The saints must give all these glories only to the Lord God. The One who is to receive all worship and praise from the saints is solely our Triune God.

The phrase, *"For the testimony of Jesus is the spirit of prophecy,"* means that the testimony and prophecy of Jesus come through the Holy Spirit.

Verse 11: Now I saw heaven opened, and behold, a white horse. And He who sat on him was called Faithful and True, and in righteousness He judges and makes war.

When the end times come, our Lord God, riding on a white horse, will fight against Satan with His righteousness and bind him by throwing him into the bottomless pit and the lake of fire.

Here, the name of Jesus Christ is "Faithful" and "True." The word "Faithful," meaning that Christ is trustworthy, expresses His truthfulness and fidelity, while the word "True," meaning that He is free from falsehood, tells us that Christ would overcome the Antichrist with the righteous judgment of God.

Verse 12: His eyes were like a flame of fire, and on His head were many crowns. He had a name written that no one knew except Himself.

That the Lord's eyes are "like a flame of fire" tells us that He has the power to judge all. The phrase *"on His head were many crowns,"* on the other hand, means that our Lord always triumphs over Satan in His fight against him, for He is the omniscient and omnipotent God.

Verse 13: He was clothed with a robe dipped in blood, and His name is called The Word of God.

Our Lord will avenge the saints on their enemies by judging these enemies of His, who had stood against Him, with His fierce wrath. This God is none other than Jesus Christ Himself. Just as He had promised with His Word, our Lord indeed came to this earth in the flesh of a man, was baptized by John to bear all the sins of the world, carried them to the Cross, and made the sins of the entire mankind disappear.

The *"robe dipped in blood"* This blood does not refer to Christ's own blood. It refers to the blood of the enemies being splattered onto the Lord's robe as He brings His fearful judgment of wrath to them and tramples them with His feet of power.

"The Word of God" refers to Jesus' character. Because our Lord does everything by His powerful Word, He is named as "the Word of God."

Verse 14-16: And the armies in heaven, clothed in fine linen, white and clean, followed Him on white horses. Now out of His mouth goes a sharp sword, that with it He should strike the nations. And He Himself will rule them with a rod of iron. He Himself treads the winepress of the fierceness and wrath of Almighty God. And He has on His robe and on His thigh a name written: KING OF KINGS AND LORD OF LORDS.

The army of the Lord God always serves His works, clothed in His glorious grace.

God will judge this world with the Word coming out of His mouth. Our Lord has always promised us with the Word of His mouth, and He always fulfills these promises with His power. The One who judges the world and destroys Satan is Jesus Christ, King of kings and Lord of lords.

Verse 17: Then I saw an angel standing in the sun; and he cried with a loud voice, saying to all the birds that fly in the midst of heaven, "Come and gather together for the supper of the great God,"
This world, along with Satan and his followers, will ultimately be destroyed by Jesus Christ. The Bible describes the destruction of this world as God's great feast.

Verse 18: "that you may eat the flesh of kings, the flesh of captains, the flesh of mighty men, the flesh of horses and of those who sit on them, and the flesh of all people, free and slave, both small and great."
This Word tells us that because the whole world and everyone in it would have been put to death by the time the great plagues of the Lord God are ended, the birds flying in the sky would fill their bellies by feeding on their carcasses. They would do so because God would have poured the great plagues of the seven bowls on this world. Our Lord told us, *"For wherever the carcass is, there the eagles will be gathered together (Matthew 24:28)."* In the end times' world, there will be only destruction, death, and the punishment of hell for the sinners. But for the saints, there will be the blessing of reigning in the Kingdom of Christ.

Verse 19: And I saw the beast, the kings of the earth, and their armies, gathered together to make war against Him who sat on the horse and against His army.
To their very end, the Antichrist, Satan's servant, and his followers will stand against the servants of God and His saints

and try to win over them. But because our Lord is the King of kings, He will seize the Antichrist and the false prophet, throw them into the lake of fire, and kill all their servants with the sword of His Word.

Verse 20: Then the beast was captured, and with him the false prophet who worked signs in his presence, by which he deceived those who received the mark of the beast and those who worshiped his image. These two were cast alive into the lake of fire burning with brimstone.

The "Beast" here refers to the Antichrist. The "false prophet" is the Antichrist's servant who, by performing miracles and signs, turns people away from faith in the Word of truth. Our Lord God will destroy Satan, the Beast (the Antichrist), the false prophet, and the followers of Satan who had worshipped the idol of the Antichrist and stood against God, against the saints, and against the gospel of the water and the Spirit.

The *"lake of fire burning with brimstone"* refers to hell. Hell is different from the bottomless pit. While the bottomless pit is where the forces of Satan are temporarily bound in, the "lake of fire" is the place of their eternal punishment. In particular, fire and brimstone have always been used in the Bible as the instrument of God's punishment and judgment.

After this world is destroyed, our Lord will return to this earth with the saints, destroy Satan and his servants first, and then open the Kingdom of Christ. The saints will then live and reign with the Lord in the Kingdom of Christ for a thousand years to come.

Verse 21: And the rest were killed with the sword which

proceeded from the mouth of Him who sat on the horse. And all the birds were filled with their flesh.

This world was created by the Word coming out of the mouth of our Lord God; likewise, the enemies of God will all be destroyed by the Word of judgment coming out of His mouth. The Kingdom of Christ will then be established on this earth. The saints, therefore, must place their hope in the Kingdom of Christ and give glory to God by fighting against Satan, the Antichrist and his followers, and by embracing their martyrdom with faith. ⊠

Only the Righteous Can Wait in Hope for Christ to Return

< Revelation 19:1-21 >

In the previous chapter, we saw how God would bring His fearful plagues to this world. In this chapter, we now see Christ and His glorious army fighting against and overcoming the army of the Antichrist, throwing the Beast and his servants into the lake of fire alive, killing the rest of the Antichrist' army with the sword of the Word coming out of the Lord's mouth, and thus finally ending all His battle against Satan.

The substance of this chapter can be divided into three main topics: 1) the raptured saints' praise of God for bringing the judgment of the great plagues to this world; 2) the proclamation for the coming of the marriage supper of the Lamb; and 3) the Lord's descent from Heaven with the army of Jesus Christ.

We must all realize that God will most certainly and soon fulfill everything that He has said to us through the Book of Revelation.

The Judgment of God!

Those who believe in the gospel of the water and the Spirit and have thus become the people of God through faith will be praising Him for saving them from all the sins of the world. Let's take a look at verses 3-5: *"Again they said, 'Alleluia! Her smoke rises up forever and ever!' And the twenty-four elders and the four living creatures fell down and worshiped God who sat on the throne, saying, 'Amen! Alleluia!' Then a voice came from the throne, saying, 'Praise our God, all you His servants and those who fear Him, both small and great!'"*

Hebrew 9:27 tells us, *"And as it is appointed for men to die once, but after this the judgment."* Man is to be judged before God once, but the sentence of this judgment is final and will not be reversed. With His one-time judgment of everyone for his/her sins, in other words, God would render His eternal judgment by throwing the sinners into the fire that burns forever. This is why the Bible tells us that *"her smoke rises up forever and ever."*

Some people might think and say, "Once you die, that's the end of it." But this is man's own thought, not God's. Because everyone has both a body and a soul, whether people believe in God or not, they all know instinctively that God exists, and that sooner or later they will all be judged for their sins before Him.

As there exists a realm of spirits for people, they know that God, though unseen by their eyes, still exists. The realm that can be seen by the eyes of the flesh does not last forever, but there exists the eternal realm of truth, unseen by our eyes. Material prosperity on this earth while thinking of only money and pursuing only material greed cannot be the mankind's reason for being; its true purpose is to enter into the eternal realm of blessing by knowing God, the Creator of the whole universe, and by knowing and believing in the gospel of the water and the Spirit given by Him.

Not only must we know what God has told us, but we must also believe in it. We must not end up in hell by believing and trusting in just our own thoughts alone. Before facing eternal suffering for our sins, we must be forgiven of all our sins and receive eternal life by believing, while on this earth now, in the gospel of the water and the Spirit given by Jesus.

For everyone, life on this earth is too short. Just as the sun rises and falls everyday, the short journey of our lives ends too quickly, fruitless and meaningless, as if we had been running like a squirrel on a treadmill. Even if you were to live for a hundred years, you couldn't really say that you've lived that long.

If you subtract the trivial rounds of your daily life, such times spent while sleeping, eating, going to washrooms, and doing other such mundane things, from your whole life span, you are actually left with very little time. While you see the things that you had already seen since your birth, and while you meet the people whom you had already met before, your hair has turned all gray, and all of a sudden you find yourself facing your own end.

The only reason as to why our life as the saints are not meaningless is because we, having been born into this world, have met the Lord who has come to us through the water and the Spirit, believed in Him, and thus received the remission of all our sins. How fortunate and thankful we are! Had it not been for the Lord who came to us through the water and the Spirit, we would all be bound to enter the eternal fire and suffer in it.

Whenever I think of this, it still gives me scares, and I come to thank the Lord once more. Hell, which came into existence because of Satan, is the most horrendous place, where the suffering is so great that one would rather wish to die, yet would not be able to do so. It is a place where fire and brimstone burn forever.

To know the gospel of the water and the Spirit given by Jesus correctly, and to thus receive the Holy Spirit, one must first meet God's servants who have already encountered this gospel of the water and the Spirit and who have already been born again. Living as a Christian, whoever wants to find the answer to the question of being born again by the water and the Spirit and of receiving the Holy Spirit can have everything resolved by believing in the gospel of the water and the Spirit.

The Bible tells us that the Spirit of God is given as a gift to all those who receive the remission of sin by believing in the gospel of the water and the Spirit (Acts 2:38). Only those who have the Holy Spirit in their hearts by being forgiven of all their sins through their faith in the gospel of the water and the Spirit can be said to have the correct faith in Jesus, and only those with this faith can enter into the eternal Kingdom of God (John 3:5). Whether one is blessed or cursed is determined by whether or not one has received the remission of sin by believing in the gospel of the water and the Spirit.

Clothed in Fine Linen, Clean and Bright

Those who think of their future and want to resolve their present problem of the remission of their sins are the ones who are wise and blessed. Though one may have lived a checkered life full of shortcomings, if he/she has believed in the gospel of the water and the Spirit and received the remission of sin and the Holy Spirit into the heart, then this person has lived the most successful life of all.

Revelation 19:4-5 says, *"And the twenty-four elders and*

the four living creatures fell down and worshiped God who sat on the throne, saying, 'Amen! Alleluia!' Then a voice came from the throne, saying, 'Praise our God, all you His servants and those who fear Him, both small and great!'"

Here, the phrase "(to) fear Him" means to accept the Word of Jesus Christ into one's heart and to live according to His guidance. Only those who have been forgiven of their sins can see and praise God in the Kingdom of Heaven. But those who have not thus received the remission of their sins will suffer in the burning fire of hell and curse God.

Let's continue with verses 6-9: *"And I heard, as it were, the voice of a great multitude, as the sound of many waters and as the sound of mighty thunderings, saying, 'Alleluia! For the Lord God Omnipotent reigns! Let us be glad and rejoice and give Him glory, for the marriage of the Lamb has come, and His wife has made herself ready. And to her it was granted to be arrayed in fine linen, clean and bright, for the fine linen is the righteous acts of the saints.'"*

It says here that the Apostle John heard the sound of praise, sounding like the voice of a great multitude, the sound of many waters, and the sound of mighty thunderings. This sound was none other than the sound of those who have received the remission of sin gathered together and praising God. This song of praise was made of, first of all, praising God for allowing them to come under the reign of the Almighty God, to be ruled by Him, and to live with Him in glory. All these things have made the saints overwhelmingly happy and joyful and give great glory to God. So, they cannot but praise Him, shouting, *"Let us be glad and rejoice and give Him glory."*

Second, the saints continue with their praise: *"for the marriage of the Lamb has come, and His wife has made herself ready. And to her it was granted to be arrayed in fine linen, clean and bright, for the fine linen is the righteous acts of the saints."* What does this mean? It means that just as He has promised the mankind, Jesus would return to this earth, marry those who have received the Holy Spirit by believing in Him and by being born again, and live and dwell with them forever.

Marriage is the union of a bridegroom and his bride. When Jesus returns to this earth, in other words, He would accept and live with only those who have been born again of the water and the Spirit. And it means that He would build His Millennial Kingdom and New Heaven and Earth to live with the saints forever and ever. The brides' glory of living with this Bridegroom is so great that it is beyond description. Just by thinking of it, our hearts swell with happiness.

When the world where Jesus Christ will reign comes, His brides will be extremely happy, beyond what words can describe. How happy would they be when they are reigned by the Good Shepherd? Because Jesus Christ is the Bridegroom of absolute goodness, so would His reign be of absolute goodness and perfection. He will reign over the Kingdom of Heaven.

The One and Only Gospel That Would Qualify You for Heaven

For one to receive the Holy Spirit and enter Heaven, he/she must believe solely in Jesus' baptism and blood. Because our Lord came to this earth to save all the sinners from all their sins by taking all such sins of the mankind onto Himself, He had to be baptized by John. Having thus received His baptism, Jesus Himself was then crucified on the Cross in our place, was judged for all our sins, rose from the dead again, and became the Lord of eternal salvation for those who believe.

This Lord will now return to the earth, embrace His people who have become His brides through faith, and live with them forever. Those who have become His brides will now live with the Lord on a new earth, a glorious and glorifying blessing for the brides. The saved children of God will thus give glory to Jesus Christ by praising Him forever. These people who are to be reigned by God will rejoice in their happiness. And for this joy, they will give all glory to the Bridegroom.

The whole mankind has been waiting for this event since the very creation. This event is fulfilled when Jesus returns, lifts up those who have received the Holy Spirit, and lives with them. God has made a new world for the mankind and is waiting for us. We exist for this, and for this we have been born into this world.

As the main passage tells us, *"His wife has made herself ready. And to her it was granted to be arrayed in fine linen, clean and bright,"* God has clothed those who believe in Jesus Christ in clean, fine linen. Those who believe in this Word, in other words, have received the remission of sin and their hearts have turned white as snow.

Like this, the brides of Jesus Christ are already prepared beforehand with the gospel of the water and the Spirit. By hearing and believing in the gospel of the water and the Spirit while on this earth, one can be born again as Jesus Christ's bride. This faith is what makes you Christ's bride, and this faith is what qualifies you to enter Heaven.

Those Who Wait in Hope

The main passage tells us, *"Blessed are those who are called to the marriage supper of the Lamb!"* With what kind of faith should those who have received the remission of their sins live? The brides who have met their Bridegroom Jesus and are living in glory must live their lives in faith and hope, looking forward to the day of their union with this Bridegroom.

As the world gets darker and darker, there is still hope for the saved brides. This hope is none other than waiting for the day when Jesus Christ, having prepared the New Heaven and Earth for His brides, would return to take them away. The Bridegroom will resurrect all His brides then, and give them eternal life. The world in which the Bridegroom and the brides are to live forever is a place that is free from evil, has no sin, and lacks nothing. The brides wait only for this day. This is why those of us who have received the remission of all our sins live with such faith and hope.

The brides who are now living in the present era, in particular, also have many shortcomings of the flesh. But as 1 Corinthians 13:13 tells us, *"And now abide faith, hope, love, these three; but the greatest of these is love,"* because the Bridegroom has thus loved His brides, He would cleanse away all their sins with His baptism and accept them as His perfect brides.

This world is running toward its final demise and has no hope left in it. But even as everything is moving ever closer to destruction, the brides must live their lives with their special hope. The time for the fulfillment of this hope is now nearing us. The whole world is now at the risk of crumbling down from earthquakes. The day has neared for everyone in this world to disappear like the extinct dinosaurs of the ancient times. All of a sudden, this world will simply fall down.

Every bride, however, has hope, for when time comes, the bodies of the brides will be transformed into perfect bodies, and they will live with the Lord, who has become their Bridegroom, forever and ever. The brides, therefore, must preach the gospel of the water and the Spirit more faithfully to the worldly people of this era.

Let Us Believe in the True Word of God!

Jesus tells us in John 3:5, *"Most assuredly, I say to you, unless one is born of water and the Spirit, he cannot enter the kingdom of God."* What, then, is the gospel of the water and the Spirit? The Bible tells us, first of all, that "water" refers clearly to the baptism of Jesus, and is the antitype of salvation (1 Peter 3:21).

When Jesus turned 30, He went to John, who had been baptizing the people of Israel in the Jordan River. Jesus tells us that John the Baptist was the representative of the mankind and the last High Priest of the Old Testament. Meeting this John, Jesus received His baptism from him, which fulfilled all the righteousness of God (Matthew 3:15, 11:11-14). The baptism that Jesus thus received was the eternal offering through which all the sins of the world were passed onto Christ Himself.

The incarnation of Jesus through the Holy Spirit, His baptism, His blood and death on the Cross, and His resurrection and ascension—all these things were the works of the Holy Spirit. When one believes that Jesus came to this earth and made, through the water and the Spirit, all his/her sins disappear at all once, he/she can then become a righteous person, freed from sin, and a bride of Christ. This is not something accomplished by man's thoughts, but it comes from the thoughts of God Himself.

The truth is that the water, the blood, and the Holy Spirit are the three essential components for the salvation of the mankind from sin, and none of them can ever be absent at all. The Bible elaborates on this clearly and exactly in chapter 5 of 1 John. It tells us that these three elements of the water, the blood, and the Holy Spirit are one in all, and that our salvation from sin cannot be whole and approved if any one of them is missing.

When we know and believe in this truth, that the perfect salvation is to believe in these three—the water, the blood, and the Holy Spirit—we can then realize and accept the love of Jesus that has saved us, and thus our hearts can actually become completely sinless. The Bible promises us in Acts 2:38, *"Repent, and let every one of you be baptized in the name of Jesus Christ for the remission of sins; and you shall receive the gift of the Holy Spirit."*

What, then, is this Word that enables us to receive the Holy Spirit? This is none other than the Word of Jesus' baptism (the water), of His death on the Cross (the blood), and of His being God, resurrection and ascension (the Holy Spirit). This Word of salvation had actually been prophesized in the writings of Moses and other prophets of the Old Testament, and was fulfilled and testified in all four Gospels of the New Testament. Also, the "eternal salvation of atonement completed at once," which is detailed in the Book of Hebrews, testifies repeatedly to the righteousness of God, which we have received through our faith.

Though everyone in this sinful world is living a life of the flesh that falls far short before God, he/she must receive the remission of sin offered by God, and live one's life by placing his/her hope in Heaven. This is the gift of God that He has given to the mankind. We must all receive this grace given to us freely. Believing in the Word that our Lord would return, build His new Kingdom, and let us live in it is our true hope. We must live with this hope, and this is what I most fervently believe.

Do you know how widespread sin is in this world? Compared to the time of Noah's flood, the sins of this era are far more spread. In Noah's time, seeing that the thoughts of the mankind were always evil, God had decided to destroy the first world with flood, told Noah to build an ark, and saved those who entered this ark by believing in His Word.

Though God had said that He would most certainly judge the world with water, only Noah's family of eight believed in His Word. They thus made the ark over a hundred-year period, and entered it to escape the flood. When they did so, God began to bring His judgment to the first world. The sky turned dark all of a sudden, and torrential rain began to rain. Perhaps in just an hour, the water might have reached as high as the third floor. So it rained for 40 days, submerging the whole world under water.

Just as Noah and his family had entered the ark believing that a new world is about to be opened, you and I must live this age in hope. Just as they could build the ark for a hundred years because they had believed in God, I believe that we, too, must persevere and preach the gospel. God told Noah, *"Make yourself an ark (Genesis 6:14)."* This Word tells us that 'for us to defend our own faith,' we must first devote ourselves to the Lord and to preach the gospel.

Though the born-again have hope, there is no hope for those who do not believe in the gospel. There is only despair for these unbelievers of the gospel. Regardless of whether people believe in the gospel of the water and the Spirit or not, we must still preach it to them with faith. The present age is the kind of time when people must believe in this true gospel as soon as possible. Those who believe in the gospel that we preach will find happiness, but those who do not believe in it will only be cursed. The latter—that is, those who do not believe in the gospel—are the fools who will receive God's eternal judgment and be thrown into hell.

Do not lose your hope. If the righteous were ever to lose their hope, only death would await them. If we have no hope, we would have neither the desire, nor the interest, nor any more reason to live on. Let us, therefore, live with hope.

In today's age, those who believe in Jesus and have thus been born again are the truly happy ones. For the mankind, its only hope left is to receive the remission of sin—that is, there is no other hope but to receive the Holy Spirit. When people are forgiven of all their sins, they can have hope and live happily forever, but if they are not, only destruction would await them, for they would not have received the Holy Spirit.

It is because I have received the remission of all my sins that I can live through today's world with hope. It is my hope and prayer that you, too, would live your life with this hope. I pray that you would not attach yourself to the vain thoughts of the world, but instead live your life as the wise bride, loving your fellow righteous brothers and sisters, helping them to stand firm in Christ, not losing your faith, waiting for the Bridegroom, and meeting Him when He finally comes to take you away.

I thank God for enabling us to live in His glory. ⊠

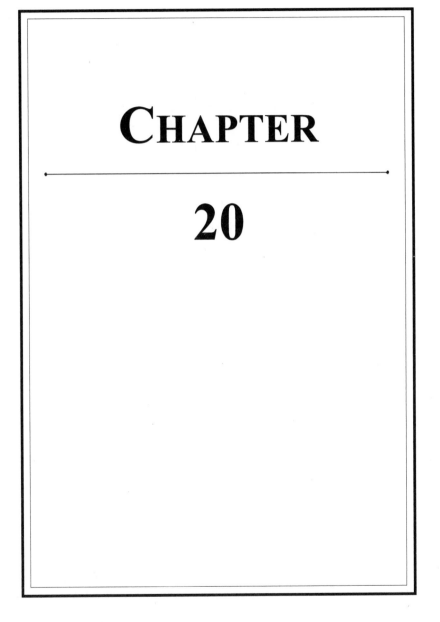

CHAPTER

20

The Dragon Will Be Confined to The Bottomless Pit

< Revelation 20:1-15 >
"Then I saw an angel coming down from heaven, having the key to the bottomless pit and a great chain in his hand. He laid hold of the dragon, that serpent of old, who is the Devil and Satan, and bound him for a thousand years; and he cast him into the bottomless pit, and shut him up, and set a seal on him, so that he should deceive the nations no more till the thousand years were finished. But after these things he must be released for a little while. And I saw thrones, and they sat on them, and judgment was committed to them. Then I saw the souls of those who had been beheaded for their witness to Jesus and for the word of God, who had not worshiped the beast or his image, and had not received his mark on their foreheads or on their hands. And they lived and reigned with Christ for a thousand years. But the rest of the dead did not live again until the thousand years were finished. This is the first resurrection. Blessed and holy is he who has part in the first resurrection. Over such the second death has no power, but they shall be priests of God and of Christ, and shall reign with Him a thousand years. Now when the thousand years have expired, Satan will be released from his prison and will go out to deceive the nations which are in the four corners of the earth, Gog and Magog, to gather them

together to battle, whose number is as the sand of the sea. They went up on the breadth of the earth and surrounded the camp of the saints and the beloved city. And fire came down from God out of heaven and devoured them. The devil, who deceived them, was cast into the lake of fire and brimstone where the beast and the false prophet are. And they will be tormented day and night forever and ever. Then I saw a great white throne and Him who sat on it, from whose face the earth and the heaven fled away. And there was found no place for them. And I saw the dead, small and great, standing before God, and books were opened. And another book was opened, which is the Book of Life. And the dead were judged according to their works, by the things which were written in the books. The sea gave up the dead who were in it, and Death and Hades delivered up the dead who were in them. And they were judged, each one according to his works. Then Death and Hades were cast into the lake of fire. This is the second death. And anyone not found written in the Book of Life was cast into the lake of fire."

Exegesis

Verse 1: Then I saw an angel coming down from heaven, having the key to the bottomless pit and a great chain in his hand.

To compensate the saints who have labored for the gospel with His rewards, our Lord God will give them the gift of the Kingdom of Christ for a thousand years. To do so, God must first command one of His angels to seize the Dragon to confine him in the bottomless pit for a thousand years. God must do this work first, because the Dragon must be seized and bound in the Abyss beforehand to enable the saints to live in the Millennial Kingdom of Christ. God thus gives His angel the key to the bottomless pit and a great chain, and commands him to begin the work of seizing and binding the Dragon in the Abyss.

Verse 2: He laid hold of the dragon, that serpent of old, who is the Devil and Satan, and bound him for a thousand years;

The one that had tempted and made Adam and Eve fall is the very serpent. The Bible calls this serpent the Dragon and Satan. God would lay hold of this Dragon and bind him in the bottomless pit for a thousand years, so that the saints could live with Christ in the Millennial Kingdom in peace.

Verse 3: and he cast him into the bottomless pit, and shut him up, and set a seal on him, so that he should deceive the nations no more till the thousand years were finished. But after these things he must be released for a little while.

In order to build the Kingdom of Christ on this earth and have the saints reign with the Lord for a thousand years, God would bind the Dragon in the Abyss for a thousand years and prevent him from deceiving the saints.

The passage says here, *"But after these things he must be released for a little while."* When the thousand years are completed, God would released the Dragon for a little while, so that when he begins to torment the saints again, He would send him to hell forever then, never to be seen again.

Verse 4: And I saw thrones, and they sat on them, and judgment was committed to them. Then I saw the souls of those who had been beheaded for their witness to Jesus and for the word of God, who had not worshiped the beast or his image, and had not received his mark on their foreheads or on their hands. And they lived and reigned with Christ for a thousand years.

In the Kingdom of Christ, the born-again Christians will receive authority to judge. The saints, having been made into Christ's priests, will reign the Millennial Kingdom with the Lord. Its inhabitants are those who were martyred to bear witness to Jesus and to defend their faith, those who neither received the mark of the Beast nor worshipped his image.

They are the ones who were martyred during the time of tribulations brought by the Antichrist, and God would resurrect them to live again and have them reign the Kingdom of Christ for a thousand years to come. Of course, all those who participated in the first resurrection will also be bestowed with the same blessing.

There are two resurrections given by the Lord: the first resurrection and the second resurrection. The saints who would live in the Millennial Kingdom are the ones who would belong to and participate in the first resurrection. All those who take part in this first resurrection will also take part in the glory of living in the Millennial Kingdom, the Kingdom of Christ. The first resurrection will take place when Jesus Christ returns to rapture all the saints (1 Thessalonians 4:15-17). But the second one will take place at the end of the Millennial Kingdom because it is prepared for the sinners to sentence them to eternal death.

The saints' authority to reign for a thousand years is given by the Almighty Lord. The Kingdom of Christ is given to them because they believed in the Lord's gospel of the water and the Spirit and gave up their lives to defend their faith in it.

Verse 5: But the rest of the dead did not live again until the thousand years were finished. This is the first resurrection.

Those who, not having received the remission of their sins from the Lord, go to Him after living on this earth as sinners will not be able to participate in the first resurrection that the Lord would give to the saints. As such, even as the saints live for a thousand years in the Kingdom of Christ in festivity, they would not receive the first resurrection, but they would instead take part in the second resurrection. The reason is because the saints who would receive the blessing of the first resurrection would have also received authority to live in the Kingdom of Christ, in wealth and glory, for a thousand years.

However, God will allow "the second resurrection" to the sinners. Why? Because at the time of the second resurrection, God would raise them from their death so that He may judge them for their sins. Their fate is such that they must be raised from the dead again to be judged of their sins. This is why the resurrection of the sinners differs from that of the saints in both its order and consequences.

Apart from those who participate in the first resurrection because of their faith in the gospel of the water and the Spirit, the Lord will not allow anyone else to live again until the thousand years are finished. Thus, the resurrection of the righteous comes a thousand years before the resurrection of the sinners. The righteous' resurrection is for them to receive eternal life and blessings, but the sinners' resurrection is for them to receive eternal punishment for their sins.

Verse 6: Blessed and holy is he who has part in the first resurrection. Over such the second death has no power, but they shall be priests of God and of Christ, and shall reign with Him a thousand years.

The Bible tells us that the second death has no power over

those who take part in the first resurrection. As such, it tells us that these participants of the first resurrection are blessed, for they would also reign in the Millennial Kingdom.

Verse 7-8: Now when the thousand years have expired, Satan will be released from his prison and will go out to deceive the nations which are in the four corners of the earth, Gog and Magog, to gather them together to battle, whose number is as the sand of the sea.

Released after being locked in the bottomless pit for a thousand years, the Dragon will try to stand against the saints once again, and so God will throw him into the fire of brimstone so that he would never be able to come out again. With this judgment, the Dragon would be seen only in hell.

We may then ask, "Does this mean that those who are not born again will still exist in this Millennial Kingdom?" The answer is, "Yes." Revelation 20:8 records that there are many people of the earth in the Kingdom of Christ. We do not know for sure whether they are the people newly created by God, or the ones who had lived on this earth beforehand. But what we do know is that God knows who they are, and that for the saints to reign, there would be a great multitude of them, as many as the sand of the sea.

The truth is that when the saints live in the Kingdom of Christ, they would still see the people of the earth. They would exist to serve the saints, and their number would be as great as that of the sand of the sea. Though they would unite with the Dragon to stand against the saints once again, they will all be destroyed by the fire brought by God, receive the eternal judgment of His great white throne, and be thrown into the forever-burning fire. With this, the Millennial Kingdom would come to its close, and from then on the saints would move to the New Heaven and Earth where they are to live forever.

Verse 9: They went up on the breadth of the earth and surrounded the camp of the saints and the beloved city. And fire came down from God out of heaven and devoured them.

The Dragon is Satan who has constantly stood against God and His saints. Although he would deceive the people of the earth living in the Kingdom of Christ and threaten the saints, because God is almighty, He would bring down fire from the sky and devour them all, and throw the Dragon into the eternal fire to never again stand against Him and His saints.

Verse 10: The devil, who deceived them, was cast into the lake of fire and brimstone where the beast and the false prophet are. And they will be tormented day and night forever and ever.

By casting the Dragon into the lake of fire and brimstone, God will ensure that he is tormented day and night. This is God's righteous judgment, the suffering that the Dragon and his followers deserve.

Verse 11: Then I saw a great white throne and Him who sat on it, from whose face the earth and the heaven fled away. And there was found no place for them.

Having completed His rewarding of the saints for a thousand years, God will now create His New Heaven and Earth and live with them forever in this place. To accomplish this, God would have to bring all the works that He had done to their conclusion and final closure. This last act, of closure, is for the Lord to sit on the white throne as the Judge and render His final judgment on all the sinners, whose deeds are recorded in the Books of Deeds, except those whose names are written in the Book of Life.

God's judgment of the sinners would all end with this, and from then on the domain of the New Heaven and Earth would open. Our Lord would make the first heaven and the first earth disappear, create the second world of the New Heaven and Earth, and allow the saints to live in this heavenly Kingdom. According to what is written in His Book of Life and the Books of Judgment, God would give the New Heaven and Earth to one group of people, and the punishment of hell to the other.

Verse 12: And I saw the dead, small and great, standing before God, and books were opened. And another book was opened, which is the Book of Life. And the dead were judged according to their works, by the things which were written in the books.

Christ's judgment at this time will determine the final punishment—that is, He will render His final sentences on the sinners with the punishment of hell. They will be judged according to their works, as recorded in the Book of Judgment. The sinners will thus die twice. Their second death is the suffering of hell, which the Bible describes as eternal death. The sinners cannot escape from the punishment of hell. They must, therefore, seek after learning the Word of the gospel of the water and the Spirit right now, while they are still living on this earth, believe in it, and thereby receive the blessing of having their names written into the Book of Life.

Verse 13: The sea gave up the dead who were in it, and Death and Hades delivered up the dead who were in them. And they were judged, each one according to his works.

"The sea gave up the dead who were in it, and Death and Hades delivered up the dead who were in them," for all sinners must receive the final condemnation for their sins. The places

described in this passage—Death and Hades, that is—particularly refer to the places where the servants of Satan who, deceived by him and being under the control of him while alive, had stood and sinned against God will be imprisoned. This verse tells us that while God had deferred His judgment of their sins for a while, now the time has come for their final judgment.

As such, wherever people may live, they must realize that to whom they belong is critically important. Those who had worked as Satan's servants while on this earth will be raised from the dead with the resurrection of punishment to receive their final judgment, but those who had served the gospel of the water and the Spirit will belong to the resurrection of eternal life and blessings.

Therefore, people must realize while on this earth that the gospel of the water and the Spirit, with which the Lord has blotted out the sins of the mankind, is of the utmost importance. Those who had worked as Satan's servants on this earth will be raised with the resurrection of punishment, but those who had served our Lord's righteous works will be raised with the resurrection eternal life and blessings. All the sinners will be judged for their iniquities and receive their final punishment in hell. It is here where we find the precise reason as to why we must, while on this earth, believe in the gospel of the water and the Spirit, the gospel with which the Lord has remitted all our sins.

Verse 14: Then Death and Hades were cast into the lake of fire. This is the second death.

This tells us of the judgment of the sins of the mankind before God, which it had committed by standing at the side of Satan. The punishment reserved for the evil ones who had led people to Satan is to be cast into the lake of fire. This is the second death that God would bring to the sinners, and is the punishment of the lake of fire. The death that the Bible speaks of here is not simply disappearing, but it is the punishment of eternal suffering in the fiery hell.

The salvation spoken of by the Scripture is not temporal, but eternal. Those who believe in the gospel of the water and the Spirit while on this earth will enter the eternal Kingdom of Heaven and live happily forever. The difference between the reward of the believers of the gospel of the water and the Spirit and the punishment of the unbelievers is as great as the difference between heaven and earth.

Verse 15: And anyone not found written in the Book of Life was cast into the lake of fire.

With the word "anyone" here, this verse tells us that whether or not people's names are written in the Book of Life depends entirely on whether they believe in the Word of the gospel of the water and the Spirit, through which all their sins are forgiven, as white as snow, regardless of whether they are good church-goers, or whether their churches belong to orthodox or heterodox denominations. Those whose names are not written in the Lord's Book of Life, therefore, will all be cast into the lake of fire without exception.

The religious people of the world have a marked tendency to put more importance on their religious rituals than on their redemption from sin. But when standing before God, if the gospel of the water and the Spirit given by Jesus is not found in one's heart, the name of this person would not be written in the Book of Life, and he/she would thus also be thrown into the lake of fire, even if he/she were a fine Christian.

Therefore, while you are still living on this earth, you must hear with your ears the Lord's gospel of the water and the

Spirit that has made all your sins disappear, and you must believe in it with all your heart. You will then receive the glory of having your name written into the Book of Life. ⊠

How Can We Pass from Death to Life?

< Revelation 20:1-15 >

God tells us that when He makes this world disappear and gives us the New Heaven and Earth instead, He would resurrect every sinner who had lived on this earth before and had been asleep in his/her tomb. Verse 13 here says, *"The sea gave up the dead who were in it, and Death and Hades delivered up the dead who were in them."* The body of a man who drowns in water would most likely be eaten by fish, while that of a man who burns to death would leave virtually no form to be recognized anymore. Yet the Bible tells us here that when the end times come, God would resurrect all back to life and judge them to send to either Heaven or hell, regardless of whether they were swallowed up by Satan, killed by Hades, or burnt to death.

Before God lies the Book of Life, in which the names of those who would enter the eternal Kingdom of Heaven are written. There also are the Books of Deeds, which record the names and sins of all those who would be cast into hell. In these Books of Deeds are written all the sins that one had committed while living on this earth. All these things have been determined by God in His providence.

The Lord Has Two Kinds of Books

God has already classified people into two mutually exclusive categories according to His own just criterion. It has been determined by God that all the dead would be resurrected, and then stand before His two books and be judged. In the Book of Life are written only the names of those who have believed in Jesus while on this earth, received the remission of their sins, and thus are determined to enter into Heaven. God's final judgment would therefore depend on in which of the two books one's name is written. God has already set, in other words, who would enter Heaven and who would be cast into hell.

God will therefore raise all the dead to live again, open His Books, and see in which of the two books their names are written. He will then send those whose names are written in the Book of Life to Heaven, but those whose names are not found in this Book of Life, in contrast, will instead be thrown into hell. We must make sure to know and believe in these established facts determined by God.

To decide who would be sent to Heaven and who would be sent to hell, God will resurrect all the dead and judge them. It has been decided by God that He would judge them according to whether their names are written in the Book of Life or the Books of Deeds (the Books of Judgment).

There are two places God has already established for all who would stand before Him. They are none other than Heaven and hell. Hell is the lake of fire where flames and brimstones are burning. God has determined that those whose names are not written in the Book of Life would be thrown into the lake of fire, while those whose names are written in this Book of Life would be welcomed into Heaven.

In Heaven, the Tree of Life stands by the river of water of life, bearing twelve different fruits according to each season. In this beautiful Heaven, the saints would have neither disease nor pain, but live happily forever with God. We must believe in the fact that God has decided to give this Heaven to the saints.

Those who do not believe in Jesus, on the other hand, have their names written in the Books of Deeds. Because all the deeds that the sinners had done while on this earth are recorded in these Books, God tells us that He would throw them all into the lake of fire, to punish them for their sins recorded in this Books, and for their sin of not believing in Jesus. What is of critical importance here is in which Book your and my names are written.

While living in this world, we must realize that life on this earth is not all that there is. As Psalm 90:10 tells us, *"The days of our lives are seventy years; And if by reason of strength they are eighty years, Yet their boast is only labor and sorrow; For it is soon cut off, and we fly away."* Even if we were to live on this earth for 70 or even 80 years, sooner or later we will all stand before God. And when we thus stand before our Lord finally, all that matters is in which Book our names are written, whether in the Book of Life or the Books of Deeds (the Books of Judgment), for this will determine whether we are welcomed to Heaven or cast into the lake of fire. We must come to the recognition that life on this earth is not everything.

The Ones Whose Names Are Written in the Book of Life

Let's take a look at Luke 16:19-26: *"There was a certain rich man who was clothed in purple and fine linen and fared sumptuously every day. But there was a certain beggar named Lazarus, full of sores, who was laid at his gate, desiring to be fed with the crumbs which fell from the rich man's table. Moreover the dogs came and licked his sores. So it was that the beggar died, and was carried by the angels to Abraham's bosom. The rich man also died and was buried. And being in torments in Hades, he lifted up his eyes and saw Abraham afar off, and Lazarus in his bosom. Then he cried and said, 'Father Abraham, have mercy on me, and send Lazarus that he may dip the tip of his finger in water and cool my tongue; for I am tormented in this flame.' But Abraham said, 'Son, remember that in your lifetime you received your good things, and likewise Lazarus evil things; but now he is comforted and you are tormented. And besides all this, between us and you there is a great gulf fixed, so that those who want to pass from here to you cannot, nor can those from there pass to us.'"*

With this passage, Jesus teaches us that Heaven and hell actually exist. Like the rich man in this passage, so many people do not believe in the existence of Heaven and hell. Abraham is the father of faith. When it says here that the beggar Lazarus was carried to Abraham's bosom, it means that, just as Abraham believed in the Word of God, Lazarus also believed in Jesus as his Savior, received the remission of his sins, and thereby went to Heaven. Living in this world, we all need to contemplate and ponder upon the fates of Lazarus and the rich man.

God tells us that for everyone in this world, life on this earth is not everything at all. No matter with how much labor one lives on this earth, not only would he/she be able to live for just 70-80 years at most, but all that would remain of him/her at the end is only labor and sorrow.

In living our lives, therefore, we must all prepare for our

afterlife. And we must also hand down our faith to our children, so that they, too, may be able to go to the good place. How tragic would it be that a man, having lived on this earth, would finally stand before God only to be judged by Him and cast into the lake of fire?

No man can change what has been decided by God, that all those whose names are written in the Books of Deeds would be thrown into the lake of fire. There is then only one way for us to avoid the lake of fire, and this is to make sure that our names are written in the Book of Life. To escape from the lake of fire, there is no other way but to have our names written in the Book of Life.

How, then, can our names be written in this Book of Life? Just as Lazarus was carried to Abraham's bosom, so must we receive the remission of our sins by knowing and believing in God's righteous act (Romans 5:18) through His Word. Only then can we enter Heaven. To have our names written in the Book of Life, we must believe in Jesus. Jesus is God Himself and our Messiah. Messiah means the One who saves those who fell in sin. Only Jesus can save us, who, because of our sins, are otherwise bound to be judged by God and cast into the lake of fire.

Who on this earth can ever not commit any sin before God, and who among us is 100 percent holy in deeds? No one! We must realize that because we are all full of shortcoming, we cannot help but fall into sin, and for these sins of ours we are all bound to be thrown into the lake of fire.

But God sent Jesus to this earth to save us, who cannot but be cast into the lake of fire for our sins. The name 'Jesus' means 'the One who will save His people from their sins' (Matthew 1:21). Therefore, we can enter Heaven only when we believe in the truth that Jesus came to this earth and saved us from all our sins with His righteous act.

Who Will Then Be Cast into the Lake of Fire?

Revelation 21:8 tells us who would be cast into the lake of fire: *"But the cowardly, unbelieving, abominable, murderers, sexually immoral, sorcerers, idolaters, and all liars shall have their part in the lake which burns with fire and brimstone, which is the second death."*

First of all, whom does the Bible refer by the word "cowardly?" This refers to those nominal Christians who have failed to receive the remission of all their sins through the gospel of the water and the Spirit, and therefore they are scared before God even though they believe in Jesus somehow. God has decided that such people would be thrown into the lake of fire. God has also determined that those who are unbelievers, abominable, murders, sexually immoral, sorcerers, idolaters, and liars would all be cast into hell.

Traditionally, there have been many idolaters in Korea. Even now, it is not uncommon to see people bowing before the images of God's own creation and offering prayers to them. People do so because they are ignorant and foolish. God hates it when people worship lifeless images as if they were divine.

God created man in His own image (Genesis 1:27). The mankind is also the master of all creation. This is why we must believe in God. Because we take after God's own image, we exist forever, just as God Himself exists forever. There is eternal world for us after our death. This is why God has told us to worship Him, the only eternal God. What, then, would happen when we bow before what are merely God's own creation? We would be committing a great sin against God, for we would be practicing what God hates the most: idolatry. The mankind can be so foolish and so stupid. God has decided, we must realize, that those who have this kind of misplaced faith would all be thrown into the lake of fire.

People who are cast into hell will die twice. This is what God Himself has determined. The first death comes at the end of their troubled lives on this earth, after walking in this weary world. It is often said that the ones who live on four feet at first, then on two feet, then lastly on three feet, only to die in the end, are none other than the mankind itself.

After dying once in this way, when people stand before God as sinners, they would all face their judgment, and it is at this time when the second death, one that would never end but last forever, would visit them, in the form of being casting into the lake of fire. Were they to just die in this lake of fire, they would at least be freed from its suffering. But in this place, though they earnestly desire to die, death will flee from them.

Everyone has a wish to live forever, never to face death. The mankind's existence, in fact, is actually eternal, just as people wish for. This is why the Bible, when one dies, does not describe it as dying, but as falling asleep. We must therefore all escape from the second death that would throw us into the lake of fire. We must all realize just what it is that we have to do in order to get our names written into the Book of Life. And to get our names into the Book of Life, we must believe in Jesus correctly.

People often think and say that Jesus, Buddha, Confucius, and Mohammad are all just men, that it is okay to just live as a good person. That's why they cannot understand why we insist that they should believe in only Jesus. But these are all mistaken thoughts. You and I, as well as everything else in this world, are nothing but mere creation and human beings before

God. But when we look at Jesus' birth and what He had accomplished while on this earth, we can all realize that He is not just a man like the rest of the four Sages. He is God Himself who, to save the mankind, came to this earth in the form of a man, took all our sin through His baptism, received all the punishment of our sins in our place, and thus completed His work of delivering the mankind from sin.

Christ' birth was different from the ordinary people's birth. Babies are born by the union of a man and a woman. This is how everyone is born into this world. But Jesus was born of a virgin who did not know man. To save us the human beings, and in fulfillment of the Word of prophecy foretold over 700 years ago through the Prophet Isaiah, Jesus, who is God Himself, was born unto this earth in the flesh of a man, through the body of a virgin (Isaiah 7:14). And while on this earth not only did He raise the dead and heal the sick and the disabled, but He also made all the sins of the world disappear.

God, the Lord of creation who made the whole universe, came to this earth and became a man Himself for a while, all to save the mankind from its sins. The reason why we must believe in Jesus is, first all, because He is God Himself. Secondly, because He took away all our sins, so that our names would be written in the Book of Life, and made us God's sinless children. Once born unto this earth, we must all die once, and after our death we must all be judged.

But Jesus came to this earth, took upon all our sins with His baptism received from John, was judged on the Cross in our place, and thereby enabled those of us who believe in Him to live with Him forever in the eternal Kingdom of Heaven. To deliver us from our judgment of sin, in other words, God Himself cleansed us of all our sins. This is why we must all believe in Jesus, the One who has become the Savior.

Jesus is not just a man. Because God promised the mankind that He would save it, and because to fulfill this promise He came to this earth in the flesh of a man through the body of a virgin, and because He did indeed save all from their sins, we must all believe in Jesus, who is God Himself. When we believe in Jesus correctly, our names are written into the Book of Life. God told us that only by being born again of the water and the Spirit could a man see and enter the Kingdom of Heaven. We must all believe in Jesus.

Jesus Who Became the Way to Heaven

We must, then, know just how exactly Jesus have made all our sins disappear. Coming to this earth, Jesus was baptized by John at the Jordan River (Matthew 3:13-17). He receive His baptism from John so that He could take upon all the sins of the mankind (including all yours and mine). Through the hands of John the Baptist, the representative of all mankind, every sin of the entire mankind was passed onto Jesus. After thus taking all the sins of the world onto Himself through John, Jesus then shed His blood on the Cross and died on it. He then rose from the dead in three days.

Our Lord has promised that whoever believes in Him will receive eternal life. God has determined that whoever believes in the truth that Jesus took upon all his/her sins on Himself and received all the punishment of these sins on the Cross would not be cast into the lake of fire, but would instead have his/her name written into the Book of Life.

Jesus says in John 14:6, *"I am the way, the truth, and the life. No one comes to the Father except through Me."* The mankind must believe in Jesus who has become the way to

Heaven. Jesus is our Savior. Jesus is our God. Jesus is the one and only real truth in this world. And Jesus is the Lord of life. To make sure that our names are written in the Book of Life and that we would thus be welcomed into the Kingdom of Heaven, we must all believe in Jesus.

Because Jesus actually took upon all our sins on Himself by receiving His baptism from John the Baptist at the Jordan River, we must believe in Him, the One who has become the Savior of atonement. And it is because Jesus completed all our salvation by being crucified and shedding His blood on the Cross as the punishment of our sins that you and I can now enter Heaven.

Jesus has decided who would be cast into the lake of fire. Those who do not believe and who are cowardly will all be thrown into the lake of fire. Not only will they themselves be cast into the lake of fire because of their unbelief, but so would their children and descendants to come. To reach one's own spiritual and physical well-being, everyone must indeed and absolutely believe in Jesus.

What If Jesus Had Not Received His Baptism?

God is the only One who gives His blessings or curses to every human being. This is why we must believe in Him. Do you know why many people's lives are so miserable, why nations of this earth fall? It is because God said that He would curse those who hate Him and worship idols for three, four generations to come. But He also said that He would bless for a thousand generations to come those who serve and love God and keep His commandments (Exodus 20:5-6).

This does not mean that if one believes in Jesus somehow,

he/she would be blessed unconditionally. One must believe in Jesus with the correct knowledge of Him. If people believe, in other words, that Jesus is God Himself who came to this earth, that He cleansed away all their sins by taking these sins upon Himself with His baptism, and that He has become their true Savior by being crucified in their place—if they believe, in short, that Jesus is their own God and their own Savior—God said that He would then bless those who believe so for a thousand generations to come.

But at the same time, God has also promised us that He would curse for three, four generations to come those who do not believe in Jesus. This is why everyone, no matter who he/she may be, must believe in Jesus, and why everyone must know and believe in the truth of being born again of the water and the Spirit. Those who have such faith will be forgiven of all their sins, receive eternal life, enter into Heaven, as well as receive, while on this earth, all the blessings that God had given to Abraham before.

We must all dwell on this Word that God has decided for us, and our faith must absolutely be in accordance to the Word as is written. We must realize and believe in the fact that those who do not believe in God would be thrown into the lake of fire, but that those who believe, in contrast, would have their names written into the Book of Life and be welcomed into the New Heaven and Earth. And we must also believe that those of us who believe will live again. That we are born again is made possible only by the gospel of the water and the Spirit.

As no one can live without water, the gospel of the water is, along with the gospel of the blood, critically important for our salvation. When Jesus was baptized, He took all our sins upon Himself. And He was submerged into the water and then emerged from the water. This meant His death on the Cross and

His resurrection. Our Lord, in other words, was judged for all our sins in our place. And the Lord's coming out of water signifies His resurrection. This also means our own resurrection, of those of us who believe.

We believe thoroughly that Jesus took upon our sins with His baptism. Had Jesus not received His baptism, what would have happened to us? There would be no way for us to escape from the lake of fire. Just as without rain no one can live in this world, the planet earth exists because of water. Likewise, this is how important Jesus' baptism is for us. Also, His death on the Cross is equally important, for this meant that He was judged for our sins in our stead. If we want to be delivered from God's curse and judgment, we must believe in Jesus absolutely. And if we want to be cleansed of our sins, we must believe that all our sins were passed onto Jesus when He was baptized.

Christian faith is never the kind of religion that makes people tremble in fear. Everyone must believe in Jesus. The born-again must come into the born-again Church and hear the Word to be nourished in faith.

Some people claim that one must believe in Jesus and do good deeds to be saved and to receive blessings, but all this is just a fraudulent claim of liars. Of course, we must live as virtuous Christians doing good deeds, but as far as the fundamental problem of our salvation is concerned, our nature is so evil that none of us can ever live our lives of the flesh in 100 percent perfection. This is why those who claim that one must be saved through good deeds are all liars who are ignorant of the gospel of the water and the Spirit and who deceive people.

When we recognize ourselves that we are fundamentally bound to commit sin, when we contemplate on the baptism that Jesus Christ received and the Cross that He carried for us from the written Word of God, and when we accept all these things, only then can we become the righteous, whose hearts are sinless, and be qualified to enter Heaven. Before the Holy Spirit dwells in us and guides us, none of us can ever be good, no matter how hard we might try.

God saved us by making all our sins disappear. Instead of throwing us into the lake of fire burning forever, He has written our names into the Book of Life, given us the New Heaven and Earth, and, as the brides have adorned themselves for the Bridegroom, He, too, has given us the cleanest and the most beautiful houses, gardens, and flowers. And He would also take away all disease from us, and would live with us forever in His Kingdom. We must believe in Jesus for the sake of our afterlife, but we must also believe in Him for our present lives. For the sake of our children, too, we must believe.

Do you want to be welcomed into Heaven, or do you want to be cast into the lake of fire? What kind of inheritance will you pass onto your own children? Even if you face some trouble and suffering for your faith in Jesus, you must still believe in Him, for doing so will bring great blessings to both you and your children.

My beloved saints, through His Word, God has told us the reason why we must preach the gospel of the water and the Spirit, and the reason why our families must also be saved. I give my thanks to God. ✉

CHAPTER

21

The Holy City That Descends from Heaven

< Revelation 21:1-27 >

"Now I saw a new heaven and a new earth, for the first heaven and the first earth had passed away. Also there was no more sea. Then I, John, saw the holy city, New Jerusalem, coming down out of heaven from God, prepared as a bride adorned for her husband. And I heard a loud voice from heaven saying, 'Behold, the tabernacle of God is with men, and He will dwell with them, and they shall be His people. God Himself will be with them and be their God. And God will wipe away every tear from their eyes; there shall be no more death, nor sorrow, nor crying. There shall be no more pain, for the former things have passed away.' Then He who sat on the throne said, 'Behold, I make all things new.' And He said to me, 'Write, for these words are true and faithful.' And He said to me, 'It is done! I am the Alpha and the Omega, the Beginning and the End. I will give of the fountain of the water of life freely to him who thirsts. He who overcomes shall inherit all things, and I will be his God and he shall be My son. But the cowardly, unbelieving, abominable, murderers, sexually immoral, sorcerers, idolaters, and all liars shall have their part in the lake which burns with fire and brimstone, which is the second death.' Then one of the seven angels who had the seven bowls filled with the seven last plagues came to me and talked with me, saying, 'Come, I will show you the bride, the Lamb's wife.' And he carried me away in the

Spirit to a great and high mountain, and showed me the great city, the holy Jerusalem, descending out of heaven from God, having the glory of God. Her light was like a most precious stone, like a jasper stone, clear as crystal. Also she had a great and high wall with twelve gates, and twelve angels at the gates, and names written on them, which are the names of the twelve tribes of the children of Israel: three gates on the east, three gates on the north, three gates on the south, and three gates on the west. Now the wall of the city had twelve foundations, and on them were the names of the twelve apostles of the Lamb. And he who talked with me had a gold reed to measure the city, its gates, and its wall. The city is laid out as a square; its length is as great as its breadth. And he measured the city with the reed: twelve thousand furlongs. Its length, breadth, and height are equal. Then he measured its wall: one hundred and forty-four cubits, according to the measure of a man, that is, of an angel. The construction of its wall was of jasper; and the city was pure gold, like clear glass. The foundations of the wall of the city were adorned with all kinds of precious stones: the first foundation was jasper, the second sapphire, the third chalcedony, the fourth emerald, the fifth sardonyx, the sixth sardius, the seventh chrysolite, the eighth beryl, the ninth topaz, the tenth chrysoprase, the eleventh jacinth, and the twelfth amethyst. The twelve gates were twelve pearls: each individual gate was of one pearl. And the street of the city was pure gold, like transparent glass. But I saw no temple in it, for the Lord God Almighty and the Lamb are its temple. The city had no need of the sun or of the moon to shine in it, for the glory of God illuminated it. The Lamb is its light. And the nations of those who are saved shall walk in its light, and the kings of the earth bring their glory and honor into it. Its gates shall not be shut at all by day (there shall be no night there). And they shall bring the glory and the honor of the nations into it. But there shall by no means enter it anything that defiles, or causes an abomination or a lie, but only those who are written in the Lamb's Book of Life."

Exegesis

Verse 1: Now I saw a new heaven and a new earth, for the first heaven and the first earth had passed away. Also there was no more sea.

This Word means that our Lord God will give His New Heaven and Earth as His gift to the saints who had taken part in the first resurrection. From this moment on, the saints will live not in the first heaven and earth, but in the new, second heaven and earth. This blessing is God's gift that He would bestow on His saints. God will give such a blessing to only the saints who had participated in the first resurrection.

The ones who are to enjoy this blessing, in other words, are the stains who had received the remission of sin by believing in the holy gospel of the water and the Spirit given by Christ. Our Lord is the saints' Bridegroom. From now on, all that awaits the brides is to be clothed in the Bridegroom's protection, blessings, and power as the brides of their Bridegroom Lamb, and live in glory in His glorious Kingdom.

Verse 2: Then I, John, saw the holy city, New Jerusalem, coming down out of heaven from God, prepared as a bride adorned for her husband.

God has prepared a holy city for the saints. This City is

the city of New Jerusalem, the Holy Palace of God. This Palace is prepared purely for God's saints. And this has all been planned in Jesus Christ for the saints, even before our Lord God created the universe. The saints therefore cannot help but thank the Lord God for His gift of grace and give all glory to Him with their faith.

Verse 3: And I heard a loud voice from heaven saying, "Behold, the tabernacle of God is with men, and He will dwell with them, and they shall be His people. God Himself will be with them and be their God."

From now on, the saints are to live with the Lord in God's Temple forever. All this is by the grace of the Lord God, a gift that the saints would receive for their faith in the Word of salvation of the water and the Spirit. All those who are clothed in the blessing of entering into the Lord's Temple and living with Him would therefore give thanks and glory to the Lord God forever.

Verse 4: "And God will wipe away every tear from their eyes; there shall be no more death, nor sorrow, nor crying. There shall be no more pain, for the former things have passed away."

Now that God dwells with the saints, there will be no more tears of sadness, nor wailing over the loss of their beloved ones, nor crying in sorrow.

All the sorrow of the first heaven and earth will disappear from the saints' lives, and all that would await the saints is to live their blessed and glorified lives with their Lord God in His New Heaven and Earth. Our Lord God, having becoming the saints' own God, will make all things and all surroundings new, so that there would be no more tears of sadness, nor crying, nor death, nor wailing, nor sicknesses, nor anything else that had tormented them on the first earth.

Verse 5: Then He who sat on the throne said, "Behold, I make all things new." And He said to me, "Write, for these words are true and faithful."

The Lord will now make all things new, and create a new heaven and a new earth. Making His creation of the first heaven and the first earth disappear, He will make new, second heaven and earth. What this verse tells us is not that God would recycle the old, but instead create a new universe. God will thus make the New Heaven and Earth and live with the saints. The saints who had taken part in the first resurrection will partake of this blessing also. This is something that the mankind could not even dream of with its man-made thoughts, but it is what God has prepared for His saints. The saints and all things therefore give all glory, thanks, honor and praise to God for this great work.

Verse 6: And He said to me, "It is done! I am the Alpha and the Omega, the Beginning and the End. I will give of the fountain of the water of life freely to him who thirsts."

Our Lord God has planned and fulfilled all these things, from the very beginning to the end. All the things that the Lord has done, He did them for Himself and for His saints. The saints are now called as "Christ's," and are made God's people. Those who have become God's saints by believing in the gospel of the water and the Spirit now realize that though they give thanks and praise to God forever, they still cannot thank Him enough for the love and works of the Lord God.

"I will give of the fountain of the water of life freely to him who thirsts." In the New Heaven and Earth, our Lord has given

the fountain of the water of life to the saints. This is the greatest gift of all that God has bestowed on His saints. Now the saints are to live forever in the New Heaven and Earth and to drink from the fountain of the water of life, from which they will never thirst again forever. The saints have now become, in other words, God's children who would have eternal life, just like the Lord God, and live in His glory. I give thanks and glory to our Lord God once again for giving us this great blessing. Hallelujah!

Verse 7: "He who overcomes shall inherit all things, and I will be his God and he shall be My son."

"He who overcomes" here refers to those who have defended their faith given by the Lord. This faith allows all the saints to overcome the world and God's enemies. Our faith in the Lord God and in the true love of the gospel of the water and the Spirit given by Him is what gives us victory over all the sins of the world, over the judgment of God, over our enemies, over our own weaknesses, and over the persecution of the Antichrist.

I give thanks and glory to our Lord God for giving us victory over all. The saints who believe in the Lord God overcome the Antichrist sufficiently with their faith. To each and every one of the saints, our Lord God has given this faith with which they can all triumph in their fight against all their enemies.

God has now allowed the saints, who have thus overcome the world and the Antichrist with their faith, to inherit His New Heaven and Earth. Our Lord God has given the faith of victory to His saints so that they could inherit His Kingdom. Because God has given us the faith that triumphs over the Antichrist, God has now become our God, and we have become His children. I give thanks and praise to our Lord God for giving us this faith of victory over all our enemies.

Verse 8: "But the cowardly, unbelieving, abominable, murderers, sexually immoral, sorcerers, idolaters, and all liars shall have their part in the lake which burns with fire and brimstone, which is the second death."

In His essence, our Lord God is the God of truth and the God of love. Who, then, are these people that are fundamentally cowardly before God? These are the ones who are born into the original sin and who have not cleansed of all their own sins with the Word of the gospel of the water and the Spirit given by the Lord. Because in their essence they worship the evil ones more than God, they have clearly become Satan's servants. It is because they worship the evil before the Lord God, and because they love and follow the darkness more than the light, that they cannot but be cowardly before the Lord God.

God in His essence is the light. It therefore is an established fact that these people who by themselves are the darkness itself would fear God. As the souls of those who belong to Satan love the darkness, they are cowardly before God who is the light Himself. This is why they must take their evilness and weaknesses to God and receive the remission of their sins from Him.

Those "unbelieving," whose hearts fundamentally do not believe in the love of our Lord God and in His gospel of the water and the Spirit, are His enemies and the greatest sinners before God. Their souls belong to the abominable, and they stand against God, love and commit every sin, follow false signs, worship all kinds of idols, and speak all kinds of lies. So, by the righteous judgment of God they will all be cast into the lake burning with fire and brimstone. This is their punishment of the second death.

God has not allowed His New Heaven and Earth to these people who are cowardly before Him, who do not believe in His gospel Word of the water and the Spirit, and who, having turned into Satan's servants, are abominable. Instead, our Lord has allowed them only His eternal punishment, casting all of them (including murders, sexually immoral, sorcerers, idolaters, and all liars) into the lake of fire and brimstone. Hell, which God would thus give them, is their second death.

Verse 9: Then one of the seven angels who had the seven bowls filled with the seven last plagues came to me and talked with me, saying, "Come, I will show you the bride, the Lamb's wife."

One of the angels who had brought one of the plagues of seven bowls said to John, *"Come, I will show you the bride, the Lamb's wife."* Here, "the Lamb's wife" refers to those who have become the brides of Jesus Christ by believing with their hearts in the gospel of the water and the Spirit given by Him.

Verse 10-11: And he carried me away in the Spirit to a great and high mountain, and showed me the great city, the holy Jerusalem, descending out of heaven from God, having the glory of God. Her light was like a most precious stone, like a jasper stone, clear as crystal.

"The great city, the holy Jerusalem" refers to the Holy City where the saints are to live with their Bridegroom. This City that John saw was indeed beautiful and fantastic. It was majestic in size, adorned by precious stones inside out, clean and clear. The angel showed John where the brides of Jesus Christ would live with their Bridegroom. This Holy City of Jerusalem descending out of heaven is the gift of God that He

would bestow on the Lamb's wife.

The City of Jerusalem shines brilliantly, and its light is like a most precious stone, like a jasper stone, clear as crystal. Therefore, to all those who live in it, the glory of God is with them forever and ever. God's Kingdom is that of light, and so only those who have been cleansed of all their darkness, weaknesses and sins can enter into this City. As such, we must all believe that for us to enter into this Holy City, we have to learn, know, and believe in the true Word of the gospel of the water and the Spirit that our Lord has given us.

Verse 12: Also she had a great and high wall with twelve gates, and twelve angels at the gates, and names written on them, which are the names of the twelve tribes of the children of Israel:

The gates of this City were guarded by twelve angels, and on them were written the names of the twelve tribes of the children of Israel. The City had "a great and high wall," telling us that the way to enter this Holy City is that much difficult. Being saved from all our sins before God, in other words, is impossible with human efforts or the material things of the world of God's creation.

To be delivered from all our sins and enter God's Holy City, it is absolutely required that we have the same faith of the twelve disciples of Jesus, the faith that believes in the truth of the gospel of the water and the Spirit. As such, no one who does not have this faith in the gospel of the water and the Spirit can ever enter this Holy City. This is why twelve angels appointed by the Lord God guard its gates.

The phrase, *"names written on them,"* on the other hand, tells us that the owners of this City have already been decided. Its owners are none other than God Himself and His people, for the City belongs to the people of God who have now become His children.

Verse 13: three gates on the east, three gates on the north, three gates on the south, and three gates on the west.

As three gates were place in the east of the City, its north, south, and west were also placed with three gates each. This shows us that only those who have received the remission of sin by believing in the gospel of the water and the Spirit with their hearts can enter this City.

Verse 14: Now the wall of the city had twelve foundations, and on them were the names of the twelve apostles of the Lamb.

Huge rocks are well used as the foundations of buildings or edifices. The word 'rock' is used in the Bible to refer to faith in our Lord God. This verse tells us that to enter the Holy City of the Lord God, we must have the faith that He has given to the mankind, the faith that believes in His perfect redemption from all our sins. The faith of the saints is more precious than even the precious stones of the Holy City. The verse tells us here that the City's wall was built on twelve foundations, and on them were written the names of the twelve apostles of the Lamb. This tells us that God's City is allowed only to those who have the same faith that the twelve apostles of Jesus Christ had.

Verse 15: And he who talked with me had a gold reed to measure the city, its gates, and its wall.

This Word means that to enter into the City built by God, one must have the kind of faith that is approved by Him, the kind that would bring him/her the remission of sin. It says here that the angel who spoke to John had a gold reed to measure the City. This means we must believe that our Lord has given us all these blessings within the gospel of the water and the Spirit. As *"faith is the substance of things hoped for (Hebrews 11:1),"* God has indeed given us the Holy City and the New Heaven and Earth, things that are even greater than what we had hoped for.

Verse 16: The city is laid out as a square; its length is as great as its breadth. And he measured the city with the reed: twelve thousand furlongs. Its length, breadth, and height are equal.

The City was laid out as a square, with its length, width, and height measuring the same. This tells us that we must all have the faith of being born again as God's people by believing in the gospel of the water and the Spirit. As a matter of fact, our Lord will not allow anyone who does not have this exact faith in the gospel of the water and the Spirit to enter into the Kingdom of God.

There are many people who have such a vague notion that they would enter the Holy City just by being Christians, even if they still have sin. But our Lord has given the salvation from sin and the Holy Spirit and has made His people only those who believe in the truth that He has forgiven them of all their sins through His baptism on this earth and He blood on the Cross. This is the faith that our Lords demands us of.

Verse 17: Then he measured its wall: one hundred and forty-four cubits, according to the measure of a man, that is, of an angel.

The biblical meaning of the number four is suffering. The faith that the Lord demands from us is not something that just anybody can have, but this faith can be had only by those who accept the Word of God, even if they cannot entirely comprehend it with their own thoughts. As a Christian, it is impossible to enter God's Holy City just by believing in Jesus' Cross, and that the Lord is God and Savior. Do you know what the Lord meant when He said in John 3:5, *"Most assuredly, I say to you, unless one is born of water and the Spirit, he cannot enter the kingdom of God"?* Do you know the meaning of our Lord coming to this earth, being baptized by John, carrying the sins of the world to the Cross, and shedding His blood on it? If you can answer this question, you would understand I am talking about here.

Verse 18: The construction of its wall was of jasper; and the city was pure gold, like clear glass.
This verse tells us that the faith that allows us to enter the Holy City of God is pure and does not have anything of the world at all.

Verse 19-20: The foundations of the wall of the city were adorned with all kinds of precious stones: the first foundation was jasper, the second sapphire, the third chalcedony, the fourth emerald, the fifth sardonyx, the sixth sardius, the seventh chrysolite, the eighth beryl, the ninth topaz, the tenth chrysoprase, the eleventh jacinth, and the twelfth amethyst.
The foundations of the wall of the City were adorned with all kinds of precious stones. This Word tells us that we can be nourished of different aspects of faith from the Word of our Lord. And these precious stones show us the kinds of blessings that our Lord would give to His saints.

Verse 21: The twelve gates were twelve pearls: each individual gate was of one pearl. And the street of the city was

pure gold, like transparent glass.
Pearl implies 'the Truth' in the Bible (Matthew 13:46). A real truth-seeker would gladly abandon all his/her possessions to possess the Truth that gives him/her eternal life. This verse tells us that the saints who would enter the Holy City need to have much patience while on this earth, standing firmly anchored to the center of their faith in the truth. Those who believe in the Word of truth spoken by the Lord God, in other words, need to have great perseverance to defend their faith.

Verse 22-23: But I saw no temple in it, for the Lord God Almighty and the Lamb are its temple. The city had no need of the sun or of the moon to shine in it, for the glory of God illuminated it. The Lamb is its light.
This passage means that all the saints would be embraced into the arms of Jesus Christ, King of kings. And the Holy City of Jerusalem has no need for the light of the first sun or moon, for Jesus Christ, the light of the world, would illuminate it.

Verse 24: And the nations of those who are saved shall walk in its light, and the kings of the earth bring their glory and honor into it."
This passage tells us that the people who had lived in the Millennial Kingdom would now enter into the New Heaven and Earth. *"The kings of the earth"* here refer to the saints who had been living in the Millennial Kingdom. These kings of the earth, the verse continues, would *"bring their glory and honor into it."* This tells us that the saints who had already been living in their glorified bodies would now move from the Millennial Kingdom to God's newly created Kingdom of New Heaven and Earth.
As such, only those who were born again by believing in

the gospel of the water and the Spirit while on this earth and thus were raptured to live in the Kingdom of Christ for a thousand years would be able to enter the Holy City of Jerusalem.

Verse 25: Its gates shall not be shut at all by day (there shall be no night there).
Because the New Heaven and Earth, where the Holy City is located, is already filled by the holy light, there can be no night in it, nor any evil ones.

Verse 26: And they shall bring the glory and the honor of the nations into it.
This tells us that through the amazing power of the Lord God, those who had been living in the Kingdom of Christ for a thousand years are now qualified to move to the Kingdom of the New Heaven and Earth, the Kingdom where the Holy City stands.

Verse 27: But there shall by no means enter it anything that defiles, or causes an abomination or a lie, but only those who are written in the Lamb's Book of Life.
Among both Christians and non-Christians of this world alike, all those who do not know the truth of the gospel of the water and the Spirit are defilers, abominable, and liars. They therefore cannot enter into the Holy City.

The Word of God here allows us to confirm just how great is the power of the gospel of the water and the Spirit that the Lord has given us on this earth. Although the gospel of the water and the Spirit has been preached to many people on this earth, there were times when this gospel was ignored and scorned even by so-called Christians. But only the faith in the gospel of the water and the Spirit given by the Lord is the key to Heaven.

Many people still remain ignorant of this truth, but you must know that anyone who realizes and believes that with the gospel of the water and the Spirit the Lord has given him/her the keys to Heaven and to the remission of sin, will have his/her name written in the Book of Life.

If you accept and believe in the truth of the gospel of the water and the Spirit, you will be clothed in the blessing of entering the Holy City. ⊠

We Must Have the Kind of Faith That Is Approved by God

< Revelation 21:1-27 >

God has given us the New Heaven and Earth. God tells us that what you see now, the first heaven and earth, and all its belongings, will all disappear, and that He will give us in their place a new heaven, a new earth, and a new sea, and renew all things in this newly created universe. This means that the Lord God would give the New Heaven and Earth as His gift to the saints who had taken part in the first resurrection. This blessing is a gift from God that He would bestow on His saints, who have received the remission of their sin.

God will therefore give this blessing to the saints who had participated in the first resurrection. This blessing is permitted only to those saints who, by believing in the holy gospel of the water and the Spirit given by Jesus Christ, have received the remission of their sins. Our Lord would thus become the saints' Bridegroom. From now on, all that remains for the brides to do is to be clothed in the Bridegroom's protection, blessings, and power as the Lamb's wives, and to live in glory in His glorious Kingdom forever.

The passage also tells us that the Holy City, New Jerusalem, descended from Heaven. This was no ordinary city, for it says that the City was as beautiful as a bride adorned for her husband, coming down from Heaven.

God has prepared a holy city for the saints. This City is the city of Jerusalem, the Temple of God. This Temple is prepared only for God's saints. And it has been planned for the saints all along in Jesus Christ, even before the Lord God created this universe. The saints therefore cannot help but thank the Lord God with their faith and give glory to Him for this gift of grace.

All these things—that saints are made the people of God and that He has thus become their God—are the grace bestowed by God and a gift that the saints have received from Him for believing in the Word of salvation of the water and the Spirit.

Therefore, all those who are blessed to enter into the Lord's Temple and live with Him will give thanks and glory to God forever, for the Scripture tells us that God would wipe away their tears, that there would be no more death, nor crying, nor suffering any longer, and that the former things would have passed away. Though sorrow, crying, pain, death, wailing, and sadness abound in this world now, in the New Heaven and Earth, all such things would have passed away. Those who live in the New Heaven and Earth given by the Lord would no longer shed any tears of sadness or cry out in sorrow for the loss of their loved ones, never again.

When this time of the saints' entrance into the New Heaven and Earth arrives, the first heaven, the first earth, and all their sorrows would simply disappear, and all that awaits the saints would be to live their lives of glory and of all the blessings with God in this New Heaven and Earth forever. God would have taken away all the imperfections of the first world and made this new world perfect.

The main passage of chapter 21 tells us of the New Heaven and Earth, which will follow the complete extermination of this world, after the Millennial Kingdom described in chapter 20 passes by. With chapter 20, anything that is even remotely related to this earth has all ended. The age of the Antichrist (the Beast), false prophets, his followers, and of the ones who had not believed in God but had stood against Him in this world, has all passed away. As they were all cast into fire when the Millennial Kingdom came to its close, now the only place where they can be seen is hell.

Thus, in chapter 21, God tells us of the New Heaven and Earth that He would give to the saints, a place of perfection where no sinner can ever be found. Just as when you want to see wild animals you go to a zoo, when this time comes, anyone who wants to see Satan and his followers will have to make a trip to hell.

In the place where God would give us the New Heaven and Earth, our Lord, too, will live with us. God has also made for us the Holy City with beautiful nature and brilliantly green gardens. When the New Heaven and Earth come, all the things of the first world and all its imperfections would have disappeared, only the truth would exist, and the perfect saints would reign the whole Kingdom of Heaven forever and ever.

Don't Be Disheartened at Your Present Condition

This present age is an age of darkness and hopelessness. Hope is not to be found anywhere in this age, whose future is only clouded in uncertainty. This is why, at times, we feel frustrated and weak even though we are preaching the gospel. As for myself, my heart had often been down because of this, but while reading the Word of Revelation and explaining its passages, I have realized that the saints and servants of God facing the end times have nothing to be saddened by. By making me realizing that the present tribulations and sufferings are only ephemeral, and that a bright world stands right before my eyes, God has strengthened my heart to never again be troubled.

If we look at only our present conditions, our lives are indeed depressing, sad and uninteresting, and we are prone to be disheartened by the ceaseless troubles that visit us while serving the gospel. But because of all the blessings of the Lord that are approaching us, though they may not be seen by our eyes of the flesh, our hearts are freed of all disorientations, and are instead filled by great hope and joy. The reason why there is absolutely no need for us to live in sadness is because our God has already given us His New Heaven and Earth.

Do you believe in the New Heaven and Earth? Though you have not experienced it, have you ever contemplated on it?

This earth, too, have some beautiful places. When we are talking about a good living environment in this world, we are usually talking about trees, green pastures besides the rivers, flowers in the fields, and good people. There must also be clear water flowing, and it must not have any bad people, nor lack in anything. When all such conditions are met, we say that it's the most fantastic environment. But in Heaven, everything is perfect, far more and better than what the best place in the whole world can boast of.

The question is, then, for whom God has prepared and would bring down from Heaven this Holy City built so perfectly. God has made this City for none other than the saints. This is why we can all forget everything about the first earth. Though we would live in glory in the Millennial Kingdom, in the next world, in the New Heaven and Earth described in chapter 21, which God truly wants to give to us, we will live with the Lord in even greater glory. To do so, God has saved us by sending us Jesus Christ, and will resurrect and rapture us. Living with the Lord in bodies made perfect like the Body of resurrected Jesus provides a picture-perfect image of the blissful and blessed life that awaits us.

To give us the Kingdom of New Heaven and Earth, God has made you and me to be born onto this earth, and He has saved us. If the saints live this world with the realization of God's profound providence, they can all live well, without facing any difficulty, suffering sadness, or facing depression. By looking at what the Lord has done and what He would do for us in the future, we can all live enterprisingly and positively.

But if we look at ourselves and the hopeless state of the politics, economics, and societies of this earth, there is no other choice but to fall into despair. You and I must never forget that God has given us the New Heaven and Earth, and that Heaven is ours. This is the reality. This is the fact. Even if this world tries to make you sad, never be saddened by it, nor angered, but only look toward the Lord. And live your life with hope, believing that the Lord has indeed given the New Heaven and Earth to His saints.

God said that He would make all things new. He told John to write these Words, that He would make all things new, *"for these words are true and faithful."* Those who take part in the first resurrection will also partake of all these blessings of living in the place where God would have made all things new. This is something that we cannot even dream of with our man-made thoughts, but it is something that God has prepared for His saints. The saints and all things would thus give all glory, thanks, honor and praise to God forever for fulfilling this great work.

The Bible says that *"faith is the substance of things hoped for, the evidence of things not seen (Hebrews 11:1)."* Though we cannot see these things with our eyes, in other words, they are all true nonetheless. We had hoped to be saved from all our sins, and by believing in our salvation we have indeed been saved. And because we have, after being saved, wanted and hoped to live forever in a whole and perfect world that lacks nothing, God has indeed fulfilled this hope for us. Everything that we have wanted and hoped for will all come true, for all our hopes are true.

In chapter 10 of Revelation, when the Lord spoke to John through His angel who stood on the sea and the earth, and when John tried to write them down, God told him not to write. Among the things that the Lord spoke, there are certain things that He did not allow to be written, for these are the mysteries that He would reveal only to us the saints.

This mystery is none other than our rapture. To know exactly at what point our rapture would happen, we must first realize that the seventh trumpet of God is the decisive clue to solving this mystery. When, then, will the seventh trumpet sound? The seventh trumpet will sound when the first three and a half years of the seven-year period of the Great Tribulation are slightly passed by. This is when the saints' resurrection and rapture will come. And when the rapture is over, the plagues of the seven bowls will shortly follow.

Some years ago, I held a revival meeting with a topic titled "the Seven Churches of Asia Minor." I also wrote a book on these seven churches of Asia Minor, and its content corresponds to what I have explained of the present passage here. Looking at the sermons in the book, I can feel that though the times have changed quite a lot, the Word of God has not changed a bit regardless of the passing times.

Do you want to live in the New Heaven and Earth, in the

place that God has prepared for you and me? The imperfections of this world are no longer found there. When God said that He would make all things new, some people could interpret this as saying that He would transform what were already there, as in recycling. But from chapter 21 and on, it absolutely is a whole new world, completely different from the past. The born-again would take part in this New Heaven and Earth made completely new by God, because they are the ones who have partaken of divine attributes. It is, in other words, because they have become the partakers of the divine realm.

Instead of basing all our thoughts on material concepts, we must think in spiritual dimensions. I pray that you would all be the kind of saints and servants that believes in what God has actually given to our souls, and that believes, in faith, that these things, though they are yet to be fulfilled, will indeed come true. God has given us great blessings.

God said that He would give the fountain of the water of life freely to those who thirst. This Word does not refer to the gospel of the water and the Spirit. When people believe that God has delivered them from their thirst by giving them His gospel on this earth and saving them from their sins, this, too, is akin to drinking the water of life. But the passage here does not refer to just this, but it refers to the actual water of life that would be drunk in the New Heaven and Earth, where whoever drinks this water of life would never die, his/her body would be turned like that of Lord, and he/she would live with Him forever.

Our Lord God has planned and fulfilled all these things, from the very beginning to the end. All the things that the Lord has done, He did them for Himself and for His saints. As such, the saints are now called by God Himself as Christ's, and have become the true children of God according to His plan. Those who have become saints by believing in the gospel of the water and the Spirit can now realize, from their faith in this great love of God and His wondrous works, that there is nothing lacking for them to forever give thanks and praise to the Lord.

As the Lord said, *"I will give of the fountain of the water of life freely to him who thirsts,"* He has indeed given the fountain of the water of life to His saints and has allowed them to enjoy eternal life. This is the greatest gift that God has bestowed on His saints. Now the saints are to live forever in the New Heaven and Earth and to drink from the fountain of the water of life, from which they will never thirst again forever. The saints have now become, in other words, God's children who would have eternal life, just like the Lord God, and live in glory. I give thanks and glory to the Lord God once again for giving us this great blessing.

The Faith in the True Gospel Enables Us to Overcome the World

The Apostle John now returns to his present time. Verse 7 says, *"He who overcomes shall inherit all things, and I will be his God and he shall be My son."* *"He who overcomes"* here refers to those who defend their faith given by the Lord. This faith allows all the saints to overcome all troubles and temptations. Our faith in the Lord God and in the true love of the gospel of the water and the Spirit given by Him is what gives us victory over all the sins of the world, over the judgment of God, over our enemies, over our own weaknesses, and over the persecution of the Antichrist.

I give thanks and glory to our Lord God for giving us victory over all. The saints who believe in the Lord God can overcome the Antichrist with their faith, because to each and every one of them, our Lord God has given this faith with which they can triumph in their fight against all their enemies. God has now allowed the saints, who have thus overcome the world and the Antichrist with their faith, to inherit His New Heaven and Earth. I give thanks and praise to our God for giving us this strong faith.

God said that to those who overcome, He would give as their inheritance His New Heaven and Earth, where there are neither tears, nor sorrows, nor worries. Only those who overcome would deserve to receive it. The faith of this victory is the faith in the gospel of the water and the Spirit that the Lord has given us. This is the faith with which we can overcome the world, our sins, our own weaknesses, and the Antichrist.

As the reward for our faith that overcomes the Antichrist, we will soon receive the New Heaven and Earth from God. Because we will receive all these blessings for our faith, when the Antichrist stands against us and tries to take away our faith, we can triumph over all the schemes of all our enemies by faith. Those who overcome believe in the Word of God no matter what others say to them, and defend their faith in the truth that the Lord has taken away all their sins. Those of us who, after having received the remission of our sins and having been born again, are now living the end times, must overcome the schemes of the Antichrist with faith.

We can overcome the short-lasting tribulations with our faith in the truth that the Lord has given us His New Heaven and Earth, as well as all wealth, splendor and glory. When a better world awaits us, would we in reality betray the gospel of this faith? When tomorrow better things will come to us, when amazingly wonderful things await us if we would only persevere through just a day, would we not be able to withstand today's hardship? We can all persevere.

The Bible tells us frequently about 'faith, hope and love' as the essential virtues that the saints should keep in their minds. Those who have hope are more than capable of overcoming their present tribulations by believing that all these blessings God has given them are their reality. And because the plagues of the end times last only a short while, and because God will also give His saints ways to escape them, we can all persevere through. I hope that you would, from this very moment and on, already enter the New Heaven and Earth and live in it in the realm of faith.

In the realm of faith, all this Word must touch your heart through faith, rather than your skin of the flesh. When it does so, your heart will become strong as it finds new strength, and it will have hope.

All the saints will be martyred in the end times. Looking at the hope that we have placed in the New Heaven and Earth, we are more than capable of embracing martyrdom with renewed strength.

In His essence, our Lord God is the God of truth and the God of love. Who, then, are the people that are fundamentally cowardly before God? These are the ones who are born with the original sin and who have not cleansed of all their own sins with the Word of the gospel of the water and the Spirit given by the Lord. Because in their essence they worship the evil ones more than they worship God, they have clearly become Satan's servants. It is because they worship the evil before the Lord God, and because they love and follow the darkness more than the light, that they are cowardly before the Lord God. All those who are cowardly before God will partake of the lake burning with fire and brimstone.

It is an established fact that these people, who by themselves are the darkness itself because of their sins in their hearts, have no other choice but to fear God. As the souls of those who belong to Satan love the darkness, they are cowardly before Jesus who has become the light. This is why they must take their evilness and weaknesses to God and receive the remission of their sins from Him. Those who do not believe in the gospel of the water and the Spirit given by the Lord are the greatest sinners before God and His enemies.

As their souls belong to the abominable, and because they stand against God, love and commit every sin that there is, follow false signs, worship all kinds of idols, and speak all kinds of lies, by the righteous judgment of God they will all be cast into the lake burning with fire and brimstone. This is their punishment of the second death.

The second death will be sentenced to the people who would be sent to hell, and these are the ones who are cowardly, who do not believe, who are abominable, who are murders, sexually immoral, sorcerers, and idolaters, who, together with the Antichrist and his followers, do not accept God's love now. The ones who do not believe in Him are the most evil ones. The Bible tells us that all these evil ones would be cast into the lake burning with fire and brimstone. This is why the Bible calls it the second death.

Those who take part in the second resurrection will not die even when they are thrown into fire, and for this very purpose of being cast into fire, they are to be resurrected in bodies that would live forever.

Unbelievers in God will be raised again to be cast into the lake of fire and brimstone. The second resurrection, which will bring eternal suffering in the fire of hell without dying, is reserved for all these people who do not believe.

Shortly after the pouring of the seven bowls containing the seven plagues, the Millennial Kingdom will be fulfilled, and when its thousand years pass by, the saints will move to the New Heaven and Earth. In the phrase, *"I will show you the bride, the Lamb's wife,"* the Lamb's wife here refers to those who have been saved by the gospel of the water and the Spirit given by Jesus Christ and by believing in it.

The Glory and Beauty of the Holy City Are Beyond Description

The city of Jerusalem refers to the Holy City where the saints are to live with their Bridegroom. This City that John saw was indeed beautiful and fantastic. It was majestic in size, adorned by precious stones inside out, clean and clear. The angel showed John where the brides of Jesus Christ would live with their Bridegroom.

Imagine living in a palace built with precious stones. In this City built with twelve different kinds of precious stones, those who are to become the Lamb's brides will live forever. This City is the gift of God that He would bestow on the Lamb's wife. The passage tells us that the city of Jerusalem shines brilliantly, and that its light is like a most precious stone, like a jasper stone, clear as crystal.

The glory of God is therefore with the City and all those who live in it. God's domain is that of light, and so only those who have been cleansed of all their darkness, weaknesses and sins can enter this City and live in it. As such, to enter this Holy City, we must all believe only in the true Word of the gospel of the water and the Spirit that our Lord has given us.

The passage says that the City has a great and high wall

with twelve gates. And it says that on the gates names are written, and that these are the names of the twelve tribes of the children of Israel. God tells us that He has indeed and actually prepared this City for His saints, surrounded by a great and high wall.

This is a spiritual indication that the way to enter this Holy City is that much difficult. It tells us, in other words, that being saved from all our sins before God is impossible with human efforts or the material things of the world of God's creation. To be delivered from all our sins and enter God's Holy City, it is absolutely required that we have the same faith of the twelve disciples of Jesus, the faith that believes in the truth of the gospel of the water and the Spirit. As such, no one who does not have this faith in the gospel of the water and the Spirit can ever enter this Holy City.

The City is guarded by twelve angels standing as gatekeepers appointed by the Lord God. The phrase, "names written on them [gates]," on the other hand, tells us that the owners of this City have already been decided, for its owners are none other than God Himself and His people, and the City belongs to the people of God who have now become His children.

This Holy City has three gates in each of its four directions of north, south, east, and west. I am sure that the Lord mentioned these three gates specifically here to tells us that they are especially related to the gospel that we believe in. 1 John 5:7-8 state that there are three that witness the true gospel both in Heaven and earth. Only those who believe in these three witnesses, both in Heaven and earth, can enter Heaven. We, the born-again, believe in Triune God and His righteous act of saving us through the water, the blood, and the Spirit.

The fact that the names of the twelve apostles are written on the twelve foundations of the City's wall tells us that the Lord has done exactly as He had promised, that He would not blot out their names from the Book of Life but write them in.

A furlong, *'Stadion'* in Greek, is a unit of measurement for distance, about 600 feet (185 m) in today's measurement. When the Bible tells us that each side of the quadrate City in Heaven measures 12,000 furlongs, it is telling us that each side measures about 2,220 km (1,390 miles). We are also told that its length, width, and height are the same. The majestic size of the City tells us just how great and glorious the Kingdom of God is.

The biblical meaning of the number four is suffering. The faith that the Lord demands from us is not something that just anybody can have, but this faith can be had only by those who accept the Word of God as it is, even if they cannot entirely comprehend it with their own, man-made thoughts.

As a Christian, it is impossible to enter God's Holy City just by believing in Jesus' Cross, and that the Lord is God and Savior. Just as our Lord Himself said, no one can enter into the Kingdom of God unless he/she is born again of the water and the Spirit. People can be born again only when they believe that all the sins of the world were passed onto Jesus when He was baptized by John the Baptist, and that He atoned for their sins by shedding His blood and dying on the Cross in their place.

The phrase, *"the city was pure gold, like clear glass,"* tells us that only those whose faith is like gold—that is, only those who truly believe in God—can enter it. It tells us that the faith that allows one to enter the Lord's Holy City is the kind of faith that believes the Word of God as it is written, one that is pure and free from all worldly things. It tells us, in other words, that one must accept God's Word of being born again of the water and the Spirit in its purity, truly believe in this Word, and have his/her faith refined.

The foundations of the wall of the City are adorned with all kinds of precious stones, telling us that we can be nourished of different aspects of faith from the Word of our Lord. We must have the disciplined faith, not just the faith in the gospel of the water and the Spirit or of hope for Heaven and the Millennial Kingdom. This trained faith also comes through the Word of God while enduring the present sufferings.

The Lord has given the saints not only His blessing of the remission of their sins, but also the blessing of the fulfillment of their hope, that those who are forgiven of their sins will enter the Millennial Kingdom and Heaven. We the saints can only thank God for qualifying us to enter the New Heaven and Earth, where neither sadness nor sorrow is ever found.

The saints who are to enter the Holy City needs to have much patience while on this earth, standing firmly anchored to the center of their faith. Those who believe in the Word of truth spoken by the Lord God, in other words, need to have great perseverance to defend their faith. When the end times come, the age of the Antichrist, the opponent of faith, will arrive.

This Antichrist will, as Satan's servant, bring great persecution to many people of faith, seeking to make them betray their faith. If people stand at the Antichrist's side and abandon their faith, not only will the Millennial Kingdom and Heaven be beyond their reach, but they will also be thrown into hell together with Satan.

Therefore, amidst the trials, persecutions, and plagues of the end times, we all need the perseverance that would allow us to defend our faith resolutely, for this unflinching perseverance is what will make the New Heaven and Earth ours.

Living in the New Heaven and Earth is like living embraced in the arms of the Lord. Because Jesus Christ, who has become the light of the new world, shines on this holy earth as its light, there is no need for the sun or the moon to shine on it. Jesus Christ is our Savior, Creator, and Judge, and in the New Heaven and Earth He is God who lives with us. By Him we enter Heaven, and from Him all blessings flow. The saints will have nothing else to do but to always praise this Lord.

In King James Version, verse 24 is written as the following: *"And the nations of them which are saved shall walk in the light of it: and the kings of the earth do bring their glory and honor into it."* When it says here that the glory of the earth are brought into Heaven, this does not mean that the ones who had reigned on the first earth, since they were wealthy, would bring their riches into the New Heaven and Earth. The earth here refers to the earth of the Millennial Kingdom.

Although the saints are saved and would enter the Millennial Kingdom all in the same manner, they would nevertheless be given different authorities, some reigning over ten cities and others over five cities, depending on their endeavor for preaching the gospel while living in the first world.

What verse 24 here tells us is that these kings who had different authorities would move to the New Heaven and Earth. Those who had reigned in the Millennial Kingdom, in other words, will enter the New Heaven and Earth as kings bringing along their faith in the Lord and all their glory and honor. It therefore has nothing to do with this first earth where all of us are living right now.

Because the New Heaven and Earth, where the Holy City is located, is already filled by the holy light, there can be no night in it, nor any evil ones. Among both Christians and non-Christians of this world alike, all those who do not know the truth of the gospel of the water and the Spirit are defilers, abominable, and liars. They therefore cannot enter the Holy City. Because whoever believes the gospel of the water and the Spirit can enter Heaven, this gospel of the water and the Spirit is the key to Heaven and the key to the remission of sin. You must realize that when you recognize and believe that God has given you this key, your name will be written into the Book of Life. And when you accept the truth of this gospel, you will be clothed in the blessing of entering this Holy City.

Believe that the Holy City has already been given to us. And live your life accordingly, with hope.

Because everything that we are facing at the present time is measured by the value system of this secular world, we cannot really figure out what true happiness is. But when we measure with God's measuring rod, we can all realize that those who have Heaven in their possession are the truly happy ones. Why? Because sooner or later, the things of the world will all disappear. Offering us nowhere to place our hope, they will all disappear as the tribulations and plagues are brought at their end, as according to God's plan. Nothing could be more foolish than placing one's hope in such things of the flesh that would simply rot away and burn down to ashes.

But in contrast, those who place their hope in the eternal Kingdom of Heaven that would neither rot away nor ever burn down are the blessed ones. Only those who are sinless can enter the Holy City of Jerusalem prepared by God. The happiest people in this world are the ones who have Heaven in their possession, whose sins have all been forgiven and cleansed away.

We must live our lives blessed by God, as the ones who

give glory to Him for giving us the New Heaven and Earth, and who dedicate ourselves to the preaching of the true gospel that enables each and every soul to enter Heaven.

Let us all live in such blessings, let us be loved by God, and, when we stand before the presence of our Lord, let us all live forever embraced in His arms. ✉

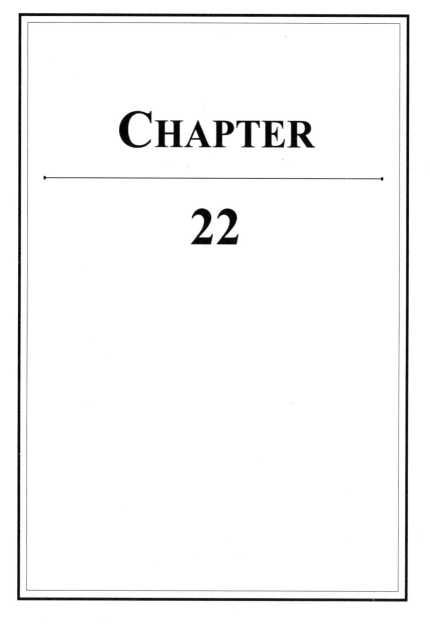

CHAPTER

22

New Heaven and Earth, Where the Water of Life Flows

< Revelation 22:1-21 >
"And he showed me a pure river of water of life, clear as crystal, proceeding from the throne of God and of the Lamb. In the middle of its street, and on either side of the river, was the tree of life, which bore twelve fruits, each tree yielding its fruit every month. The leaves of the tree were for the healing of the nations. And there shall be no more curse, but the throne of God and of the Lamb shall be in it, and His servants shall serve Him. They shall see His face, and His name shall be on their foreheads. There shall be no night there: They need no lamp nor light of the sun, for the Lord God gives them light. And they shall reign forever and ever. Then he said to me, 'These words are faithful and true.' And the Lord God of the holy prophets sent His angel to show His servants the things which must shortly take place. 'Behold, I am coming quickly! Blessed is he who keeps the words of the prophecy of this book.' Now I, John, saw and heard these things. And when I heard and saw, I fell down to worship before the feet of the angel who showed me these things. Then he said to me, 'See that you do not do that. For I am your fellow servant, and of your brethren the prophets, and of those who keep the words of this book. Worship God.' And he said to me, 'Do not seal the words of the prophecy of this book, for the time is at

hand. He who is unjust, let him be unjust still; he who is filthy, let him be filthy still; he who is righteous, let him be righteous still; he who is holy, let him be holy still. And behold, I am coming quickly, and My reward is with Me, to give to every one according to his work. I am the Alpha and the Omega, the Beginning and the End, the First and the Last. Blessed are those who do His commandments, that they may have the right to the tree of life, and may enter through the gates into the city. But outside are dogs and sorcerers and sexually immoral and murderers and idolaters, and whoever loves and practices a lie. I, Jesus, have sent My angel to testify to you these things in the churches. I am the Root and the Offspring of David, the Bright and Morning Star.' And the Spirit and the bride say, 'Come!' And let him who hears say, 'Come!' And let him who thirsts come. Whoever desires, let him take the water of life freely. For I testify to everyone who hears the words of the prophecy of this book: If anyone adds to these things, God will add to him the plagues that are written in this book; and if anyone takes away from the words of the book of this prophecy, God shall take away his part from the Book of Life, from the holy city, and from the things which are written in this book. He who testifies to these things says, 'Surely I am coming quickly.' Amen. Even so, come, Lord Jesus! The grace of our Lord Jesus Christ be with you all. Amen."

Exegesis

Verse 1: And he showed me a pure river of water of life, clear as crystal, proceeding from the throne of God and of the

Lamb.

It says here John was shown *"a pure river of water of life, clear as crystal."* The word water is used in this world as synonymous to life. The verse here tells us that this water of life flows in the New Heaven and Earth where the saints will live forever. Flowing from the throne of the Lamb, the river of the water of life moistens the Kingdom of Heaven and renews all things. In the phrase, *"the throne of the Lamb,"* "the Lamb" refers to Jesus Christ, who has saved the mankind with the gospel of the water and the Spirit while on this earth.

In the New Heaven and Earth that God has given to His saints, the water of life flows. Since this garden is as clear and clean as a beautiful watercolor painting, it can only be described as fantastic. The water of life that God has given us is not just an ordinary river, but it is the water that gives life to all living things there. As such, life thrives in everything that comes in contact with this river of life. The saints who are to live along the riverside of this water of life will drink this water, enjoy eternal life and live forever.

The river of the living water flows from the throne of God and of the Lamb. The saints cannot help but praise the grace of God and of the Lamb in the new Kingdom of Heaven, for God has bestowed on them His grace of life. I am thankful that all the grace of this new life flows from the throne of the Lord.

Verse 2: In the middle of its street, and on either side of the river, was the tree of life, which bore twelve fruits, each tree yielding its fruit every month. The leaves of the tree were for the healing of the nations.

The parade of the Lord's wonderful blessings on His saints in Heaven continues, for the Word tells us here that the Lord will give us the tree of life on either side of the river and allow us to eat from its fruits. The tree of life, which bears twelve kinds of the fruits, yields its new fruits each month, bringing the strength of new life. It is also said here that its leaves are for the healing of the nations.

Because the grace that the Lord has bestowed on His saints is so great and grateful, all that we can do is just praise Him and God the Father. Now, all that the saints should do is not trying to do something valuable for the Lord on their own, but rather only praising the Lord with their thankful hearts for giving them the New Heaven and Earth and new life. I praise the Lord for making the saints' hearts to only shout, "Thank you, Lord! Hallelujah!"

Verse 3: And there shall be no more curse, but the throne of God and of the Lamb shall be in it, and His servants shall serve Him.

To the saints living in the Kingdom of Heaven, God has given the blessing of eliminating curse forever. That the throne of God and the Lamb is among the saints shows us that the saints who live in the Kingdom of Heaven place the Lamb at the center of their hearts. Therefore, the saints' hearts are always overflowing with beauty and truth, and their lives are filled with joy.

From the phrase, *"His servants shall serve Him,"* we see that the saints living in the Kingdom of Heaven are clothed in the glory of serving the Lord very close to Him. The Kingdom of Heaven, where our Lord lives, is the most beautiful and splendid Kingdom.

As such, His servants who serve Him right next to the Lord can enjoy all His glory closely. This tells us that in the Kingdom of Heaven also, there would be the servants of the Lord. The word servant is a word that symbolizes lowliness, but the servants who can serve our glorious Lord close to Him are the most blessed in the Kingdom of Heaven also, for they are clothed in such an unspeakably great splendor. Those who have become the Lord's servants in the Kingdom of Heaven and on this earth also are the ones who would be clothed in all Heaven's glory and who are the happiest of all.

Verse 4: They shall see His face, and His name shall be on their foreheads.

To whom do all the saints and servants of the Lord belong? They belong to the Lord. They are the people of the Lord and the children of God. Those who serve the Lord in the Kingdom of Heaven, therefore, have the Lord's name written on their foreheads. The Lord protects and blesses them always, for they have become His. That the saints have become His means that they have become clothed in one of the happiest and most glorious splendors. Those who are ashamed of being His and the Lord's servants are those who are ignorant of His splendor, and they can never become the citizens of Heaven.

On the foreheads of the saints living in Heaven, the Lord's name is written. This is a blessing bestowed by the Lord. From now on, the saints have become His. As such, even Satan cannot harm the saints who have become the Lord's. The saints and the Lord are to live forever in all the splendor of Heaven. That the saints would see the Lord's glorious face everyday means that they would live in His love and wondrous blessings forever and ever.

There is one more thing that the saints need to know: Along with the Lord Jesus, God the Father and the Holy Spirit would also be with them as their family. We must not forget that in the Kingdom of Heaven, God the Father, His Son Jesus, the Holy Spirit, the saints, and the angels and all things would live together as one family and in perfect peace. I praise the Lord for making us His.

Verse 5: There shall be no night there: They need no lamp nor light of the sun, for the Lord God gives them light. And they shall reign forever and ever.

As the Bible tells us here, the saints will reign the New Heaven and Earth with the Lord. Those who have become His saints by believing in the gospel of the water and the Spirit have received the salvation that would enable them to reign in Heaven with the Lord and live in His wealth, splendor and authority forever. We are amazed once again by this gospel, for what a gospel of wondrous power and blessing we have!

I praise our God of Trinity for all these blessings and glory. The saints who believed in the gospel of the water and the Spirit while on this earth will reign the Kingdom of Heaven. How marvelous this blessing is! We cannot help but praise the Lord. It is only most right and proper that they should so praise God.

In the New Heaven and Earth where the saints are living, there is no need of lamps, electric bulbs, or the sun. Why? Because God Himself has become the light of the New Heaven and Earth, and there shall be no night there. God has allowed the saints to reign in there forever as His children. This blessing reminds us once again just how great the grace that the saints have received from the Lord is.

We the saints must realize how great the blessings of Heaven bestowed on us after our salvation are. The grace that our Lord has bestowed on His saints is higher and greater than the sky. The saints must not let this wondrous blessing that the Lord has given them pass them by. The saints can only give eternal thanks and praise to the Lord for His greatness, glory, and the blessing that He has bestowed on them, and live in wealth and splendor forever. Amen! Hallelujah! I praise our God!

Verse 6: Then he said to me, "These words are faithful and true." And the Lord God of the holy prophets sent His angel to show His servants the things which must shortly take place.

"These words are faithful and true." The Lord will surely fulfill all His promises that He has revealed to the saints through Revelation. This is why our Lord has told everything to all His saints beforehand speaking as the Holy Spirit through the servants of God. What is the most blessed Word in the Book of Revelation? There are many blessed Words in Revelation, but the most blessed Word is that God will allow the saints to reign with the Lord in the New Heaven and Earth and live in authority and glory.

Because God will most certainly fulfill this work soon, the saints can never allow their faith to fall apart or be trapped in despair. The saints must overcome all trials and tribulations with their faith of hope. Our Lord will not fail to make all His prophecies and promises made to the saints and God's Church come true. Our Lord sent His servants to this earth and made them speak the Words of prophecy, so that He could tell His saints and Church about all these blessings.

Verse 7: "Behold, I am coming quickly! Blessed is he who keeps the words of the prophecy of this book."

Because the Words of the prophecy of this Book of Revelation tell us of the saints' future martyrdom, it reveals to us that the time will come when the saints would be persecuted by the Antichrist and would have to defend their faith to death.

Because it is God' will, the saints must embrace their martyrdom. They will then participate in their resurrection and rapture, reign in the Kingdom of Christ for a thousand years to come, and then live in the New Heaven and Earth forever. As such, the saints must trust in all the Word of God that our Lord has spoken to them and keep their faith. The most blessed ones of the end times are those who believe in the Word of our Lord and live by faith.

God has told His saints that He would come quickly. The Lord will come to us without any more delay. To fulfill all the blessings of God flowing from the Word of the water and the Spirit, the Word that brings to the saints their salvation from sin, our Lord will come to this earth quickly.

After being saved, the saints must hold onto to the Word of the blessings of the Lord promised to them, and keep their faith. If their hearts ever lose their faith in the Word of the Lord, they would be losing everything, and this is why they must defend their faith in the Lord's Word. God tells the saints, in other words, to keep their faith in the Lord.

Verse 8: Now I, John, saw and heard these things. And when I heard and saw, I fell down to worship before the feet of the angel who showed me these things.

It is the prophets and the saints who spread God's Word of prophecy. We must therefore praise God who works as He has spoken to them, and we must worship only Him. At times some people try to raise themselves high as God and be treated as such. They do so because they are either frauds or the false prophets. Only God is worthy to receive all praise, worship, glory, and service.

Verse 9: Then he said to me, "See that you do not do that.

For I am your fellow servant, and of your brethren the prophets, and of those who keep the words of this book. Worship God."

What must we do to become God's true prophets? We must first believe in the mystery of the gospel of the water and the Spirit given by the Lord. We would then become God's people, saints, and brothers and sisters to each other. Only after this can God charge them with His works. Those who have become the servants of the Lord must also believe in His Word and keep it with their faith. These are the ones who give all glory to God instead of keeping it for themselves. Our Lord is worthy to receive all worship and glory from everyone in this world. Hallelujah!

Verse 10: And he said to me, "Do not seal the words of the prophecy of this book, for the time is at hand."

The Word of promise written in Revelation must not be kept hidden. Because it is soon to be fulfilled, it must be testified to everyone. Amen! Let us all believe in the Word of prophecy in the Book of Revelation and preach it.

Verse 11: "He who is unjust, let him be unjust still; he who is filthy, let him be filthy still; he who is righteous, let him be righteous still; he who is holy, let him be holy still."

When the day of the Lord's return nears, He will let those who seek after sin continue to seek after sin, those who are holy to continue to be holy, and those who are filthy to continue to be filthy. When the end times come, those whose hearts have become sinless by believing in the Lord's gospel of the water and the Spirit will still serve the gospel on this earth, and those who have kept their holiness given by the Lord and lived their lives with faith will continue to live so. Our Lord advises us to keep the faith that we have now.

Verse 12: "And behold, I am coming quickly, and My reward is with Me, to give to every one according to his work."

Our Lord will come soon, in other words, and give the Paradise on earth and the New Heaven and Earth to the saints who have served and labored to spread the gospel of the water and the Spirit, to reward them for their sacrifices. When the saints believe in the Word of prophecy in Revelation, they will be able to defend their faith until the very end, for they would have placed their hope in the Lord. We must realize and believe that the Lord will reward the saints' labor with far greater blessings, for our Lord is glorious and merciful.

Verse 13: "I am the Alpha and the Omega, the Beginning and the End, the First and the Last."

Our Lord is the beginning and the end of everything. He is our Savior and God Himself, who will bring us the completion of the salvation that only He can give us. All history in the entire universe, the history of both Heaven and earth, began from the Lord and will be ended by Him.

Verse 14: Blessed are those who do His commandments, that they may have the right to the tree of life, and may enter through the gates into the city.

Because what the Lord has spoken to us is all life, the saints believe in His Word, preach and defend it. They do so because the Word that our Lord has spoken to His saints and to all things in the universe are all true. This is why the saints and servants of God keep the Lord's Word in their minds. They defend their faith by believing the Word of God even more strongly, so that they would have the right to eat the fruits of the tree of life planted in the New Heaven and Earth.

The saints who have become sinless by believing in the

gospel of the water and the Spirit given by the Lord try to defend their faith, for they have the right to eat the fruits of this tree of life in Heaven.

Verse 15: But outside are dogs and sorcerers and sexually immoral and murderers and idolaters, and whoever loves and practices a lie.

Those who are mentioned in the above passage are the ones who do not believe in the gospel of the water and the Spirit, and thus are not born again even until the end times. The Antichrist and his followers, misleading people with his signs and miracles, have deceived them time after time by falsely proclaiming that the Antichrist is the Savior. They had led people to their own destruction by making them worship the Antichrist's image. Our Lord keeps such people outside the gates of the Holy City, so that they may never enter the New Heaven and Earth. The Lord's City is open only to the saints who have defended their faith that believes in the gospel of the water and the Spirit.

Verse 16: "I, Jesus, have sent My angel to testify to you these things in the churches. I am the Root and the Offspring of David, the Bright and Morning Star."

For the sake of God's Church and the saints, our Lord has sent us God's servants, and He has made them testify all the things that would come to pass. The One who made them testify these things is Jesus Christ, God Himself who has become the saints' Savior.

Verse 17: And the Spirit and the bride say, "Come!" And let him who hears say, "Come!" And let him who thirsts come. Whoever desires, let him take the water of life freely.

To all on this earth who hunger and thirst after the righteousness of God, our Lord has invited them into the Word of the water of life. Anyone who thirsts and hungers after the righteousness of God has been given the blessing of coming to the Lord, believing in gospel of the water and the Spirit given by Him, and thereby drinking the water of life. This is why our Lord says to everyone to come to Jesus Christ. Anyone can receive the truth of the gospel of the water and the Spirit freely. But the water of life is excluded from those who do not have this desire. If you desire, you, too, can drink the water of life given by the Lord by believing in the gospel of the water and the Spirit.

Verse 18: For I testify to everyone who hears the words of the prophecy of this book: If anyone adds to these things, God will add to him the plagues that are written in this book;

The Scripture is the Word of God. As such, when we believe in this Word, we can neither add to nor subtract from it. This verse tells us that because the Word of the Scripture is the Word of God, no one can believe in it by adding or subtracting from the written Word of truth, nor believe by leaving the written truth out. We must therefore be careful. Every Word spoken by God is important; none can ever be left out as unimportant.

Yet people still continue to ignore the gospel of the water and the Spirit given by the Lord. This is why they are yet to be delivered from their sins, why they still remain sinners, and why are entering into their own destruction—even as they claim to believe in Jesus as their Savior. To deliver the sinners from sin, our Lord has given them His water and blood (1 John 5:4-5, John 3:3-7). Yet many people place importance only on Jesus' blood on the Cross; as such, they still have not been delivered from their sins, and will thus face all the plagues written in the Book of Revelation.

Those who claim to believe in Jesus and yet continue to ignore the truth that Christ took care of all the sins of the world with His baptism from John will face the even more fearful punishment of hell. Why? Because they do not believe in the gospel of the water and the Spirit that the Lord has given them, and therefore have not been born again yet. Anyone who ignores the gospel of the water and the Spirit given by the Lord will enter into the lake of fire burning forever and face eternal suffering—the day of regret will surely come to all such people.

Verse 19: and if anyone takes away from the words of the book of this prophecy, God shall take away his part from the Book of Life, from the holy city, and from the things which are written in this book.

Is there anyone among us whose Christian faith leaves out the Word of truth, that Jesus took upon all the sins of the mankind upon Himself by receiving baptism from John, and that at once He cleansed away all the sins by being crucified? If so, such people will surely all lose the right to enter God's Holy City, for they do not believe in the baptism that our Lord received from John to take upon the sins of the mankind upon Himself all at once. They are ultimately committing the sin of ignoring the gospel of the water and the Spirit given by the Lord.

As such, Christians must take to their hearts the truth that Jesus took upon the sins of the mankind with His baptism received from John. Unless they do so, they will all be excluded from the glory of entering the Holy City given by the Lord. If you believe that Jesus is your Savior, you must then be cleansed of all your sins by wholeheartedly believing that Jesus came to this earth, was baptized by John at the Jordan River to wholly save all the mankind from the sins of the world, and that He thereby cleansed away all the sins committed by the mankind by so taking them upon Himself. The spring whereupon you can be cleansed of all your filthiness is the baptism that our Lord received. Having thus taken upon Himself our sins of the world, our Lord shed His blood and died on the Cross to pay the wages of all our sins with His own death.

The baptism that Jesus received from John is the confirmed evidence of our salvation from sin. 1 Peter 3:21 tells us, *"There is also an antitype which now saves us—baptism (not the removal of the filth of the flesh, but the answer of a good conscience toward God), through the resurrection of Jesus Christ."* We must realize that Jesus carried the sins of the world to the Cross and shed His blood in order to pay the wages of the sins of the mankind with His own death, all on our behalf.

This is why God is once again giving His Word of warning to the entire mankind in verse 19. We must believe in the Word of the gospel of the water and the Spirit as it is, without adding to or subtracting from it.

Verse 20: He who testifies to these things says, "Surely I am coming quickly." Amen. Even so, come, Lord Jesus!

Our Lord will soon come again to this world. And the saints, who have received the remission of their sins by believing in the Lord and are clothed in the glory of Heaven, are earnestly waiting for the Lord's second coming. Because those who believe in the gospel of the water and the Spirit are all prepared to meet the coming Lord even now, they are waiting for the Lord to return and clothe them in His blessings promised to the saints. As such, the saints are hoping ardently for the Lord's second coming, in faith and thankfulness.

Verse 21: The grace of our Lord Jesus Christ be with you all. Amen.

The Apostle John concludes the Book of Revelation with a benedictory prayer for the grace of our Lord Jesus Christ to be with those who desire to enter the Holy City given by God. Let us, too, become the saints who enter the Holy City given by Jesus Christ through faith without fail. ⊠

Be Joyful and Strong in the Hope of Glory

< Revelation 22:1-21 >

Revelation 22:6-21 shows us the hope for Heaven. Chapter 22, the concluding chapter of the Book of Revelation, deals with the confirmation of the faithfulness of the Scriptural prophecies and God's invitation to the New Jerusalem. This chapter tells us that the New Jerusalem is a gift of God given to the saints who have been born again by believing in the gospel of the water and the Spirit.

God made the born-again saints praise Him in the House of God. For this, I am deeply thankful to the Lord. Words cannot express how thankful we are for allowing us to be the saints who, by believing in the gospel of the water and the Spirit, have been forgiven of all our sins before the Lord. Who on this earth would ever receive a greater blessing than what we have received? There is none!

Today's main passage is the last chapter of Revelation. In the Book of Genesis, we see God making all the blueprints for the mankind, and in the Book of Revelation, we see our Lord fulfilling all these plans. The Word of Revelation can be described as a destroying process of this world in order to complete all God's works for the mankind according to His design. Through the Word of Revelation, we can see the Kingdom of Heaven beforehand as revealed by God.

The Shape of God's City and Its Garden

Chapter 21 speaks of God's City. Verses 17-21 tell us: *"Then he measured its wall: one hundred and forty-four cubits, according to the measure of a man, that is, of an angel. The construction of its wall was of jasper; and the city was pure gold, like clear glass. The foundations of the wall of the city were adorned with all kinds of precious stones: the first foundation was jasper, the second sapphire, the third chalcedony, the fourth emerald, the fifth sardonyx, the sixth sardius, the seventh chrysolite, the eighth beryl, the ninth topaz, the tenth chrysoprase, the eleventh jacinth, and the twelfth amethyst. The twelve gates were twelve pearls: each individual gate was of one pearl. And the street of the city was pure gold, like transparent glass."*

This Word of Revelation describes the New Jerusalem that God would give to His born-again people. This City of Jerusalem in Heaven, we are told, is built with twelve different kinds of precious stones, with twelve gates made of pearls.

Chapter 22 then speaks of the nature found in the garden of the City of Jerusalem. Verse 1 says, *"And he showed me a pure river of water of life, clear as crystal, proceeding from the throne of God and of the Lamb."* In the City of God, a crystal river flows through its garden, just as God made four rivers flow in the Garden of Eden at the beginning. God tells us that this is the garden that the righteous would enjoy in the future.

The main passage also tells us that the tree of life stands in this garden; that it bears twelve kinds of fruits, yielding its fruits every month; and that its leaves are for the healing of the nations. It appears to me that the nature of Heaven is such that not only are its fruits eaten, but also its leaves, since the leaves have healing power.

The Blessings Received by the Righteous!

The Bible tells us that in the City of God, *"There shall be no more curse, but the throne of God and of the Lamb shall be in it, and His servants shall serve Him. They shall see His face, and His name shall be on their foreheads."* It tells us that those of us who have been forgiven of our sins will reign forever with God who has saved us.

Those whose sins have been blotted out by believing in the gospel of the water and the Spirit while living on this earth will not only receive the blessing of having all their sins disappear, but they will also be God's own children, have many angels serving them when they go to the Kingdom of God, and reign with the Lord forever. The passage tells us that the righteous would receive from God such eternal blessings as standing at the river of life and eating the fruits of life, and that as a part of these blessings there would be no more disease.

It also tells us that they would need neither the light of this earth nor of the sun, for in God's glorious Kingdom they would live forever with God, who Himself is its light. The children of God who have received the remission of their sins through the gospel of the water and the Spirit, in other words, will live like God. This is the blessing received by the righteous.

The Apostle John, one of the twelve disciples of Jesus who wrote the Book of Revelation, also wrote the Gospel of John and the three Epistles of the New Testament—First, Second, and Third John. He was exiled to the Island of Patmos for refusing to recognize the Roman emperor as a god. During this exile, God sent His angel to John and showed him what would come to pass on this earth, revealing to him the destruction of the world and the place where the saints would eventually enter and live in.

If we were to describe the Book of Genesis as the blueprint of creation, we may describe the Book of Revelation as the completed miniature of the blueprint. For 4,000 years, our Lord has told the mankind that He would make all its sins disappear through Jesus Christ. And in the age of New Testament, when the time came, God fulfilled all His promises, that He would send Jesus the Savior to this earth, that He would have Jesus be baptized by John, and that He would make the sins of the world disappear through Christ's blood on the Cross.

When the mankind fell into the Devil's deception and was trapped in its destruction because of sin, our Lord promised that He would deliver it from its sins. He then sent Jesus Christ, had Him be baptized and bleed, and thereby saved the mankind perfectly from its sins.

Through the Word of Revelation, God has recorded in detail what kind of glory awaits those who have received the remission of their sins, and what kind of judgment awaits the sinners on the other hand. God tells us, in other words, that there are many who would end up in hell even though they have claimed to believe in Him faithfully (Matthew 7:21-23).

Our Lord has saved the sinners from their sins, and He has told us not to seal the Word of the blessings that He has prepared for the righteous.

Who Are the Unjust and the Filthy?

Verse 11 states, *"He who is unjust, let him be unjust still; he who is filthy, let him be filthy still; he who is righteous, let him be righteous still; he who is holy, let him be holy still."* Who are the "unjust" here? The unjust are none other than those who do not believe in the love of the gospel of the water and the Spirit given by the Lord. Because people commit sin all the time, they must believe in the gospel of the water and the Spirit that the Lord has given them and thereby live their lives glorifying God. Because only God is the One who is to receive glory from the mankind, and because only He is the One who has clothed us in His grace of salvation, we must all live a life that gives all glory to God. Those who disobey God are filthy, for they do not always believe in His Word.

In Matthew 7:23, our Lord told the religionists who profess to believe in Him only by lips, *"I never knew you; depart from Me, you who practice lawlessness!"* Our Lord called them as *"you who practice lawlessness."* He rebuked them because these people believe in Jesus only through their deeds, instead of believing in the gospel of the water and the Spirit wholeheartedly. Lawlessness is sin, and not believing in the Word of God with one's heart. Therefore, when people practice lawlessness before God, it means that they do not believe in the love and the salvation of the water and the Spirit that God has given them. Lawlessness is none other than changing the Word of God at one's own whim and believing it arbitrarily in whatever way that one feels like.

Those who truly believe in Jesus must accept whatever God has established as it is. We believe in Jesus, but in no way does this allow us to alter God's plan and the completion of His salvation. The message of the main passage is that God would give eternal life to those who believe in His salvation as it stands on its own, but send to hell those who make changes to God's Law and believe in whatever way that suits their own tastes.

"He who is unjust, let him be unjust still." This tells us that such people, in their stubbornness, do not believe in the

salvation as set by God. They are the unjust. And this is why the sinners are always unjust.

The passage continues, *"he who is filthy, let him be filthy still."* This refers to those who, although they are sinful, and despite the fact that Jesus has made their sins disappear with the water and the Spirit, have no intention whatsoever to cleanse their sins with faith. As such, God would leave alone these faithless people as they are, and then judge them. By giving people conscience, God has made it possible for them to clearly recognize sin in their hearts. And yet they still have no intention to cleanse the sins in their hearts, nor to know the gospel of the water and the Spirit. God tells us that He would let these people be as they are.

Proverbs 30:12 says, *"There is a generation that is pure in its own eyes, yet is not washed from its filthiness."* The religionist-Christians today are such people who do not even want to be cleansed of their sins. However, Jesus, who is God Himself, came to this earth to save the sinners, cleansed away all their sins by taking the sins of the mankind upon Himself with His baptism all at once, was at once judged for all these sins by being crucified, and thereby has indeed saved from sin those of us who believe.

To whomever knows and believes in the Word of the gospel of the water and the Spirit with which Jesus Christ has saved the sinners, our Lord has permitted this person to be forgiven of all his/her sins, regardless of what kind of sinner he/she might be. And yet there are still people who have not received this remission of sin through faith. These are the one who have resolved themselves to not even try to get their sins cleansed away. God will let them be as they are.

This is to fulfill the justice of God. It is to show that God is the God of justice. These people will be cast into the fire of brimstone that burns forever. They will then realize who the God of justice really is. Although they confess Jesus as their Savior, they are not only deceiving their own conscience, but they are also defiling the conscience of others. Because they have rejected the gospel of the water and the Spirit, God will pay them back according to what they have done. When the day comes, God will bring His wrath to those who deserve His wrath.

Give to Everyone According to His Work

There are two kinds of people on this earth: those who have met the Lord, and those who have not. Our Lord will pay everyone back according to his/her work.

No one can be justified on his/her own, but justification comes from Jesus. He took all the sins of the mankind upon Himself with His baptism all at once, carried the sins of the world to the Cross, and on the Cross faced all the judgment of sin that the mankind itself should be facing. The mankind could become righteous by believing in this truth. Those who believe in this truth are the ones who have met the Lord.

God asks those who are sinless, who know and believe in this truth, to preach the gospel on this earth and keep His holy Word as they live on. God says, *"he who is holy, let him be holy still."* We must keep this command in our hearts, defend our holy faith, and always preach the perfect gospel. Why? Because too many people in this world remain ignorant of this true gospel, and as a result their faith is all wrong.

There are those on this earth who unconditionally support the doctrine of incremental sanctification. Although our Lord has already made the mankind's sins disappear, these people still pray for the forgiveness of their sins daily, even as now. Offering their prayers of repentance on a daily basis, they try to cleanse away their sins, to be incrementally sanctified so that they would finally become the righteous who no longer commit any sin, and to thus be a match for Jesus. But Jesus Christ, the Son of God, is the King, the Prophet and the High Priest.

The true servants of God not only carry out their task of making sure that everyone is truly forgiven of sin, but they also lead everyone to the truth as the co-workers of God. God's servants are the ones who, through the written Word, have the exact knowledge of the things that would come to pass.

Verse 12-13 say, *"And behold, I am coming quickly, and My reward is with Me, to give to every one according to his work. I am the Alpha and the Omega, the Beginning and the End, the First and the Last."* Our Lord indeed is the Alpha and the Omega, the Beginning and the End, the First and the Last. We must believe in everything that the Lord has spoken to us in fear.

Our Lord will reward the saints with the blessings that are far greater than their works, for He is glorious and merciful. He is the merciful and compassionate One who has saved us from all our sins, and, as the Word of Revelation tells us, the God of power and justice who would complete His work of salvation. And this completion of salvation, which is soon to come, is permitting to the saints the glorious entrance into the City of the New Jerusalem, the generous and sufficient rewards of our Lord for their works.

Blessed Are Those Who Do His Commandments

Continuing on with verse 14, the main passage tells us,

"Blessed are those who do His commandments, that they may have the right to the tree of life, and may enter through the gates into the city." There are many people who claim, based on this verse, that salvation comes by deeds—by observing, in other words, His commandments.

But in fact, "doing His commandments" means believing in and keeping all the written Word of God with faith. John the Apostle wrote, *"And this is His commandment: that we should believe on the name of His Son Jesus Christ and love one another, as He gave us commandment" (1 John 3:23).* So, when we believe in the true gospel of the water and the Spirit, and devote ourselves to preaching the gospel to save all the lost souls throughout the whole world, we are doing His commandments in His presence.

The truth is that all the sins we commit throughout our lives have already been blotted out through the baptism that Jesus received from John the Baptist. Following this baptism, our Lord's blood on the Cross, His resurrection, and His ascension have made us be born again and allowed us to live a new life in His truth.

Whenever we fall into sin after being born again, we must return to the Word of truth that has cleansed us of all our sins; realize that our roots are such that we cannot help but sin; and, returning once again to the faith of the Jordan River where our Lord took upon all our weaknesses, shortcomings, and sins, be baptized together with the baptism of Jesus and be buried together with Christ who died on the Cross. When we do so, we can finally be freed from the sins committed after being born again, and be washed clean. Holding onto the righteous of God by reaffirming our eternal salvation of atonement and thanking Him for His permanent and perfect salvation.

Jesus has already washed away all the sins of this world.

The problem is found with our conscience. Although our Lord has already taken care of the sins of the world with His baptism, because we the human beings do not realize that the Lord has thus cleansed away all our sins with His baptism and crucifixion, our conscience remains troubled as sinners. We therefore are apt to feel that we still have sin left in us, when in fact all that we have to do is just believe that all our sins have actually been washed away already through the gospel of the water and the Spirit given by Jesus Christ.

If our hearts have been hurt by our sins, with which truth can we then heal the wounds of these sins?

These wounds, too, can all be healed by believing in the gospel of the water and the Spirit—that is, by believing that our Lord took all the sins of the world upon Himself by being baptized by John at the Jordan River, and that He made all these sins disappear by carrying them to the Cross of Calvary and shedding His blood on it. In other words, the sins of our deeds that we commit after receiving the remission of sin can also be washed away when we confirm once again our faith in the gospel that Jesus Christ has already cleansed away all our sins, including these sins of our deeds.

The sins of this world were washed away all at once when Jesus Christ received His baptism and was crucified. As such, neither the sins of the world nor the personal sins of ours need to be washed away twice or thrice, as if they must be cleansed continuously. If someone teaches that the remission of sin is attained little by little, then the gospel that he/she is preaching is a false gospel.

God has made the sins of the world disappear at all once. Hebrews 9:27 tells us, *"And as it is appointed for men to die once, but after this the judgment."* As we die once because of sin, it is God's will that we should also receive the remission of sin at once. Coming to this earth, Jesus Christ took all our sins upon Himself at once, died once, and was judged in our place at once as well. He did not do these things for several times.

When we receive the remission of sin by believing in Jesus Christ with our hearts, then, it is also right for us to believe all at once and receive the eternal remission of all our sins. Because the sins that we commit from then on hurt our hearts from time to time, all that we have to do is go before the Word of this salvation, that our Lord has washed away our sins all at once, and cleanse and heal our tainted hearts with faith: "Lord, I am so full of shortcomings. I've committed sin again. I was unable to live a whole life according to Your will. But when You were baptized by John at the Jordan River and bled on the Cross, did You not take care of all these sins of mine also? Hallelujah! I praise You, Lord!"

With such faith, we can confirm our remission of sin once again and thank the Lord always. This last chapter of Revelation tells us that by going before Jesus Christ, who is the tree of life, and by believing that the Lord has already washed away all the sins of the world, those who have received the remission of sin have earned the right to enter the Kingdom of God, the Holy City, through their faith.

Whoever wants to enter the city of God must believe that Jesus Christ atoned for the sins of the mankind eternally by receiving His baptism at once and shedding His blood. Though we all have many acts of shortcomings, by believing in the baptism and the blood of Jesus Christ our Savior, our faith can be approved by God as true, and we can all go before the tree of life.

Only by believing in Christ's baptism and blood can we have the right to drink the water of life flowing in the city of New Jerusalem and to the fruits of the tree of life. Because the qualification to enter the New Heaven and Earth, which can never be allowed to be taken away by anyone, comes only from the gospel of the water and the Spirit, we must defend our faith and also preach it to many others. Likewise, the phrase "(to) do His commandment" means for us to overcome the world by faith—that is, to believe in and keep the gospel of the water and the Spirit, and to devote ourselves to preaching the true gospel all over the world.

In Matthew 22, Jesus tells us "the parable of the wedding feast." The conclusion of this parable is that those who do not have their wedding garments on should be cast into outer darkness (Matthew 22:11-13). How can we wear our wedding garments to participate in the marriage supper of the Lamb, and what are the wedding garments? The wedding garments that enable us to enter the marriage supper of the Lamb is the righteousness of God given to us through the gospel of the water and the Spirit. Do you believe in the gospel of the water and the Spirit? If so, you are then beautifully clothed in His righteousness so that you can enter Heaven as a sinless bride of the Son.

We, the born-again, also commit sin every day. However, only the righteous who have been forgiven of their sins before God are qualified to wash away their daily sins from their garment of righteousness with faith. Because those whose sins have not been forgiven are not qualified to wash away their sins, they would never be able to cleanse themselves of their sins with their daily prayers of repentance. That we have been saved from the sins of the world by believing in the Lord was all made possible by knowing and believing that the Lord has washed away all our sins of the world by coming to this world, being baptized, and shedding His blood.

We can confirm, in other words, that our daily sins have

already been washed away only in His true gospel. Those who have received the remission of sin from the Lord through the Word of the water and the blood can also have the conviction of their salvation from the sins that they commit as they go on with their lives.

It is because our Lord has made our sins disappear all at once that we can also wash away the sins that we commit with our own acts by believing in this salvation of eternal atonement. If this were not the case, if our Lord had not washed away all our sins at once, in other words, how could we ever become sinless?

How could we ever enter into the Holy City of Heaven? How could we ever go before Jesus Christ, the tree of life? By believing in our Lord who has made all our sins disappear, we can enter the Kingdom of Heaven as the clean and spotless people; and whenever we sin in our lives, by going before our Lord and confirming that He has made these sins disappear also, we can be freed from all such sins. That's why I tell you that only the born-again are privileged to be forgiven their daily sins by faith.

King David committed great sins before God, even though he was a servant of God. He committed adultery with a married woman, and killed her husband who was a faithful subject of his. Nevertheless, he praised God for His merciful forgiveness like this:

"Blessed is he whose transgression is forgiven,
Whose sin is covered.
Blessed is the man to whom the LORD does not impute iniquity,
And in whose spirit there is no deceit (Psalm 32:1-2)."

Who is the most blessed in this world and before God? The blessed are none other than those of us who have been born again; who have been saved; and who, whenever sin is committed in our lives, look toward the fact that the Lord has made all our sins disappear, go to the spring of life everyday, and wash away our tainted hearts daily. This is ruminating on our deliverance and confirming our Lord's great grace of salvation.

Only the righteous have received the remission of sin, making all their shortcomings whole. Their acts are whole, and so are their hearts. Having thus become the righteous without blemish, we can then enter the Kingdom that God has prepared for us, the Kingdom of Heaven. If we would only accept what Jesus Christ, the gate of salvation and the tree of life, has done for us, His power would be revealed, and we would therefore all receive the remission of sin and enter Heaven.

Those Who Go before the Tree of Life

The reason why those of us who have received the remission of sin always go before the Lord is to confirm that our Lord has made all our sins disappear, to ruminate on the grace of salvation once more, to remember it, and to praise God for it, so that we may all be more than able to enter His Kingdom. This is why we preach the gospel.

A countless number of Christians, unable to meet God's servants who can guide them by teaching the Bible correctly, are stuck in their misunderstanding of the Word and mistaken beliefs. Even now, there are people who are preoccupied with their acts, offering prayers of repentance every morning and all night long. Why do they do these things? Because they believe that by doing so, their sins would be forgiven. And they believe so because they have been taught erroneous doctrines. But these are unrighteous acts before God. Such people are the pitiful ones who know neither the righteousness of God nor His unconditional love.

The Bible is not something that can be taken lightly, as if it can be interpreted in whatever way one wishes to. And yet because people have interpreted, taught, and believed in it based on their own man-made thoughts, the result has been like the above—that is, they remain ignorant of God's righteousness and love. Each passage of the Bible has the exact meaning, and this can be interpreted correctly only by God's prophets who have received the remission of sins.

Going before the tree of life is for us to believe in the Lord while on this earth, to remember everyday that our Lord has made our sins disappear, to praise Him, and to preach this gospel. We, the born-again, are also to remember that He took our sins upon Himself, to confirm this truth everyday, to worship Him with the joy of thanksgiving, and to go before our Lord.

However, it is not an exaggeration to say that Christians throughout the entire world have misinterpreted this passage and mistakenly believe that they can enter the Kingdom of God by having their sins washed away on a daily basis through the prayers of repentance. But this is not what the passage means.

After receiving the remission of sin, our hearts can remain in peace by confirming that our Lord has made all the sins that we commit with our acts disappear. By confirming the remission of ALL our sin, we are no longer bound by sin. This is the way to go before the tree of life in Heaven.

The Scripture is on a whole different dimension from the man-made thoughts. As such, to know the truth, we must first learn and hear the truth from the born-again servants of God.

Those Who Are Outside the City

Verse 15 says, *"But outside are dogs and sorcerers and sexually immoral and murderers and idolaters, and whoever loves and practices a lie."* This Word refers to all those of the end times who are not born again. It is simply amazing that our Lord would depict these people with such accuracy.

One characteristic of dogs is that they regurgitate—that is, they throw up what they had eaten, eat it again, and then throw up again, and then once again eat what they just vomited out. Our Lord says here that these "dogs" would not be able to enter into the City.

To whom do these dog refer then? There are people who cry out, "Lord, I'm a sinner; please wash away my sins," and then praise God singing, "I've been forgiven, you've been forgiven, we've all been forgiven!" But the next moment, these people once again cry out, "Lord, I'm a sinner; if you would just forgive me one more time, I'll never sin again." They then sing again, "I've been forgiven by the Blood of Calvary!"

These people go back and forth so much that no one is sure whether they were actually forgiven or not. None other than this kind of people are the "dogs" that the Bible speaks of. Dogs bark everyday. They bark in the morning, they bark in the afternoon, and they bark at dawn. These people do not bark exactly in this way, but they do cry out that they are sinners, even though they have been forgiven of their sins. They become the righteous one minute, they turn into sinners the next minute.

In this way, they are like the dogs that vomit out what's inside and eat it again, and then vomit it out again only to eat it one more time. In short, the Bible refers to Christians who still have sin in their hearts as the "dogs." These dogs can never enter Heaven, but must remain outside the City.

Next, who are the "sorcerers?" These are the ones who, taking advantage of the innocent church-goers' emotions, robs them of their money with their sweet-talking, and the ones who deceive people with false signs and miracles claiming to heal their diseases. Because they all take the name of God in vain, they cannot enter into the Holy City.

Also, the sexually immoral, murderers, idolaters, and whoever loves and practices a lie cannot enter into the City. When the end times come, dogs and sorcerers would deceive people, and the Antichrist would emerge. The Antichrist who deceives many people with false miracles and signs, steals their souls, stands against God, and seeks to raise himself higher than God and to be worshipped, and all his followers would never be able to enter into the City.

As such, if we fall into the deception of those who claim that we still have sin, or if we fall into the deception of signs and miracles that stir up our emotions, we would all end up outside the City along with the Antichrist and Satan, wailing and gnashing our teeth, just as the Word warns us.

Verses 16-17 says, *"'I, Jesus, have sent My angel to testify to you these things in the churches. I am the Root and the Offspring of David, the Bright and Morning Star.' And the Spirit and the bride say, 'Come!' And let him who hears say, 'Come!' And let him who thirsts come. Whoever desires, let him take the water of life freely."*

Have you received your remission of sin freely? Through the Holy Spirit and God's Church, our Lord has given us the gospel of the water and the Spirit that enables us to drink the water of life. Whoever hungers for the righteousness of God, whoever thirsts after the Word of truth, and whoever wants desperately to receive the remission of sin—to all such people,

God has offered to clothe them in His mercy and extended His invitation into His Word, the water of life of His salvation. Receiving the remission of sin is the only path to respond to this invitation to the New Heaven and Earth where the water of life flows.

Amen, Come Lord Jesus!

Verse 19 says, *"and if anyone takes away from the words of the book of this prophecy, God shall take away his part from the Book of Life, from the holy city, and from the things which are written in this book."* Before God, we cannot believe in whatever way we wish to based on our own thoughts. If it is written in the Word of God, all that we can say is just "yes," for if anyone were to say "no" to the Word, our Lord would also take him/her away, saying, "You are not My child." This is why we must believe in Him according to the Word. We can neither add to nor subtract from any of the Word of God, but we must believe in it as it is written.

Holding onto the servants of God and believing in what the Holy Spirit speaks through God's Church are what the true faith is all about. Yet many people, as they have excluded the gospel of the water and the Spirit from their faith, still have sin remaining in their hearts. Even when the Word repeatedly tells them that only those who are sinless can enter God's Holy City, they still leave out Jesus' baptism from their faith, and instead add to it their insistence on such acts as giving prayers of repentance and material offerings.

Those who believe in Jesus as their Savior must be able to confess with their faith that all the sins of the mankind were passed onto Jesus through the baptism that Jesus received from

John the Baptist at the Jordan River. If you omit Jesus' baptism you are essentially abandoning your own faith. In other words, if you do not believe in the gospel of the water and the Spirit, even the blood of the Cross is meaningless, and the resurrection of Christ, too, is irrelevant to you. Only those who believe that God has made all their sins disappear freely are relevant to the resurrection of Jesus, and only they can shout out loud for the coming of the Lord Jesus, as the Apostle John does in verse 20.

Verse 20 says, *"He who testifies to these things says, 'Surely I am coming quickly.' Amen. Even so, come, Lord Jesus!"* Only the righteous can say this. Our Lord will soon come back to this earth, according to the prayers of the righteous. Only the righteous, who have received the perfect remission of sin by believing in the gospel of the water and the Spirit, would rejoice and wait eagerly for the quick coming of the Lord. This is because those who are prepared to receive the Lord are only those who are clothed in the garment of the gospel of the water and the Spirit—that is, those who are sinless.

Our Lord is waiting for the day when He would respond to the righteous' waiting, the day when He comes to this earth. He will reward us with the Millennial Kingdom, and clothe us, who are the righteous, in His great blessings of entering the New Heaven and Earth where the water of life flows. This waiting of our Lord is not that long. As such, all that we can do is just say, "Amen. Even so, come, Lord Jesus!" And, with faith and thanksgiving, we earnestly long for the Lord's return.

Finally, verse 21 says, *"The grace of our Lord Jesus Christ be with you all."* The Apostle John ended the Book of Revelation with his last prayer of blessings for everyone. He offered his prayer of blessing at the end, with his heart hoping for everyone to believe in Jesus, be saved, and enter the city of God.

My beloved saints, that we have been saved by God means that He has loved us, delivered us from all our sins, and made us His people. It therefore is simply wonderful and thankful that God has made us righteous so that we may enter His Kingdom.

This is the core of what the Bible speaks to us. To make us live forever in His Kingdom, God has allowed you and me to be born again by hearing this true gospel, and He has delivered us from all our sins and judgment. I praise and thank our Lord for His salvation.

It is so fortunate that we have safely received the remission of our sins. We are all people who have been greatly blessed by God. And we are His prophets. As such, we must spread the gospel of the remission of sin to all those souls that are yet to hear this gospel, and also preach to them the Word of Revelation, the completion of the gospel.

I hope and pray that everyone would believe in Jesus, who is the Creator, the Savior and the Judge, and, when the end times come, thereby enter the holy place of the New Heaven and Earth given by the Lord. May the grace of our Lord Jesus be with you all. ✉

Appendix

Questions & Answers

Questions & Answers

1) Is the number 144,000 in chapter 7 literally the number of the people of Israel who would be saved, or is it just a symbolic figure?

The number 144,000 that appears in chapter 7 tells us literally how many Israelites would be saved in the end times, 12,000 from each of the twelve tribes of Israel for a total of 144,000. This is fulfilled by the special providence of God through which some of the descendents of Abraham, whom God loved, would be saved. God remembers the promise that He made to Abraham, and so to fulfill this promise, He would now allow the gospel of the water and the Spirit to be spread not only to the Gentiles, but also to the people of Israel, the descendants of the flesh of Abraham.

As such, God has determined that through the tribulations of the end times and the two witnesses whom God would specially raise for the Israelites, they would come to believe that Jesus Christ, whom they had persecuted and crucified, is in fact their true Savior. Through God and the faith of Abraham, the Israelites have become the recipients of God's special love.

God has decided that He would especially deliver 12,000 from each of the twelve tribes of Israel from their sins and destruction, and has sealed them with the seal of God through His angel. Among the people of Israel, therefore, 144,000 have received the mark that shows that they have become the people of God. This number is divided equally among the twelve tribes, for God's love for them is not based on favoritism for any particular tribe, but He clothes them all in the same grace of becoming His people. Though people at times let their own emotion cloud their judgement, God works in all things with absolute justice and fairness.

After sealing 144,000 of the Israelites with the seal of salvation, God would then bring down the great plagues on this earth. God has made a total of 144,000 Israelites His people, 12,000 from each of its twelve tribes—from the tribes of Judah, Reuben, Gad, Asher, Naphtali, Manasseh, Simeon, Levi, Issachar, Zebulun, Joseph, and Benjamin. This to keep the promise that God made to Abraham and His descendents that He would become their God.

God has thus decided to save 144,000 of the Israelites. The number 14 here, as it appears in Matthew 1:17, has a special meaning for us, telling us that God would begin His new work among the Israelites. This number contains the will of God that He would now conclude the history of the first world on this earth and allow those Israelites that are saved to live in the New Heaven and Earth.

When we look at the genealogical line from Abraham down to Jesus Christ, we can find out that from Abraham to David span 14 generations, from David to the captivity in Babylon span another 14 generations, and from the captivity in Babylon to Christ span yet another 14 generations. In other words, we can find out that God begins His new work in every 14 generations. God has sealed 144,000 Israelites with the will that He would make them live a new life, not in this present world, but in the Kingdom of God. As can be seen, God is the faithful One who surely fulfills what He once promised and set for the mankind.

2) Who are the two witnesses that appear in chapter 11?

The two witnesses that appear in chapter 11 are the two servants of God whom God would especially raise to save the people of Israel in the end times. To keep His promise made to Abraham, God would make these two prophets, who are sent to deliver the Israelites from sin, perform signs and miracles, and make the Israelites, led by them, return to Jesus Christ and believe in Him as their Savior. These two witnesses would feed the Word of God to the people of Israel for 1,260 days—that is, the first three and a half years of the seven-year period of the Great Tribulation. By spreading the gospel of the water and the Spirit to the Israelites and making them believe in it through the two witnesses, God would give the Israelites the same salvation that He has given the Gentiles, just as the latter were saved from all their sins through faith.

Revelation 11:4 says, *"These are the two olive trees and the two lampstands standing before the God of the earth."* There are many different interpretations on the two olive trees; some people even claim that they are the olive trees. The two olive trees refer to the anointed ones. In the age of the Old Testament, people were anointed when they were appointed as prophets, kings, or priests. The Holy Spirit descended on them when they were anointed. As such, the olive tree also refers to Jesus Christ, who was conceived of the Holy Spirit (Romans 11:17).

However, looking at Revelation 11:1—*"Then I was given a reed like a measuring rod. And the angel stood, saying, 'Rise and measure the temple of God, the altar, and those who worship there.'"*—we should realize that the focus of chapter 11 is on the salvation of the people of Israel. In other words, from this time would begin the work of spreading the gospel of the water and the Spirit to the Israelites, of their deliverance from all their sins through the grace of salvation given by Jesus Christ, and of their becoming of the true people of God. Therefore, the two witnesses are the two prophets of God whom He would raise in the end times to save the people of Israel.

In the Bible, the lampstand refer to God's Church. As such, the two lampstands refer to God's Church founded among the Gentiles and the Church permitted to the Israelites. God is not only the Israelites' God, but He is also the Gentiles' God, for He is God of everyone. As such, among the Israelites and the Gentiles alike, God has established His Church in both of them, and through His Church He does the work of saving souls from sin until the very last day.

Since the Old Testament's time, the Israelites had prophets established by God's Law, and through them they heard the Word of God. They have the Law of Moses and the Prophets. As such, they know everything about the sacrificial system and the prophecies of the Old Testament, and this is why they require God's prophets who are appointed from their own people.

They also believe that they are the chosen people of God, and they therefore do not take it seriously nor listen when the Gentiles tell them of the Word of God. Thus, only when the prophets believing in the gospel of the water and the Spirit and appointed by God rise out of their own people would they finally accept and believe in Jesus Christ as their Savior.

This is why God Himself would establish the two prophets from the people of Israel and send them to the Israelites. These prophets would actually do many wonders that the well-known servants of God in the Old Testament had done before. Revelation 11:5-6 tells us, *"And if anyone wants to harm them, fire proceeds from their mouth and devours their enemies. And if anyone wants to harm them, he must be killed in this manner. These have power to shut heaven, so that no rain falls in the days of their prophecy; and they have power over waters to turn them to blood, and to strike the earth with all plagues, as often as they desire."*

Unless these servants of God for the people of Israel have such power, the Israelites would not repent, and God would therefore clothe the two witnesses in His power. God would give the two witnesses His special power, so that they may preach all the Word of prophecy to the Israelites, and testify to them and make them believe that Jesus Christ is their long-awaited Messiah. Seeing the wonders actually performed by the two witnesses, the Israelites would then listen to them and return to Jesus Christ.

When the two witnesses complete their work of spreading the gospel to the Israelites, the Antichrist would emerge in this world, stand against their preaching of the gospel, and make them be martyred. Revelation 11:8 tells us, *"And their dead bodies will lie in the street of the great city which spiritually is called Sodom and Egypt, where also our Lord was crucified."*

Having preached the gospel to all the Israelites and thus completed all the works of their calling, the two witnesses would then be killed in the place where Jesus was crucified before. This fact backs the interpretation that these two witnesses are from Israelites. For the people of Israel, they are the servants of God.

In conclusion, God would raise His two prophets to testify to the Israelites, who have refused to believe in Jesus Christ and have rejected Him, and who are like Sodom and Egypt spiritually, that Jesus is in fact their long-awaited Messiah, and through these two witnesses clothed in His power, God would make the Israelites believe in Jesus.

3) Who is the woman in chapter 12?

The woman in chapter 12 refers to God's Church in the midst of the Great Tribulation. Through the woman persecuted by the Dragon, chapter 12 shows us that God's Church would be greatly harmed by Satan when the end times come. However, through the special protection of God, His Church will overcome Satan and the Antichrist with its faith, and receive the glory of being clothed in His great blessings.

Because the saints who remain in God's Church would receive the nourishment of faith even in times of the Tribulation, they will overcome the Antichrist and triumph by embracing their martyrdom with their faith in the gospel of the water and the Spirit. God explains this fact to us through the metaphor of the woman in chapter 12.

Revelation 12:13-17 tells us, *"Now when the dragon saw that he had been cast to the earth, he persecuted the woman who gave birth to the male Child. But the woman was given two wings of a great eagle, that she might fly into the wilderness to her place, where she is nourished for a time and times and half a time, from the presence of the serpent. So the serpent spewed water out of his mouth like a flood after the woman, that he might cause her to be carried away by the flood. But the earth helped the woman, and the earth opened its mouth and swallowed up the flood which the dragon had spewed out of his mouth. And the dragon was enraged with the woman, and he went to make war with the rest of her offspring, who keep the commandments of God and have the testimony of Jesus*

Christ."

Satan, who is often described as the Dragon in the Bible, was originally an angel that was driven out of Heaven for seeking to take over God's place. Because the Devil, together with other angels that followed him, was cast out of Heaven as a result, and knowing that he would soon be bound in the bottomless pit, he then came down to this earth and persecuted God's Church and His saints.

Although Satan tried to prevent Jesus Christ from doing what He came to this earth to do—that is, saving the mankind from sin—Christ nevertheless took upon the sins of the mankind Himself with His baptism, bled His blood on the Cross, rose from the dead again, and thereby has indeed saved the mankind from all its sins. Jesus therefore completed the Father's will. In spite of Satan's attempts to interfere with the work of Jesus to carry out God's will to save the mankind from sin, Christ overcame the Devil's disturbance and fulfilled all of the Father's will.

However, by deceiving many people and turning them into his allies, Satan has made them stand against Jesus Christ and the saints. Knowing that his days are numbered, he incites the people of this earth to stand against God and persecutes His saints. By making sure that the world is overrun by sin, Satan has made everyone pursue after sin and hardened their hearts to stand against God with their iniquities.

Satan attacks the beloved saints of God endlessly with sin, for he knows very well that he is running out of time. He has made everyone of this world pursue after sin and hardened their hearts to stand against God and His saints with their sins. As such, when the end times come, the saints must defend their faith and fight against and overcome Satan.

But God has a special blessing in store for His saints, for

He loves the saints who remain inside His Church. This blessing is that He would nurture the saints with the nourishment of faith in God's Church during the first three and a half years of the Tribulation, before the Antichrist makes his appearance in this world, deceives people and makes them into his servants to stand against and persecute God and His saints. Why? Because when the time of rampant sin comes and the Antichrist makes his appearance, the saints must be martyred. To do so, God would nurture His saints through His Church and enable them to be martyred with their faith for three and a half years—that is, *"for a time and times and half a time"* (Revelation 12:14).

4) What is Babylon?

The word Babylon is used in the Bible to refer to this world that has parted from God. In the Old Testament, the story of the "Tower of Babel" can be found. As people garnering together their power sought to build the Tower of Babel to leave God, God prevented them from building the Tower, brought it down, confused their language, and scattered them around.

Likewise, this world is like the time of the Babel Tower. The kings of the earth have fornicated and lived in luxury with the things of this world, and all the merchants have ignored God in their lives, too busy selling and buying everything that He has given them. Using religion, the false prophets have lived their lives while talking loud, turning themselves into merchants who trade in people's souls, and amassing a fortune with the material possessions of this world. They have loved the world, saying that no world built by the mankind thus far has ever been better than the present one.

Like this, when the end times comes, this world would be so filthy before God and sin would be so widespread in it that God would have no choice but to bring down the world that He Himself made. Loving the world too much, the people of this world have regarded it as their God, believing and following it as such. This world has thus become a hotbed of sin, the people living in this hotbed of sin have become drunk in all kinds of sin, and these sins therefore have resulted in the fall of the world. The earth will therefore face its final demise brought by the plagues of the seven bowls of God.

Another reason why this world would face the plagues of the seven bowls from God is because its people, as they love the world, have turned into the servants of Satan and the Antichrist, and uniting their effort with the Antichrist, they have murdered the born-again saints who believe in the gospel of the water and the Spirit given by the Lord.

When the end times come, people would surrender to the Antichrist, receive the mark of Satan given by him, and thus turn into the servants of the evil one. Because the people of this world, conspiring with the Antichrist, have stood against God and murdered His saints, God would pay them back just as they had brought persecution, suffering, tribulation, and death to the saints.

5) When will the Millennial Kingdom begin? (Is it pre-tribulation or post-tribulation Kingdom?)

Many people believe that the saints would be raptured before the advent of the Great Tribulation of seven years, and that during this period of the Tribulation they would already be in the Millennial Kingdom of Christ, rather than on this earth. However, when we verify this belief with the Word of God, we can easily find out that it is a false belief.

Our Lord God gives the Kingdom of Christ to His saints for a thousand years as a gift to reward them for laboring and giving up their own lives for the sake of the gospel. As Revelation 20:4 tells us, *"And I saw thrones, and they sat on them, and judgment was committed to them. Then I saw the souls of those who had been beheaded for their witness to Jesus and for the word of God, who had not worshiped the beast or his image, and had not received his mark on their foreheads or on their hands. And they lived and reigned with Christ for a thousand years."*

The above passage explains to us who are the one that would be able to enter the Millennial Kingdom. These are the ones who, amidst the Great Tribulation, fought against the Antichrist, were martyred to defend their faith, and neither received the mark of the Beast nor worshipped his image. To separate the wheat from the chaff, God has allowed the mankind the choice to either receiver or not receive the mark of the Beast. To rapture the saints and to reward them for their faith and their victory over Satan with the Kingdom of Christ of one thousand years, God wants to clearly separate the wheat from the chaff.

For the Antichrist, the biggest obstacle to standing against God, idolizing himself, and making people receive his mark will be the people of God. As such, the Antichrist will devote all his efforts to their elimination. But the saints will not surrender to the Beast, fight against him with faith, embrace their martyrdom, and thereby glorify God. A countless number of the saints, looking toward their afterlife, will willingly embrace their martyrdom to defend their faith in God. As the

Antichrist will thus bring much suffering to the saints during the time of the Great Tribulation, God has prepared for him and his followers the plagues of the seven bowls and the punishment of hell that burns forever.

As such, this world would be completely destroyed and brought down by the plagues of the seven bowls, with great earthquakes, the likes of which have never been seen before, striking the earth. As a result, the first world would disappear without a trace. God would then command his angel to seize the Dragon and bind him in the bottomless pit for a thousand years, for our Lord would have to first confine the Dragon in the Abyss before He can allow His saints to live in the Millennial Kingdom of Christ.

Because Satan is not found in the Millennial Kingdom where the saints are to reign with Christ, there are neither deceivers nor curses anymore. Isaiah 35:8-10 explains the Kingdom of Christ that would come to the saints who participate in the first resurrection as the following: *"A highway shall be there, and a road, And it shall be called the Highway of Holiness. The unclean shall not pass over it, But it shall be for others. Whoever walks the road, although a fool, Shall not go astray. No lion shall be there, Nor shall any ravenous beast go up on it; It shall not be found there. But the redeemed shall walk there, And the ransomed of the LORD shall return, And come to Zion with singing, With everlasting joy on their heads. They shall obtain joy and gladness, And sorrow and sighing shall flee away."*

The Kingdom of Christ, lasting for a thousand years as the above, will come after this earth goes through the seven-year period of the Great Tribulation and after the world ruled by Satan and the Antichrist is completely destroyed. This Kingdom, therefore, is the reward that our Lord would give to

His saints for being persecuted and martyred to defend their faith in the gospel of the water and the Spirit, and for laboring to preach this gospel.

6) What is the City of New Jerusalem?

The City of New Jerusalem is the Holy City in the New Heaven and Earth that God has prepared for the saints who will participate in the first resurrection. After ending the plagues of the seven bowls on this earth, God would bind Satan in the bottomless pit for a thousand years, bestow the blessing of reigning with the Lord in the Millennial Kingdom on the saints who would have participated in the first resurrection, and after the thousand years are ended, make the first heaven and the first earth disappear and give the saints the gift of the New Heaven and Earth.

Those who are to receive these blessings are the saints who have received the remission of their sins by believing in the holy gospel of the water and the Spirit given by Jesus Christ. The Lord would become the saints' Bridegroom, and the saints, as the brides of the Lamb who has become their Bridegroom, would live in glory clothed in the Bridegroom's protection, blessing, and power in His glorious Kingdom.

God has prepared for these saints the Holy City in the New Heaven and Earth. This city is none other than the City of New Jerusalem. This is prepared solely for the saints of God. And this has all been planned for the saints in Jesus Christ even before the Lord God created the universe. Those who, by the amazing power of the Lord God, would live in the Millennial Kingdom of Christ are qualified to move to the New Heaven and Earth where the Holy City is found.

From this moment and on, the saints are to live with the Lord forever in the Temple of God. Because God is with them, there would no longer be death, nor sorrow, nor wailing, nor suffering, for the first heaven and the first earth would pass away, and God would make all things new.

The City of New Jerusalem shines, as it has the glory of God, and its light is like the most precious stone, like jasper stone, clear as crystal. God's glory is therefore with the city and those who are to live in it. The City has a great and high wall with twelve gates, three in each direction; the gates are guarded by twelve angels, and the names of the twelve tribes of Israel are written on the gates. The City's wall has twelve foundations, and on them the names of the twelve apostles of the Lamb are written.

The city is laid out as a gigantic square, with one side measuring 12,000 furlongs—equivalent to about 2,220 km (1,390 miles). Its wall measures 144 cubits, approximately 72 m. This wall is built with jasper, and the City is pure gold, like clear glass. The foundations of the wall are adorned with all kinds of precious stones, and the city's twelve gates are made of pearl.

Because the Lord God and the Lamb are in the City, there is no need for the sun or the moon to shine. Also, the river of the water of life flows from the throne of God and of the Lamb, wetting the Kingdom of Heaven and renewing all things. On both sides of the river stands the tree of life, bearing twelve fruits and yielding its fruits every month, and its leaves are for the healing of the nations. There are no more curses, but only eternal blessings are found there.

7) What is the mark of the Beast?

During the time of the Tribulation, to bring everyone under his control, the Antichrist will force all to receive his mark on either their right hands or foreheads. This mark is the mark of the Beast. The Antichrist will demand people to receive his mark so that He could turn everyone into his servant. He will proceed with his political scheme by using people's lives as his leverage. If people do not have the mark showing that they belong to the Beast, he will prevent them from buying or selling anything. This mark is the name of the Beast or his number. When the Beast appears in this world, its people will be coerced to receive this mark made of either his name or number.

When counted, the number of the Beast on this mark is 666. This means that the Beast, who is the Antichrist, proclaims himself as God. In other words, it shows the arrogance of a human being trying to be God. As such, anyone who receives this mark on his/her right hand or forehead would be serving and worshipping the Antichrist Beast as God.

When the world faces immense difficulties from the plagues of the seven trumpets, the Antichrist, empowered by Satan, would bring the whole world under his reign with great force. Healing himself from his mortal wounds and performing such miracles as bring down fire from the sky, he will make everyone of this world follow him. As heroes emerge in times of trouble, the Antichrist, a man who received his power from Satan, will resolve the difficult problems that the world faces with great authority, and thereby be revered by all the people of the world as God. As Satan thus makes people serve the Antichrist as God, many will end up worshipping him as such.

The Antichrist therefore does his final works with the help

of another beast coming up out of the earth. The second beast forces people to make an image after the first Beast, the Antichrist; gives breath to this image of the Beast with the power of Satan and makes it speak; and kills everyone who does not worship the Beast' image. He makes everyone receive his mark on either the right hand or the forehead, and prevents anyone who does not receive the mark from buying or selling anything.

Receiving the mark of the Beast means surrendering to him and becoming his servant. The mark is not received by physical coercion, but by a personal and rational decision. But as without receiving this mark no one can buy or sell anything, or even live on, all the people of the world who have not received the remission of sin would stand at the Beast's side and end up surrendering to him.

Those who thus surrender to the Beast and receive his mark will all be cast, together with the Devil, to the lake burning with fire and brimstone. The nominal Christians who have not yet been born again will, because their hearts are not dwelt by the Holy Spirit, capitulate before Satan in the end, receive his mark on their right hands or foreheads, and worship him as God. At this time, only those who have received the remission of sin and who has the Holy Spirit in their hearts will be able to resist the Beast's demand to receive his mark, and fight against and overcome the Antichrist with faith.

8) Who or what are the four living creatures standing before the throne of God?

Revelation 4:6-9 describes the four living creatures as the following: *"Before the throne there was a sea of glass, like crystal. And in the midst of the throne, and around the throne, were four living creatures full of eyes in front and in back. The first living creature was like a lion, the second living creature like a calf, the third living creature had a face like a man, and the fourth living creature was like a flying eagle. The four living creatures, each having six wings, were full of eyes around and within. And they do not rest day or night, saying: 'Holy, holy, holy, Lord God Almighty, Who was and is and is to come!' Whenever the living creatures give glory and honor and thanks to Him who sits on the throne, who lives forever and ever....* "

The four living creatures around the throne of God are, together with the 24 elders, the faithful ministers of God who always serve His will and praise His holiness and glory. When God works, He does not work by Himself, but He always works through His servants. The four living creatures, the ministers who are closest to God, have received the ability to always carry out all His wills.

Each of the four living creatures has a different form, signifying that the four living creatures serve God in different capacities. They are full of eyes around and within, meaning that these living creatures constantly pay close attention to God's purposes. As such, the four living creatures are the faithful ministers of God who always serve and carry out His will.

In addition, the four living creatures do not rest in their praise of God's glory and holiness, just as God never sleeps. They praise the holiness of God the Father and our Lord Jesus, who is God and the Lamb, and His almighty power. In this way, the four living creatures standing before God's throne praise Him out of their sincere hearts, not out of obligation. Why? Because for what Jesus Christ has done—that is, lowering

Himself even to the form of a man and being born into this world through the body of the Virgin Mary; taking all the sins of the mankind upon Himself by receiving baptism from John; carrying these sins to the Cross and dying on it; and thereby saving all the mankind from sin—He now sits on the throne of God, and for these beautiful works of His, He is worthy to receive glory from all the creatures forever and ever.

The four living creatures thus exalt God high above by giving Him, along with the 24 elders, sincere praise out of the depth of their hearts.

9) Which one is right: pre-tribulation rapture, or post-tribulation rapture? Would the saints still be on this earth during the Great Tribulation?

Looking at the history of Christianity, we can see that a countless number of liars have risen till the present time. Interpreting the Book of Revelation and calculating the time of rapture with their own methods, these liars have set a particular date as the day of rapture and used to teach that the Lord would return and the saints would be raptured on this day of their choosing.

However, all such claims ended up as a dud. One characteristic common to all of them is that across the board, they all advocated the theory of pre-tribulation rapture. Saying to their followers that their worldly possessions would serve no use at all since they are all to be raptured and lifted up to the air before the Great Tribulation, these lairs deceived many people and robbed them of their material possessions.

We must realize that this is Satan's shrewd trickery, trying to deceive all the people of this world and turn them into his servants through these lairs.

What is the most important to the saints, and what they are most curious about, is the question of when the rapture of the saints would come. Revelation 10:7 tells us, *"but in the days of the sounding of the seventh angel, when he is about to sound, the mystery of God would be finished, as He declared to His servants the prophets."* What does it mean when it says here, *"the mystery of God would be finished"*? "The mystery of God" refers to none other than the rapture of the saints.

After the sixth of the plagues of God's seven trumpets ends, the Antichrist emerges on this earth, rules over the world, and demands everyone to receive the mark of the Beast. From his persecution the saints are martyred. This is shortly followed by the sounding of the seventh trumpet, at which point both the martyred saints and the surviving saints who defended their faith are resurrected and raptured.

When the seventh trumpet sounds, God does not bring a plague to this earth; but rather, this is the time when the rapture of the saints occurs. Following the rapture, God immediately proceeds to pour the plagues of the seven bowls on this earth. As such, when the time of the plagues of God's seven bowls comes, the saints are not found on this earth, but rather in the air with the Lord. We must all realize that the rapture of the saints comes when the seventh angel sounds the last trumpet.

However, even now many Christians still continue to believe in the theory of pre-tribulation rapture. Because their faith is not prepared for the coming of natural disasters and the emergence of the Antichrist, they would ultimately lose their spiritual war against Satan and the Antichrist, turn into their servants, and be destroyed along with the world.

The first three and a half years of the seven-year period of the Great Tribulation are the time of the plagues of the seven trumpets, when this earth is ravaged by natural disasters. A third of the sun and a third of the stars would be darkened; a third of this earth's forests would be burnt down; a third of the sea would turn into blood, killing a third of its life forms; meteors would fall from the sky, turning a third of water into wormwood; and many people, as a result, would die from all these. The world would fall into chaos from these plagues, with nations rising against nations, states against states, and war breaking out incessantly everywhere.

As such, when the Antichrist emerges and resolves all these problems in such chaotic circumstances, many people would follow him, and thereby bring the most terrifying plague on this earth.

This world will therefore see the rise of a politically integrated international organization, a management system that pursues the common interests of the nations. This internationally united state will fall into Satan's hands with the emergence of the Antichrist, and turn into a state that stands against God and His saints. The ruler of this internationally united state would control and reign over all nations, and ultimately work as the Antichrist. He, who works with the power of Satan, is the enemy of God and a servant of the Devil.

The Antichrist now reveals his true color, forbidding people from believing in the true God and forcing people to worship himself as God instead. For this, he would perform many signs before them, resolve the world's intractable and chaotic state of affairs single-handedly with the power of Satan, and thereby capture everyone's heart.

In the end, he would make idols after his image and demand people to worship it as God. And to put everyone under his control in this time of tribulations, He would force people to receive his mark on either their right hands or foreheads, and forbid all those who do not have this mark from trading. He would also kill all those who refuse to worship him, no matter how many they might be. As such, everyone whose name is not written in the Book of Life would all end up receiving the mark and worshipping the Beast.

However, the saints will neither surrender to the Antichrist nor receive his mark. Because the Holy Spirit dwells in their hearts, no one but the Almighty God can ever be the object of their worship and their Lord. The saints will therefore refuse to worship Satan and the Antichrist and to become their servants, instead be martyred with their faith, and thereby overcome them.

As Revelation 13:10 tells us, *"He who leads into captivity shall go into captivity; he who kills with the sword must be killed with the sword. Here is the patience and the faith of the saints."* When the Antichrist makes his appearance and forces people to receive his mark, the first three and a half years of the Great Tribulation would have passed, and the second three and a half years would have begun. This is when the saints would be persecuted by the Antichrist and be martyred.

But the Antichrist's seizing of power and his persecution of the saints are permitted by God for only a very short while, for the Lord would shorten the time of tribulation for His saints. At this time, the saints would give glory to God by fighting against the Antichrist to defend their faith and overcoming him with their martyrdom.

After going through the first three and a half years of the Great Tribulation, the born-again saints are to remain on this earth until the time of their martyrdom when the second half of the Tribulation begins. They must therefore fight against Satan and the Antichrist and overcome them with their faith. This is why Revelation tells us that God would give Heaven to those who overcome. As such, before the first three and a half years of the Great Tribulation pass by and the Antichrist emerges, the saints must have their faith nurtured within God's Church, in the protection and guidance of our Lord.

People must therefore be freed from this false doctrine of Satan widespread in Christian communities, called the theory of pre-tribulation rapture, and by believing in the gospel of the water and the Spirit now, they must all receive the remission of their sins, be born again, and join God's Church. Only then would their faith be nourished through God's Church for the first three and a half years of the Great Tribulation, and only then would they be able to have the kind of faith with which they can fight against the Antichrist and embrace their martyrdom when the time of the extreme tribulation comes.

10) When you say that the rapture of the saints would come after the seventh angel sounds his trumpet, are you not contradicting what the Lord said, that no one knows the day and hour of the rapture, not even the Lord Himself?

Not at all! What our Lord has told us is not the exact day and hour of the saints' rapture, but the background and signs leading up to this remarkable event. Only then can the saints who love the Lord prepare their faith, and only then can they participate in the rapture by fighting against the Antichrist and embrace their martyrdom when the time comes.

Through His revelation, God showed the Apostle John, who was exiled to the Island of Patmos at the time, everything that would come to pass in the end times of this world. Like this, when God plans and fulfills all His works, He makes sure to let his servants know.

Of all the Word of God, the Book of Revelation in particular is written with many metaphorical expressions. Because of this, only the servants of God who are saved from all their sins by believing in the gospel of the water and the Spirit and thus have the Holy Spirit dwelling in their hearts can solve these metaphors and explain them to people. To the servants of God and His saints, the Word of Revelation reveals in detail everything about the plagues of the seven trumpets, the appearance of the Antichrist, the martyrdom of the saints, their resurrection and rapture, the Millennial Kingdom of Christ, and the New Heaven and Earth.

The rapture of the saints is intimately related to their martyrdom. Revelation 11:10-12 tells us about the death of the two prophets, and their resurrection and rapture in three and a half days. These two witnesses are martyred by the Antichrist and then resurrected in three and a half days from their death. What we can find out from this account is that when the Antichrist emerges on this earth and makes people worship the Beast by receiving his mark on their right hands or foreheads, the saints would fight against the Antichrist and be martyred with their faith, but with the return of the Lord that follows shortly, they would also participate in the first resurrection and be raptured.

The Apostle Paul also spoke of rapture in 1 Thessalonians 4:16-17: *"For the Lord Himself will descend from heaven with a shout, with the voice of an archangel, and with the trumpet of God. And the dead in Christ will rise first. Then we who are alive and remain shall be caught up together with them in the clouds to meet the Lord in the air. And thus we shall always be with the Lord." The Apostle Paul, in other words, also told us that the time of rapture would come after the martyrdom of the saints and when the seventh angel sounds his trumpet."*

When the Antichrist's reign of this world begins, when he tries to force us to receive his mark, and when he demands to be worshipped as God, we the saints must all realize that the time of our martyrdom is at hand, and we must also believe that shortly after our martyrdom would come our resurrection and rapture. We do not know exactly on what month and day this would happen. But what is clear to us is that the rapture of the saints would come when the seventh angel sounds his trumpet. All the saints must prepare to receive the Lord's Day by believing in this truth.

11) You say that Jesus would return to rapture the saints, and that He would descend on this earth to wage the war of Armageddon as well. Are you then saying that the Lord would descend on this earth twice? What's the difference between these two?

Descent of Jesus from Heaven to the air to rapture the saints and His return to the earth to judge the Devil through the war of Armageddon are different from each other.

When the first three and a half years of the Great Tribulation end, and shortly after the martyrdom of the saints with the appearance of the Antichrist, the Lord would descend from Heaven. At this time, the saints who had been asleep in their tombs and the saints who have survived through the Tribulation without receiving the mark of the Beast and by defending their faith will all be resurrected and lifted up to the sky, and meet the Lord in the air. From this moment on, the saints will always be with the Lord. The Lord does not descend to the earth at this time. Why? Because the plagues of the seven bowls that would judge Satan and the Antichrist still remain to be poured on this earth.

The Apostle Paul thus told us in 1 Thessalonians 4:17, *"Then we who are alive and remain shall be caught up together with them in the clouds to meet the Lord in the air. And thus we shall always be with the Lord."* The saints who fought against the Antichrist and were martyred to defend their faith would participate in the first resurrection, meet the Lord in the air, not on this earth, and enter Heaven's marriage supper of the Lamb with Jesus Christ, who has become their Bridegroom.

After this, God would command His angels to pour the plagues of the seven bowls filled with the wrath of God, which He had held in patience since the creation, on the Antichrist, his followers, and all the sinners of this world still remaining on this earth. The world will therefore face plagues of immense proportions, the likes of which it had never seen before. The saints who meet the Lord in the air would now praise the Lord in the air for the plagues of the seven bowls that would be poured on this earth.

Having taken part in their resurrection and rapture through the Lord, they would stand in a sea of glass mingled with fire to praise the righteous judgment that God brings to this earth. Therefore, the saints who were martyred and participated in their resurrection and rapture through the power of the Lord would praise the Lord endlessly, for the salvation that He has given them, and for His judgment of the Antichrist and his servants brought by His omniscient and omnipotent power.

As the angels holding the seven bowls pours each of the bowls, everyone on this world would suffer greatly, from the plague of foul and loathsome sores; the plague of the sea turning into blood; the plague of the water turning into blood;

the plague of being scorched by the heat of the sun; and the plague of darkness and pain. When the sixth angel pours his bowl on the great river Euphrates, its water would be dried up, preparing the way for the kings from the east. A great famine would ravage throughout the earth from this plague, bringing the greatest suffering to the mankind. And demons would run rampant, inciting people's hearts through the Antichrist and the false prophet.

Then, the spirits of demons would incite the kings of the earth for war and gather them to a place called Armageddon to battle against the Almighty God. It is here that the last war between Satan and God is waged. But because Jesus is God the Almighty, He would descend from the air sitting on a white horse with His army, overcome Satan, and throw the Beast into the lake burning with fire and brimstone (Revelation 19:11-21). Because Jesus Christ now has the absolute power as the Lord of the second coming, He appears on this earth to judge the world and to destroy the Beast.

As such, we must realize that when Jesus Christ descends from Heaven at the time of the saints' rapture, He does not descend onto this earth, but rather He comes into the air to lift up the saints to His place, allowing them to meet Him in the air and to enter the marriage supper of Heaven. When the Lord returns onto this earth, He does so to triumph over Satan and his army standing against God with His Word of power through the Battle of Armageddon, to cast the Devil into the lake of fire and brimstone, and to kill off all his remaining followers. This is the second coming of the Lord. We need the correct knowledge and faith that can differentiate between the Lord's descent to the air and His second coming onto the earth.

Yet many people think that the Lord would make a nonstop descent to this earth when the rapture happens. This is factually incorrect. When the rapture happens, the Lord does not come onto the earth, but to the air. In other words, He lifts up and receives the saints in the air.

As such, you must shed yourself of the thought that the Lord would come again onto this earth at the rapture's time, and instead realize, based on the written Word, that the rapture of the saints would come when the seventh angel sounds his trumpet.

12) Does the "great multitude which no one could number (Revelation 7:9)" refer to the raptured saints?

Yes, that is correct. Revelation 7:9 says, *"After these things I looked, and behold, a great multitude which no one could number, of all nations, tribes, peoples, and tongues, standing before the throne and before the Lamb, clothed with white robes, with palm branches in their hands."* From the phrase, *"of all nations, tribes, peoples, and tongues... clothed with white robes,"* we can see that with their faith in the gospel of the water and the Spirit, a countless multitude among the Gentiles would fight against and overcome the Antichrist, be martyred, and participate in the first resurrection and the rapture.

Although in these last days the Antichrist runs amok with impunity, we can also recognize that at the same time, there would rise even more people who believe in the gospel of the water and the Spirit given by God. As such, a great multitude would rise among the Gentiles also, a multitude so great that no one could even number, who would be saved from sin by believing in the gospel of the water and the Spirit and embrace their martyrdom with their faith.

Revelation 7:14 says, *"So he said to me, 'These are the ones who come out of the great tribulation, and washed their robes and made them white in the blood of the Lamb.'"* As the Great Tribulation came upon this earth, these people were saved from sin by believing in the gospel of the water and the Spirit preached by God's Church with all their hearts. They therefore were martyred, for they neither worshipped the Antichrist nor received the mark of the Beast on their right hand or the forehead, and thereby joined in the saints' resurrection and rapture. This is why they stand before the throne and before the Lamb and praise; *"Salvation belongs to our God who sits on the throne, and to the Lamb!"*

God, therefore, is not just the God of the Jewish people, but He is also the God of the Gentiles. As such, He will make sure that when the last days of the Great Tribulation come, a countless number of Gentiles from all nations, tribes, peoples, and tongues would believe in the gospel of the water and the Spirit, receive the remission of sin, and stand among the martyrs' file.

13) The two witnesses are resurrected and lifted up to heaven after completing their testimony. How is this different from the rapture of the saints with the second coming of Christ?

As I explained with my answer for Q. 2, these two witnesses are God's special servants whom He would raise from the people of Israel to save the Israelites. There is an important work that God must do before destroying this world, and that is to save the people of Israel from sin and make them participate in the first resurrection and the rapture.

The Apostle Paul said in Romans 3:29-30, *"Or is He the God of the Jews only? Is He not also the God of the Gentiles? Yes, of the Gentiles also, since there is one God who will justify the circumcised by faith and the uncircumcised through faith."* The way to be saved from sin before God is the same for both the Jews and the Gentiles. For both the Jews and the Gentiles alike, justification comes only through their faith in the gospel of the water and the Spirit. To be saved from all their sins, the Jewish people must also accept Jesus Christ as their Savior and believe, just as the Gentiles believe, that Jesus Christ took all their sins upon Himself with His baptism, and that He died on the Cross to be judged of these sins on their behalf.

God treats both the Jews and the Gentiles alike, and has permitted both of them the same salvation through faith. This is why God allowed His two witnesses to the Jewish people during the time of the first three and a half years of the Great Tribulation, and why He allowed these witnesses to preach the gospel of the water and the Spirit to them.

In connection with these two witnesses, chapter 11 of Revelation refers to the two olive trees and the two lampstands. The two olive trees refer to these two servants of God whom He would allow for the salvation of the Israelites, and the two lampstands refer to God's two Churches, which are of the Israelites and of the Gentiles. God would allow, in other words, His two Churches alongside each other to preach the gospel of the water and the Spirit to the Israelites and the Gentiles during the first three and a half years of the Great Tribulation.

Right now, God's Church is not found among the Israelites. But when God searches their hearts and when His time comes, He will prepare their hearts to receive His Word, raise the two servants for them, and make them accept Jesus Christ as their Savior.

God therefore will save both the Israelites and the Gentiles during the time of the Great Tribulation. He will also allow the persecution and martyrdom of the born-again saints to both the Israelites and the Gentiles alike. The fact the two witnesses are martyred after completing their testimony and then are resurrected and lifted up to heaven in three and a half days—this ultimately contains the fact that just like these two witnesses, the servants of God and His people among the Gentiles would also fight against the Antichrist, be martyred, and thereby participate in their resurrection and rapture.

14) I believe that the saints would be raptured before the Great Tribulation. But the Bible makes frequent references to the saints who still remain on this earth during the time of the Great Tribulation. Are they the ones who compromised with the world, and whose faith turned lukewarm as a result?

First of all, you must realize that the theory of pre-tribulation rapture that you believe in is in fact a false doctrine. This is the part where many Christians have misunderstood. They think that because the saints would already have been raptured before the Great Tribulation, when its time comes there would only be sinners on this earth. However, the problem is that the Bible makes frequent references to the saints who, while still remaining on this earth during the time of the Great Tribulation, overcome persecution with perseverance and are martyred.

Many people therefore mistakenly think that these saints that are left behind and persecuted in the Tribulation's time are the ones who had compromised with the world and whose faith were only lukewarm.

People who hold this view live in such confusion because they do not know the exact time of the rapture from the Word of God. When, then, is the exact time of the rapture? On this issue, Paul spoke to us in 2 Thessalonians 2:2-4 as the following: *"Now, brethren, concerning the coming of our Lord Jesus Christ and our gathering together to Him, we ask you, not to be soon shaken in mind or troubled, either by spirit or by word or by letter, as if from us, as though the day of Christ had come. Let no one deceive you by any means; for that Day will not come unless the falling away comes first, and the man of sin is revealed, the son of perdition, who opposes and exalts himself above all that is called God or that is worshiped, so that he sits as God in the temple of God, showing himself that he is God."*

"The man of sin... the son of perdition" here refers to the Antichrist who would emerge in the midst of the Great Tribulation. In other words, the Antichrist would make his appearance in the world before the rapture and raise himself high as God. He would therefore make idols of himself and force people to worship and serve him. To bring everyone under his control, he would also make people receive the mark of the Beast's name or number on either their right hands or foreheads, and forbid anyone who does not have this mark from buying or selling anything.

When this Beast appears in the world, the people of this world will be coerced to receive the mark made of his name or the number of his name. As such, everyone whose name is not written in the Book of Life since the creation would all end up receiving the mark and worshipping the Beast.

However, because the saints who have become God's people have the Holy Spirit dwelling in their hearts, they cannot worship any creature as God apart from their true Lord God. The Holy Spirit living in their hearts would therefore give them the strength to resist the coercion of Satan and of the Antichrist and to defend their faith with their martyrdom. And the Holy Spirit would also give them the words with which they can stand against their enemies.

Revelation 17:12-13 tell us, *"The ten horns which you saw are ten kings who have received no kingdom as yet, but they receive authority for one hour as kings with the beast. These are of one mind, and they will give their power and authority to the beast."* The Antichrist would receive authority to persecute the saints and reign the nations of the world for only a very short while. The Antichrist's demand to receive his mark, therefore, will shortly be followed by the martyrdom of the saints.

Revelation 11:11-12, on the other hand, tell us, *"Now after the three-and-a-half days the breath of life from God entered them, and they stood on their feet, and great fear fell on those who saw them. And they heard a loud voice from heaven saying to them, 'Come up here.' And they ascended to heaven in a cloud, and their enemies saw them."* From this fact, that the two martyred witnesses were resurrected and raptured in three and a half days, we can also see that the interval between our martyrdom and rapture is not such a long time either. These two witnesses were raptured simultaneously with their resurrection. When the Lord returns, the martyred saints and the surviving saints who did not receive the mark of the Beast will all be resurrected, lifted up to the air, and receive the Lord in the air.

Therefore, we can realize that the appearance of the Antichrist, the saints' martyrdom and resurrection, and their rapture are all closely interrelated with each other. Paul and

John thus explained to us the time of the saints' rapture in such detail. All the saints will go through the first three and a half years of the Great Tribulation. Until the plagues of the seven trumpets are all over, in other words, they would all be still remaining on this earth.

And with the appearance of the Antichrist, the saints would enter into the second three-and-a-half-year period of the Great Tribulation, and they would remain on this earth until they are martyred for refusing to receive the mark of the Beast. Realizing this, we must all receive the nurturing of faith in God's Church now, at this very present time. ⊠

HAVE YOU TRULY BEEN BORN AGAIN OF WATER AND THE SPIRIT?

PAUL C. JONG

Among many Christian books written about being born again, this is the first book of out time to preach the gospel of the water and the Spirit in strict accordance with the Scriptures. Man can't enter the Kingdom of Heaven without being born again of water and the Spirit. To be born again means that a sinner is saved from all his lifelong sins by believing in the baptism of Jesus and His blood on the Cross. Let's believe in the gospel of the water and the Spirit and enter the kingdom of heaven as the righteous who have no sin.

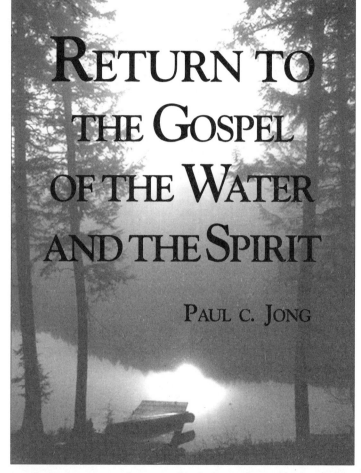

RETURN TO
THE GOSPEL
OF THE WATER
AND THE SPIRIT

PAUL C. JONG

Let's return to the gospel of the water and the Spirit. Theology and doctrines themselves can't save us. Many Christians still follow them and are not born again. This book clearly tells us what mistakes theology and doctrines have made and how to believe in Jesus in the most proper way.

The Holy Spirit who Dwells in Me

A Fail-safe Way for You to Receive the Holy Spirit

Paul C. Jong

In Christianity, the most significantly discussed issue is salvation from sins and the indwelling of the Holy Spirit. However, few people have the exact knowledge of these two things, while they are most important issues in Christianity. Nevertheless, in reality people say that they believe in Jesus Christ while they are ignorant of redemption and the Holy Spirit.

Do you know the gospel that makes you receive the Holy Spirit? If you want to ask God for the indwelling of the Holy Spirit, then you must first know the gospel of the water and the Spirit and have faith in it. This book will certainly lead all Christians worldwide to be forgiven of all their sins and to receive the Holy Spirit.

The Righteousness of God that is Revealed in Romans

Our LORD
Who Becomes the
Righteousness
of God
(I)

PAUL C. JONG

The words in this book will satisfy the thirst in your heart. Today's Christians continue to live while not knowing the true solution to the actual sins that they are committing daily. Do you know what God's righteousness is? The author hopes that you will ask yourself this question and believe in God's righteousness, which is revealed in this book.

The Doctrines of Predestination, Justification, and Incremental Sanctification are the major Christian doctrines, which brought confusion and emptiness into the souls of believers. But now, many Christians should newly come to know God, learn about His righteousness and continue in the assured faith.

This book will provide your soul with a great understanding and lead it to peace. The author wants you to possess the blessing of knowing God's righteousness.

The Righteousness of God that is Revealed in Romans

Our LORD
Who Becomes the
Righteousness of God
(II)

PAUL C. JONG

The words in this book will satisfy the thirst in your heart. Today's Christians continue to live while not knowing the true solution to the actual sins that they are committing daily. Do you know what God's righteousness is? The author hopes that you will ask yourself this question and believe in God's righteousness, which is revealed in this book.

The Doctrines of Predestination, Justification, and Incremental Sanctification are the major Christian doctrines, which brought confusion and emptiness into the souls of believers. But now, many Christians should newly come to know God, learn about His righteousness and continue in the assured faith.

This book will provide your soul with a great understanding and lead it to peace. The author wants you to possess the blessing of knowing God's righteousness.

Commentaries and Sermons on the Book of Revelation

IS THE AGE OF THE ANTICHRIST, MARTYRDOM, RAPTURE AND THE MILLENNIAL KINGDOM COMING? (I)

PAUL C. JONG

After the 9/11 terrorist attacks, traffic to "www.raptureready.com," an Internet site providing information on the end times, is reported to have increased to over 8 million hits, and according to a joint survey by CNN and TIME, over 59% of the Americans now believe in apocalyptic eschatology.

Responding to such demands of the time, the author provides a clear exposition of the key themes of the Book of Revelation, including the coming Antichrist, the martyrdom of the saints and their rapture, the Millennial Kingdom, and the New Heaven and Earth—all in the context of the whole Scripture and under the guidance of the Holy Spirit.

This book provides verse-by-verse commentaries on the Book of Revelation supplemented by the author's detailed sermons. Anyone who reads this book will come to grasp all the plans that God has in store for this world.

The TABERNACLE:

A Detailed Portrait of

Jesus Christ

(I)

PAUL C. JONG

How can we find out the truth hidden in the Tabernacle? Only by knowing the gospel of the water and the Spirit, the real substance of the Tabernacle, can we correctly understand and know the answer to this question.

In fact, the blue, purple, and scarlet thread and the fine woven linen manifested in the gate of the Tabernacle's court show us the works of Jesus Christ in the New Testament's time that have saved the mankind. In this way, the Old Testament's Word of the Tabernacle and the Word of the New Testament are closely and definitely related to each other, like fine woven linen. But, unfortunately, this truth has been hidden for a long tome to every truth seeker in Christianity.

Coming to this earth, Jesus Christ was baptized by John and shed His blood on the Cross. Without understanding and believing in the gospel of the water and the Spirit, none of us can ever find out the truth revealed in the Tabernacle. We must now learn this truth of the Tabernacle and believe in it. We all need to realize and believe in the truth manifested in the blue, purple, and scarlet thread and the fine woven linen of the gate of the Tabernacle's court.

Paul C. Jong's Christian book series, which is translated into English, French, German, Spanish, Portuguese, Dutch, Greek, Danish, Swedish, Italian, Hindi, Malagasy, Malayalam, Telugue, Kannada, Nepali, Bengali, Bermese, Urdu, Thai, Japanese, Chinese, Taiwanese, Mongolian, Vietnamese, Indonesian, Arabic, Iranian, Javanese, Tagalog, Russian, Ukrainan, Hebrew, Slovak, Czech, Georgian, Albanian, Polish, Hungarian, Bulgarian, Romanian and Turkish, is also available now through e-book service.

E-book is digital book designed for you to feel a printed book on screen. You can read it easily on your screen in your native language after download the viewer software and a text file. Feel free to visit our web site at http://www.bjnewlife.org for e-book service, and you can get the most remarkable Christian e-book absolutely for free.

And, would you like to take part in having our free Christian books known to more people worldwide? We would be very thankful if you link your website to our site so that many people get an opportunity to meet Jesus Christ through the literature. Please visit our site at http://www.bjnewlife.org/english/nlmbanner.html to take our banners. In addition, we would be also very thankful if you introduce our website to the webmasters around you for adding our link.

The New Life Mission
Contact: John Shin, General Secretary
E-mail: newlife@bjnewlife.org